MIXED MATCHES

June Duncan Owen has an MA in history from the University of Sydney and a diploma in social science from the University of Adelaide. She has worked as a social worker in Adelaide and Singapore, and as a teacher in South Australia and Victoria and as a farmer in Tasmania. She has written professionally for more than twenty years and has had two other books published, *The Heart of the City* (1987), a history of the Sydney City Mission, and *Writing and Selling Articles* (1997) based on years of teaching professional writing courses. June's first novel, *Looking for a Mail Order Bride* will be published in 2002.

INSIDE FRONT COVER **1** Teri and Allan **2** Kayleen, Kevyn and Gavin **3** Bill and Pat **4** Li Li, Colin and their daughters **5** Tom and Luz **6** Herb and Eileen **7** Ted and Taeko **8** James and Tomoko **9** Manjeet, Frank and Oscar **10** Andrea, Bernard and their daughter INSIDE BACK COVER **11** Hiroe and Cornel **12** John, Yvonne and their children **13** Nuli and Margaret **14** John, Heckyung and their son Patrick **15** Joan and Bandhu **16** Felix, Louise and their daughter **17** Elizabeth and Tony **18** Padma and Peter

A UNSW Press book

Published by
University of New South Wales Press Ltd
University of New South Wales
UNSW Sydney NSW 2052
AUSTRALIA
www.unswpress.com.au

National Library of Australia
Cataloguing-in-Publication entry:

Owen, June Duncan.
Mixed matches: interracial marriage in Australia.

Bibliography.
Includes index.
ISBN 0 86840 581 7.

1. Interracial marriage — Australia.
2. Interracial marriage — Australia — History. I. Title.

306.8460994

Cover illustration Barbara Hanrahan 'Generations', 1991
UNSW Art Collection
Reproduced with kind permission of Mr Jonathon Steele

Printed in Hong Kong through Bookbuilders

MIXED MATCHES

INTERRACIAL MARRIAGE IN AUSTRALIA

June Duncan Owen

UNSW PRESS

CONTENTS

FOREWORD

There has been much writing on intermarriage between women and men of different ethnic origins in post-war Australia. Some has concentrated, as does this work by June Duncan Owen, on marriage between persons of different races. Such writings, however, have been demographic (such as my own work — counting the numbers involved in different kinds of intermarriage). Some have been sociological, discussing the social settings of such marriages. Some have been religious, discussing the outcomes of marriages between persons of Anglo-Celtic Catholic or Protestant and persons of Buddhist or Islamic background.

All these studies are valuable but they often lack what June Duncan Owen's study has in abundance — a deep understanding by the author of what can happen between individual persons, and in particular families, when interracial marriages occur. June Duncan Owen is very well qualified to carry out this study, as she is an Anglo-Celtic Australian with a Sinhalese-Indian husband.

The hundred or more cases covered by this study include a great variety of relationships, some being Anglo-Celtic men marrying non-white wives and some, like the author, being Anglo-Celtic wives with non-white husbands. The study also discusses the children of twenty or so such marriages. The non-white partners come from many different racial backgrounds: Afghan, African, Chinese, Japanese, Philippine, Pacific Island, Indian, Sri Lankan, West Indian and also some mixtures. There are also a few cases where the white partner is not Anglo-Celtic but Scandinavian, Dutch, Italian, Greek or Jewish.

The study also covers marriages between white persons and Aboriginal or part-Aboriginal persons. I find these cases very interesting, especially in the light of the present controversy within the Aboriginal community.

A very important matter emerging from the study is the great variety of reactions within interracial marriages. Some Anglo-Celtic wives adopt their husband's culture while others stay firmly 'Australian'. Likewise, some non-white partners keep close links with their non-white relatives overseas or in Australia, while others do not. This diversity of response to interracial marriage is a most interesting and valuable theme of this study and demonstrates that writers must refrain from making simple generalisations about such an complex subject.

The one thing that can be said with certainty is that successful interracial marriages require much hard work by both partners, a very strong commitment to the marriage and a determination to work through difficult times without ending the marriage. Where breakdown does occur among the interviewees the author is very understanding and non-judgmental.

A very unusual and exciting element of this book is the involvement of the author in her study. Her life and those of her Sinhalese-Indian husband and their Singaporean-born daughter and Australian-born son are interesting in themselves. The author brings her experiences into the interviews so that she and her experiences become part of the interview. By doing this she is able to encourage the interviewees to speak in real depth about themselves. (In my experience this is often difficult to achieve in traditional, often quite formal, interview situations.) In this study the persons interviewed ask the author meaningful questions about herself, and her replies add greatly to the quality of the interview and the study.

Altogether this is a most important and valuable study, and UNSW Press is to be highly commended for publishing it. Additionally it is accompanied by a valuable bibliography that will enable the reader to pursue matters of particular interest.

I have much pleasure in writing this foreword and hope — indeed, I am sure — that those who read June Duncan Owen's fine work will gain as much enjoyment from it as I have.

Charles A Price, Professorial Fellow (retired)
Department of Demography
Australian National University, Canberra

PREFACE

When Australia opened its doors to all people regardless of racial origin, it opened its doors to interracial marriage on a large scale. Research figures released by demographer Charles Price early in 2000 are surprising, even to people who have been attuned to changes in the ethnic mix of Australia, not least because we are actively involved in it. Price maintains that 'at least 60% of the Australian people are ethnically mixed while about 20% have at least four distinct ancestries'.[1]

In 1996 Peter Davis, the Mayor of Port Lincoln, echoed the sentiments of *The Bulletin* writers who, one hundred years earlier, had been so influential in forming, as well as expressing, public opinion. Davis said that he believed all children of mixed-race marriages were 'mongrels'. Later, defending his choice of words, he repeated the animal imagery of the nineteenth-century writers: 'If you are a child of a mixed race ... you are a mongrel and that's what happens when you cross dogs or whatever'.[2]

Ten of Davis's council members walked out in protest, and there was a public outcry, but a few months later, when Port Lincoln elected its new council, Davis was re-elected. Port Lincoln is in South Australia, where the statue of Colonel Light, a mongrel according to Davis's definition, still looks down from the slopes of North Adelaide upon the splendid capital city he planned.

Davis's disparaging remark about the children of mixed-race marriages was the spark that began this book.

Over one hundred mixed-race couples told me their stories between 1997 and 1999, and this book is largely composed of their thoughts and experiences that followed their choice to marry a person from another race. They speak of the difficulties and the special joys they encountered as they learned to build a family starting with two people from often vastly different backgrounds, within a not-always-welcoming society.

Some of the interviewees were well known to me, others were introduced by mutual friends, and most were incredibly open in sharing their lives. Discretion curbed my pen and suggested the use of first names only and, in some cases, anonymity.

Interviewees were chosen on the basis that to an ordinary Australian onlooker, each couple would be seen as 'mismatched'. Some of the interviewees laughed at my use of that word and protested that they felt they were very well matched indeed; that skin colour, shape of face and whether one has crinkly hair or straight simply does not matter. And, of course, they are right. It was a clumsy way of describing how these marriages are seen by Australian society; clumsier than poet Billie Livingstone's 'cross-coloured'.[3]

The name signifying these marriages does not matter, but, as Kenneth Rivett pointed out in *Australia and the Non-White Migrant*, 'visible difference can offer a focal point for prejudice and perhaps augment it'.

In this book I hope to highlight that segment of society that seems to have been forgotten in the rush towards multiculturalism; those mainstream Australians who have chosen their partner from the 'other' group. I believe they will become a very important slice of our society in the process of building a cosmopolitan yet united Australia, because every couple and their descendents will play a vital role of bridging some of the fissures within our nation.

June Duncan Owen

ACKNOWLEDGMENTS

This book would not exist without the participation of the interviewees, their frankness, their willingness to share their experiences. I am wholly in their debt. I also wish to thank the many people who encouraged me in the planning, researching and writing of this book, and reading the manuscript in its various stages. My thanks go to Peter Stewart who was there at the beginning, Emeritus Professor AH Willis, and to Yvonne Chamberlain who was there at the end — and throughout, to my daughter, Charmaine Clements. Through the months of travelling and the many more months while I sorted and worried and wrote, and tore up and wrote again, my husband, Joshua, was there with suggestions, cups of tea, curry dinners and encouragement. Thank you, one and all.

I
INTRODUCTION

> If we are all descended from one common stock, we all have an equal right to the soil of the globe; but this right is never to be exercised to the prejudice of others or in injustice ...
>
> *Colonial Times*, 1830[1]

Despite present-day Australia's cosmopolitan population, the spectre of the 'yellow peril' or the 'nigger in the woodpile' still lies, not quite buried, in the consciousness of many Australians. I met an undercurrent of this fear and disgust late one Saturday afternoon, as I stood at a bus stop near Sydney's Central Station with my Sinhalese-Indian husband and our children. It was winter, and with grubby khaki overcoat flapping a man circled us slowly, hawking and flicking his rheumy eyes over us, up and down, up and down. Then, with deliberate and exact aim, he expectorated upon my skirt.

Many of us have inherited an element of anger or fear of familial links with people who are different — those who in some way are not like us, those who are the 'other'. Sometimes it is religion that is perceived as a barrier to keep us apart. More often nowadays it is the colour of our skin. Over the centuries and across cultures marriages, or proposed marriages, between people from different racial groups cause small explosions of irritation, disappointment or anger, even in the most harmonious societies. Four hundred years ago Shakespeare aired contemporary attitudes towards mixed-race marriages in *Othello*. The black Moor marries Desdemona over the fierce objections of her father, Brabantio, who rages that his daughter's marriage is 'against all the rules of nature', even though Othello, a powerful and much-admired general, is a suitable husband in every way for the high-born Desdemona, except for his black face.

I heard echoes of Brabantio in my own father's response to my marriage, and several Chinese wives told me their fathers responded in the same terms when the proposed son-in-law was white. The spitting at Central Station was a protest against what that particular Australian man saw as an unwanted tainting of his racial family. There are different kinds of protests. Many Aboriginal Australians marry outside their racial/cultural group, but even after several generations of such intermarriage and despite the fact that they may live among and be physically indistinguishable from the white population, they cling to their Aboriginality. Indian citizens of this country may happily call themselves Australians but also shout their desire to retain the so-called purity of their Indian blood by seeking spouses from India for years, even generations, after deciding to call Australia home.

Throughout most of Australia's history, interracial marriage has been a highly-charged, emotional issue for the families of the couples involved, and also for the nation, but it was not always so. In the eighteenth century ideas of tolerance and the equality of man were widely accepted, and early plans for the first settlement included balancing the sex ratio of the new colony by bringing a shipload of Pacific Islander women as wives for the convicts. Captain Phillip ignored instructions to pick up the women on his way to Botany Bay only because he felt that, if removed from their island home, the women would 'pine away in misery'.[2]

In the early years after settlement at Port Jackson, the convict women were the only companions available for the much greater number of male convicts and also for the single men from the barracks, because Phillip discouraged friendships, or indeed any unofficial contact, with the Aborigines. However, convicts sent to work on outlying farms and those who, having earned their tickets-of-leave or emancipation, acquired their own lonely plots of land, soon found companionship with Aboriginal women.

Within a few years there were marriages or permanent liaisons between white men and Aboriginal women. There were also other mixed-race marriages, such as the union of Chinese free settler Mark O'Pong and Englishwoman Sarah Jane Thompson in 1823. In Tasmania, a Chinese convict from Mauritius married fellow convict Hannah Howard, and when he was pardoned in 1833, she was released into his care.[3] In the half-century following Australia's first European settlements, small numbers of people from many different nations and races came as sailors, whalers, workers, tradesmen, small businessmen, or landholders like O'Pong, fitting in unobtrusively and, if they could find a wife, marrying. Mixed-race marriages were also accepted in the upper levels of early colonial society during the broad-minded years of the early nineteenth century. The Colonial Office selected Colonel William Light, the son of a British Army officer and his Malay wife, as surveyor-general to plan the experimental South Australian settlement and its new city of Adelaide that was settled in 1836. But by mid-century ideas of racial purity had begun to spread.

The gold rushes of the 1850s brought large numbers of people from all over the world, far too many to integrate inconspicuously. Of these, Chinese were the most bitterly resented because they were the most numerous by far and they looked different, dressed differently, spoke their own language, lived separately and, perhaps most importantly, they gave their allegiance not to the colonial governments, nor even to the general population of miners, but to their own headman. It was his rules they obeyed. This made them seem a strange and powerfully cohesive group, evoking fear and anger among the straggly groups of men of many nationalities who had come alone to the diggings. Marriages between Chinese miners and Australian women exacerbated this anger, for white miners saw such marriages as not only a defection from their own racial family, but a depletion of the already small pool of marriageable women available to them.

Stories abounded of white girls being lured to the Chinese camps, and cartoons in popular journals depicted cunning Orientals pursuing white women or carrying them off by guile or force. The lot of any white woman who married a Chinese miner could not have been easy, for not only did she become an outcast on the diggings, living in primitive conditions among people whose language she did not understand, but she was blamed and ostracised for her defection and lost the respect previously accorded her. Manning Clark wrote that in a riot a 'European woman, married to a Chinese, was assaulted and her clothing and that of her children was torn to pieces while her tormentors took counsel on how to rape her ...'.[4]

Describing a fight in a mining camp during which the white wife of a Chinese miner 'was beaten up by the mob', a contemporary reporter offered the opinion that 'Any white woman who would marry a Chinese showed a character of such moral degradation as to warrant not the slightest confidence being placed in her evidence'.[5]

Such women needed courage to withstand the depressing effect of the almost universal disapproval, even the repugnance, of their fellow countrymen and women. I spoke to two Australian-born Chinese men, descendants of two white women who were brave enough to flout convention and community disapproval by taking Chinese husbands in the second half of the nineteenth century. Both men regard themselves as wholly Australian except that, yes, they still have Chinese faces.

Herbert calls himself an 'Ockercidental/Oriental' and was well known as 'Australia's Bobby Breen' in the 1940s and 1950s, before becoming an artist and establishing his own advertising agency. Now in semi-retirement, he paints and runs art classes.

HERBERT Yes, I'm an ABC (Australian-born Chinese). My great-grandfather, Samuel Hand, was born in China in 1837, came to Australia and in 1863 married a Londoner, Eliza Cross, in Ipswich. Their daughter Jane married Samuel Ah Warr, an itinerant Chinese baker in Dubbo, when she was only fifteen years old. She brought up nine children just as Eliza had brought her up — as Australians.

My father, Chun Yun Nin, came from Canton and married one of Jane and Samuel's daughters, who promptly re-named him Harry. They had ten children (I am the seventh). We were an ordinary Australian family, even if we had Chinese faces. We ate Australian food — just what my mother had learned to cook from her mother, who had learned from that Englishwoman, Eliza. But Dad could not give up his rice, so he always cooked the evening meal, and if we went out for a celebration it was always to a Chinese restaurant.

Our home was a rented terrace house in Waterloo, then a poor neighbourhood in Sydney. Our neighbours were Australians, both black and white, Italians and Greeks, and I don't remember any racism. Chinese were called Charlie, but without malice and no offence was taken. Chow was different; that was an insult.

My father worked in a Chinese furniture factory, but once when he was out of work, I suppose it was during the Great Depression, he turned to catering. He made minced pork and prawn buns and took them in to the markets to sell. We all learned how to cook pork and prawn buns and we sold the excess around the neighbourhood. That was about the only Chinese thing in our childhood.

We never thought of ourselves as anything but Australian, never learned to speak Chinese, and we all married Australians, except one sister and of course myself. I married an Englishwoman, but I've turned her into an Australian too. My father never acquired a lot of English, and he remained close to the Chinese community and the Joss House all his life.

Records suggest that Eliza, and later her daughter Jane may have been ostracised in the country towns where they lived, but Englishwoman Eileen, who married Eliza and Samuel Hand's great-grandson in the 1950s, says she has never felt discrimination from other Australians.

The importation of the Kanakas from Vanuatu and other Pacific islands began in 1863 and within twenty years 10 000 were employed in the sugar plantations of Queensland.[6] Since only about 5 per cent were women, it was not long before many of the young islanders married Aboriginal or white Australian women. Faith Bandler is a well-known Australian descended from just such a match.[7]

Many letters to the press made it clear, as did this 1899 protest by JB Drake MLA, that though Kanakas were welcomed on the canefields for their labour, their marriages with white women were hotly resented: 'These are the men who lease land, marry white women … it is an army of semi-civilised barbarians who have settled down in Queensland … it is mud and filth entering into the stream of a nation's pure life-blood'.[8]

Another *Bulletin* writer of June 1899 suggested: 'It would be interesting to know how many white women are living on the proceeds of Tommy Tanna's labour — also how many half-castes are added annually to the population of Mongrelia'.[9]

It was the white women and their children who were the targets of hate, rather than the Islanders, just as nearly a hundred years later it was I who was spat upon, not my 'other' husband. Tanna is one of the islands of Vanuatu and 'Tommy Tanna' a nineteenth-century colloquial, but not necessarily abusive, nickname for a niVanuatu. Contemporary newspapers, journals and public announcements very often used loaded language when referring to Chinese, Indians, Kanakas or Aborigines, and cartoons commonly depicted them in a degrading posture or as a personified animal or monster such as a dragon or octopus.

In 1901 the new Commonwealth Parliament legislated that all Pacific Islanders who wished to return home should be repatriated by 1906, but allowed anyone who had forged permanent links with Australia, particularly by establishing themselves on the land or by marriage to Australians, to stay. About 2000 Islanders did.

Henry Lawson, the storyteller best remembered for his tales of the privations of life in the bush, felt that liaisons with Aboriginal women were the ultimate hardship suffered by lonely drovers and stockmen in Australia's bush. In 'Out Back Hell' he wrote:

> And away on far outstations, seldom touched by Heaven's breath,
>   In a loneliness that smothers love and hate —
> Where they never take white women — there they live the living death
>   With a half-caste or a black gin for a mate.

Despite the passionate nationalist's belief, records — and families — show that many of these liaisons, when there was some degree of permanence, were not viewed as a 'living death' or a last resort by the men engaging in them. From the earliest days white convicts, settlers and even bushrangers fathered many children with Aboriginal women. Some of the men gave the women no recognition or support, but there were lasting marriages, such as that of James Bugg, a shepherd who married an Aboriginal woman in the early 1830s and sent their children to school in Sydney to ensure that they would not be disadvantaged by their mixed-race parentage.[10] The marriage of Bugg's eldest daughter, Mary, to the bushranger Frederick Ward, famous as Captain Thunderbolt, can perhaps be seen as a union of two outcasts, though today many amateur genealogists are surprised and delighted to find that one of their great-great-grandmothers was Aboriginal.

At a time when xenophobia and patriotism were so often confused, such marriages must have called for extraordinary strength. It was almost certainly fraught with difficulty then, as now, for a white woman to marry 'out'. The male-dominated Australian culture more easily accepts any wife of a regular white Australian man. If she is different, she is likely to be seen as exotic, exciting, whereas a woman marrying 'out' gives up her position in the dominant culture. A story told in explanation of Aboriginal Jimmy Governor's murderous rampage is that he was incensed at the way his white wife was ostracised by the 'big house' and the rest of the white population after she married him.

The commonsense and hormones of ordinary people have always travelled in advance of the intelligentsia in Australia. In literature and art, from 1850 until very recently, depiction of marriage or even sexual love between people of different races was taboo. In Katharine Suzannah Prichard's 1937 prize-winning novel *Coonardoo*, the love between the Aboriginal girl and the white squatter is doomed, for though he loves her, he is not strong enough to withstand the disapproval of his society and so destroys them both. As recently as 1986 a film critic wrote in *The Australian* that 'On stage and screen miscegenation remains tricky if not actually taboo'.[11]

From the United States, usually even stricter than Australia in segregating the races, came a notable exception — the 1967 film *Guess Who's Coming to Dinner*. The film required a brave producer and the universally-popular stars Spencer Tracy and Katharine Hepburn, with Sidney Poitier playing the romantic lead as a handsome, intelligent and successful American professional — just the kind of husband the parents would have chosen for their daughter, except for his black face.

Yet those of us who have taken this step in Australia know that it is not only a different skin colour, a different set of facial features, that we take into our family; we also have to embrace a different set of cultural values, different expectations, different habits and courtesies, a different history, different cultural memories and sometimes a different faith. Even now it seems to demand extra determination to step across a racial barrier in choosing a partner, and often even more determination to forge a lasting marriage.

Hardly a day goes by that 'multiculturalism', 'discrimination', 'reconciliation', 'diversity', 'non-English-speaking background', 'racism', 'Asian migration' are not mentioned in the media. There are estimates and statistics to enlighten Australians about our various backgrounds. We are urged to be 'tolerant' of all differences, as if those differences were not minor compared to the great bond of our common humanity. Australians have lived in an open-to-the-world society for more than a generation now and are, by and large, welcoming and tolerant. However, welcoming a visitor, a new neighbour, or a work colleague of a different race differs vastly from welcoming them into one's family. The 'as long as they don't marry my sister' syndrome still exists, though a gradual mingling of races is surely a natural consequence of today's fast worldwide transport and communication and, more particularly, immigration.

As the years go by, each incoming group will add a little to the mix that will become the typical Australian, until our population is richer still, but it would be foolish to pretend that this mixing is always harmonious. Though pressures against interracial marriage still exist in today's cosmopolitan Australia, there are compensations for marrying into another race. Rather like migrating to another country, it is an act of adventure, a stepping out into another world, an act of consciously choosing to change one's life, to become someone else. Just as in migrating, if one dwelt upon fears of leaving the known, one would never step out into the unknown. Most mixed-race marriages, therefore, are between adventurous, positive-thinking men and women, whose marriages have a better than average chance of being full of surprises and joy rather than trepidation and disappointment.

Some mixed-race couples lean towards fitting seamlessly into mainstream Australian culture; some have decided to accentuate their difference by adapting to the non-Australian partner's lifestyle and culture, albeit within the Australian community; some have chosen a third culture — theirs alone.

Some couples do refer to their union as 'odd' or 'not normal'. One Chinese wife told me that she feels so strongly that her marriage is abnormal, that after many happy years with her Australian husband, she still feels uncomfortable walking down the street with him. In contrast, most couples are continually astonished by the community's view, signalled in various ways, that they do not belong together.

The spitter at Central Station saw me as an Australian woman (one of his mob) married to an outsider; he saw my husband as an intruder from the Indian subcontinent. He did not see the things we had in common. He did not see our whole family stifling giggles in church as we listened to a sermon about how married couples grow to look alike; he did not see our small son look pointedly from his father's dark brown skin to mine — very fair under the freckles and the sunburn — nor hear his stage-whispered 'How long do you think it will take?'.

Remembering how my marriage brought unhappiness to my mother and anger and a sense of betrayal to my father, I paid attention to how parents felt when their children chose a marriage partner of another race. I also listened to more than twenty of the adult or near-adult children of those 'mixed' families, some of whom happily called themselves 'mongrels', turning Mayor Davis's insult into a comradely nickname.

Descendants of early miners and Afghan camel drivers told me their stories, and so did descendants of Chinese and Indians who came alone to Australia during the darkest days of the so-called White Australia Policy, and Japanese brides of the Occupation Forces who came after World War 2. Colombo Plan students who married here and stayed, and more recent migrants and refugees from various countries within Asia, Africa, the Pacific Islands and the West Indies, told me their experiences, as well as Aborigines who intermarried with all manner of later settlers in our country. In Darwin and Katherine in the far north, in Esperance on the Great Australian Bight, in Perth and Adelaide and Melbourne and Canberra and Sydney, representatives of this particular segment of the Australian community spoke of how their marriages are stitching up gaps between Australia's people.

Sometimes such couples still provoke unwanted attention, but as their children grow and marry into, perhaps, another wave of migrants that we in Australia have come to expect, then they will become less and less noticeable. They will merge, not sink into a general coffee-coloured Australia, but merge as bright spots of paint merge in a painting, giving a new sparkle and texture to what would be a flatter, duller picture without them.

2
_____

INTERRACIAL MARRIAGES
FROM 1788 TO 1900

The need for common action on immigration by the six colonies was
one of the more urgent reasons for federation in 1901.

AC Palfreyman[1]

Chinese and Indian and Sri Lankan and other non-European workers — gardeners, shepherds, carpenters, cooks — arrived regularly in
the Australian colonies from the beginning of settlement. They came
in small enough numbers to slip unnoticed into the cities and
become an accepted part of small towns, where they sometimes married into the local population. Not until the gold rushes of the early
1850s did great waves of non-Europeans begin to arrive, and these
arrivals were overwhelmingly Chinese.

The number of Chinese entering the Australian colonies rose
steadily, peaking at 40 000 in 1858.[2] In the poorer goldfields of New
South Wales, Chinese diggers often outnumbered all others, thus a
large percentage of the workers on the diggings looked different,
dressed differently and spoke a different language. Despite the fear
and prejudice this caused, it was never as bad as in California, where
Chinese were considered to be outside the law. In Australian
colonies, in all aspects of law, migrants of any race were equal to citizens before the courts. If European miners or other Australians
were caught and identified committing robbery or assault against
the Chinese, charges were laid and jail sentences for such crimes
were common. One member of the bench in Castlemaine, Victoria,
admonished the diggers: 'All men are equal ... and you have no right

to attempt to drive any away because they do not work as you please'.[3]

For economic reasons, very few Chinese women came to Australia during this period and, in contrast to California where the Chinese had to import their own prostitutes, local prostitutes served all races in Australia's colonies.[4] (Later, in the Queensland gold-fields, Japanese prostitutes came to serve their countrymen.)

Victoria was the first state to restrict Chinese immigration, in 1855. New South Wales and South Australia followed with similar legislation, but they all repealed these laws a few years later when the flood of immigrants had eased. Queensland enacted restrictive legis-lation in 1877, when there were 17 000 Chinese miners on the Palmer River goldfields, and two years later the First Intercolonial Trades Union Conference condemned the importation of Chinese workers.[5] At that time, Western Australia was still importing Asian labour, but in 1886 it too became frightened by the flood of Chinese immigrants to its newly-discovered goldfields. Public outcry follow-ing the arrival of shiploads of smallpox-infected Chinese passengers, and the discovery that a high proportion of them carried forged papers, forced all colonial governments to pass legislation for tighter controls on immigration.

Despite these restrictions there were strong feelings that all Australians should be equal. Under the New South Wales Naturalisation Act anyone could declare himself a British subject after living in the colony for five years, and this included Chinese and others, who once naturalised no longer had to pay the occasional tax on arrival.[6]

In May 1888 the New South Wales premier, Henry Parkes, said:

> I contend that if this young nation is to maintain the fabric of its lib-erties unassailed and unimpaired, it cannot admit to its population any element ... of an inferior character. I have maintained at all times that we should not encourage or admit amongst us any class of persons whatever whom we are not prepared to advance to all our franchises, to all our privileges as citizens, and all our social rights, including the right of marriage.

In fact, marriage between people of different races was never illegal in the Australian colonies. All immigrants, including the Chinese, had full legal rights of citizens once accepted into an Australian colony, including the right to marry whomever they pleased. In Victoria during the gold rush, fifty marriages were recorded between Chinese men and white women in just five years, whereas in San Francisco, in the twenty-five years from its first gold rush there were only five such couples, all of whom had been married outside California.[7]

Though in the Australian colonies Chinese had all rights, their access to justice was often restricted by fear and distrust, as well as language problems. Even if they spoke English or had an interpreter, they often did not understand how the law worked. In *Sojourners*, Eric Rolls tells the story of Sun San Lung, who came to Australia in 1863, bought land in Castlemaine, married Lizzie, a European, and had a son. Lizzie died, Sun San Lung married another white woman, and then in 1887 took his eldest son back to visit China. Sun San Lung returned to Australia wearing European clothes and speaking fluent English, but despite his extensive property holdings and his white Australian wife waiting for him in Castlemaine, neither he nor his son was allowed to disembark in Melbourne.

In Sydney, Quong Tart was more successful in his relations with authority, or perhaps Sydney was less aggressively anti-Chinese. Brought to Braidwood as a child by his uncle, a headman in charge of a group of miners, Quong Tart was befriended by local townspeople and settlers and was already wealthy when he moved to Sydney at the age of twenty-four. There he expanded his wealth by dealing in silks and tea, and establishing restaurants and tearooms. He had reached a position of influence in the city by 1887 when he married Margaret Scarlett, but despite the esteem in which he was held and the lavish home he provided for her in Randwick, the Scarlett family did not approve.[8]

Quong Tart, acting as an unofficial Chinese ambassador, campaigned against the importation of opium. While checking opium users in the goldfields, he found seventy-three white Australian women, most of them already addicted, living with Chinese men in the mining camps. Quong Tart failed to stop the flow of opium, and at the time of his death in 1903 — after being attacked in his warehouse by Chinese robbers — there were still a hundred Chinese gambling houses with opium dens in their back rooms in central Sydney. Many of Sydney's prostitutes and homeless women fleeing from brutal husbands found shelter in these back rooms and, resisting persuasion by city missionaries to go back to their families, stayed and married their benefactors.[9]

Reverend Francis Hopkins explained the women's preference not on their probable addiction, but on the belief that 'a Chinaman's Anglo-Saxon wife is almost his God, a European's is his slave. This is the reason why so many girls transfer their affections to the almond-eyed Celestials'.[10] Compare this view with the way in which many of the Asian wives of today speak of deliberately choosing white Australian husbands because such a marriage allows them freedom, whereas marriage within their own race and culture would 'enslave' them. This was mentioned by Chinese, Japanese, Korean and Indian women interviewed.

Though many of the Chinese businessmen and miners went

back home when the gold ran out, those who stayed left their mark on cities and country towns, not least in the families they founded. Russell Jack, who runs the Golden Dragon Museum in Bendigo, is the great-grandson of one of those early miners. His family has lived in Bendigo for five generations, ever since his great-grandfather came from China to seek gold on Dai Gum San — the Big Gold Mountain — and in 1870 married a young Englishwoman.

I spoke with Russell, and expressed a wish that his great-grandmother could speak to me across the years about her experiences as the white wife of a Chinese digger on the Bendigo goldfields.

RUSSELL She would have met racism then, I guess, just as I did eighty years later.

I was a young man in the 1950s and I was only ever interested in Australian girls, because they're the most beautiful women in the world. I was keen on a girl — very keen. But her mother put an end to it. She disapproved because I was Chinese, and that was the end of my first love affair.

A while later, a good mate I worked with said to me, 'I can't understand this racism business. I think any race is as good as another'.

Well, I was fancy-free then and looking around, so I said, 'I believe you've got a couple of good-looking daughters at home. One evening I might come knocking on your door'.

End of conversation. End of friendship. I couldn't believe it! I'd thought of that man as a friend. It was okay for me to be his mate at work, but he certainly didn't want me as a son-in-law.

The Chinese mix well in Bendigo, but there has always been racism — here and everywhere else. If you scratch hard enough, you'll find a racist.

In the 1950s of Russell's youth much of white Australia's population felt prejudice against other races. *The Bulletin* still carried the front cover slogan 'Australia for the white man', and continued to carry it until 1961. But in the 1870s, and for the rest of their lives, Russell's great-grandparents would have faced racism wherever they turned. In the late nineteenth and early twentieth centuries there was an Anti-Chinese League, and newspapers frequently printed anti-Chinese — and indeed anti-any-other-race — cartoons, jokes and stories.

In 1888 *The Boomerang* of Bathurst published a story by William Lane, the socialist visionary who later led a party of Australians to their ill-fated Utopia in Paraguay. His serialised story *White or Yellow?* was set twenty years into the future, when Lane believed that the Chinese would be the new landed gentry of Australia. In the story John Saxby, the president of the Farmers' Union, tells his daughter Cissie's sweetheart that their neighbour, Stella Stibbins, has been seen associating with Wong, a wealthy Chinese man. Because of that association, Saxby calls

Stella the 'vilest of the vile' and says he expects the friendship will lead to marriage and ... 'you know what that means. In a generation after that marriage there won't be a pure-blooded white man in Australia'.[11]

Enraged by this vision of an Oriental-tainted Australia, the younger man urges Saxby to lead the Farmers' Union into armed battle against the Chinese. 'If we can't save it [Australia] we can die for it ...', adding, 'Cissie can die as well ... I'd sooner kill her with my own hands than have her live to raise a brood of coloured curs'.

William Lane's story reflected official, as well as popular, opinion of the day. The British Government, mindful of its treaty obligations with the Chinese Emperor, tried to persuade the colonies to soften their stance towards immigrating Chinese, but most officials agreed that interracial marriage would lead to degeneration. The Colonial Office's Sir James Stephens thought all non-Europeans should be excluded from Australia because any intermixture of other races would debase the 'noble European race'.[12]

In his poem 'To Be Amused' Henry Lawson voices the widespread fear of leprosy, which many believed the Chinese were spreading, as well as his hatred of mixed-race marriages:

> I see the stricken city fall ...
> The pure girl to the leper's kiss
> God give us faith, for Christ's own sake,
> To kill our womankind ere this

In both these examples by popular contemporary writers of the time, as in most other contemporary expressions of prejudice against interracial marriage, it is the white woman who is the real target of hate, rather than the interloping, 'other' man. The up-to-date version of this narrow targeting is the confidence with which many interviewees offered their opinion that there is still much more prejudice against an Australian woman who marries an 'other' man than an interracial marriage where the husband is white.

White Australians were not the only ones to fear dilution of their 'pure' blood. During the 1890s and the early years of the twentieth century, Chinese-language newspapers circulating in Sydney regularly referred to white Australians in insulting terms. Since very few Australians then, as now, read Chinese, it is unlikely that the general population ever knew the Chinese press was calling them 'barbarians' and 'foreign devils' and 'the laziest race on earth'.

The Chinese believed themselves to be culturally superior to other races and, like most Anglo-Celtic Australians, were concerned with racial purity, openly disapproving of mixed-race marriages.

Most references to Australian women were derogatory, sweeping generalisations were made that incest was widespread and one particularly scurrilous article claimed that all white women, even 10-year-old girls, were sexually promiscuous and carried sexual diseases. One newspaper reported, quite seriously, that infanticide was more prevalent in Australia than in China and was the prime cause of Australia's small population.[13] All this was to show the moral superiority of the Chinese and, most particularly, to convince the newspaper's almost totally male Chinese readership that they should not marry Australian women. Notice that, even from this 'other' side, it is the white Australian women who are attacked, rather than the Chinese men who, by intermarriage, could have been said to cause the dilution of their 'pure' blood.

Chinese antipathy to this 'diluting' of the race still exists among Chinese from all parts of Asia. Among the Chinese/Australian couples I interviewed, a far greater number of the Chinese partners told me their parents disapproved of their marriage than did their Australian spouses.

In nineteenth-century Australia there was little public outcry against people from the Indian subcontinent, probably because they did not come in large groups. Even though the Indian Government prohibited emigration in 1839, people from the different countries of that subcontinent were among the Australian colonies' earliest immigrants, coming singly or in small groups to take up work as tailors, gardeners or merchants. In 1860 three camel men and twenty-four camels were brought from Peshawar to accompany Burke and Wills in their crossing of the continent, and when it was realised how well the animals coped with the dry inland, more camels and their handlers were brought from Peshawar and the Punjab to assist in building the Overland Telegraph Line and to work as hauliers over long dry stretches of the inland. The camels were fattened and quartered outside outback towns such as Marree in South Australia, Broken Hill and Bourke in New South Wales and Coolgardie in Western Australia.

Though many of the camel men came from northern India and what is now Pakistan, they were mostly Muslim and were all labelled Afghans. Very few women came and many of the cameleers remained single, or, having married before they left home, travelled back every few years to visit their families. Some married white Australian women who went through Muslim wedding ceremonies and adopted Muslim customs and social restrictions. This meant a lonely life for the women in the Ghantowns during the long periods when their husbands were away with the camel teams, for no other Afghan man was permitted speak to them. Some Afghans married Aboriginal women, and reconciliation between Muslim exclusivity and the tribal social life Aboriginal women were used to must have been even more difficult, though in large Ghantowns such as that in Marree, the women would have had many other wives for company.

In the early 1900s Gool Mahomet met and married Desiree Ernestine Adrienne Lesire, a Frenchwoman who had come to Australia to work as a governess. Re-named Miriam Bebe by her husband, she educated their six children while travelling almost constantly between Western Australia, outback South Australia and Broken Hill.[14] Miriam Bebe seems to have led a life rare among the wives of Afghans, as she travelled among, and probably mixed with, outback communities. Most Afghan men travelled alone and were well respected among the station-owners whose wool they delivered to the river or rail-heads. My mother remembers the camel team drivers as courteous men who were fond of children. They must have gained the trust of my grandfather, for my mother and her sisters were allowed to visit the camel drivers' camp to take gifts of fresh fruit and vegetables from the homestead gardens, and were rewarded by being taught the intricate string knotting of macramé and also to speak a little of the drivers' language (Pushtu, I think). This childhood trust lingered and thirty years later my mother — otherwise the most timid of women — would scoff at our fear of the strange bearded and turbaned hawkers who appeared at our gate once or twice a year. She would then buy goods at wildly inflated prices because 'what else can the poor men do, now there's no more camel driving?'.

The Afghans led abstemious lives and usually made good husbands, but there were exceptions. Annie Grigo met Dost Mahomet in Coolgardie and fled with him on a swift camel to Port Headland to escape her father's anger. After her father's death, Annie's mother and brother went to live with Annie and Dost, but when Annie's brother saw Dost punch his wife, a fight erupted. Annie's brother hit Dost over the head with a jarrah post. Dost died and Annie's brother was charged with murder, but found not guilty. Annie, obediently following her dead husband's wishes, took her five children back to India to meet their grandparents. There, Dost's family blamed their son's foreign wife for his death and had her murdered — 'cut to pieces' — in the colourful words of Winifred Steger who related this tale in her book *Always Bells: Life with Ali*. Steger herself had a much happier time with her Afghan husband. They had three children and travelled to Mecca together. After Ali died, Winifred wrote novels and worked in an Afghani store in Marree to support herself and her children.[15]

Some Afghans became legends. Born in 1857, Mahomet Allum came to Australia as a young man and, after working for many years in the inland, settled in Adelaide to become a well-respected businessman and herbalist. In 1938, when he was 80, Mahomet Allum married Jean, a 20-year-old Australian woman. Their marriage was reportedly happy, and she became a Muslim. They had a daughter, but while Jean was still a young woman, she contracted smallpox while visiting Pakistan and died.[16]

In 1870 Sinhalese pearl-divers were brought from Sri Lanka, then known as Ceylon, to far north Queensland where they replaced Aboriginal women as pearl-shell divers. Twelve years later another shipload of Sinhalese, including a few wives and families, came to work on the sugar plantations. Unaccustomed to such hard physical labour, most of the men found other work locally or drifted north to work in the pearling industry. By that time Thursday Island already had Australia's only distinct Sinhalese community of over one hundred Sinhalese families, though many of the wives were black or white Australian women.[17] However, no sign of this community remains today. Sinhalese names have disappeared from the shopfronts as the Sinhalese families moved south when the pearling industry declined.

Indians continued to come to Australia in small groups as cane-cutters and farm labourers; some of these men and their descendents eventually owned their own farms and later moved to banana plantations in Woolgoolga on the New South Wales north coast. Augmented by more recent arrivals, Sikhs of this best-known Indian enclave in Australia have established two temples and play a significant role in the town. Members of this community almost invariably send back to India for spouses for their children, and this is still the preferred option for many Indians in Australia today.

'None of us could marry a girl from Woolgoolga. It would be like marrying your own sister', a Sikh schoolteacher in that town told me, making the assumption that all other young women in Australia, including hundreds of young Indian women, were off-limits.

The grandson of a Sikh who had brought horses out from the Punjab in 1887 told me that most of the brides brought out from India to Woolgoolga are uneducated girls who have led very sheltered lives in India, and he believes they face enormous problems in Australia:

> Once here, they rarely leave the house. They hide in an inner room when others come to the house — even tradesmen. They cannot speak English, and find it difficult to learn because the husband, who speaks English well, wants to practise his Punjabi so he won't forget it. He also wants his children to learn Punjabi, so he insists on the language in the home being Punjabi, thus the wives take many years to feel at home in the wider community

Woolgoolga families also import husbands from India for their daughters. Pamela, a young Indian woman who came out to

Australia as a small child with her family, resented being married off to a stranger from India. When she asked to see a photo of the chosen bridegroom, she was told it was none of her business. She believes the strain of the early months of her marriage to a stranger permanently undermined her health.

Pamela's experience can be compared with that of Manjeet, a young Sikh student from Malaysia, who met and fell in love with Frank, an Australian student.

MANJEET I had done what my parents wanted. I'd got my degree. I expected them to be anything from angry to disappointed when they learned about Frank. They were.

My mother flew out immediately to put things right. She'd take me home, she said, and buy me a new car. Once they understood that I wasn't going to be interested in anyone else, their focus switched to Frank. 'He is a white man, and who knows what his intentions are? He's probably highly dishonourable and we'll be left with a dishonoured daughter when he dumps you!'

Finally Frank went home with me to be thoroughly looked over by the rest of the family. They decided he wasn't too bad, but he had to agree to marry me before we returned to Australia.

FRANK A bit earlier than we'd have chosen, that's all. I knew they were worried. They had to see that Manjeet was treated right.

MANJEET Half a dozen years have passed and now my mother agrees that it was the right decision, and mine to make.

In Woolgoolga, Pamela and her husband are happy now too, but she says she will not arrange a marriage in twenty years' time for her little daughter and, most particularly, she will not bring out a bride for any son she might have. 'Young men who are brought out, like my husband, are treated well. But brides just become servants to the rest of the family.'

Part of the reason that Indian parents put pressure on their children to enter traditional arranged marriages is the Indian belief that modern Australian love-marriages are 'unstable'. Parents feel, as parents do everywhere, that they know what is best for their now adult child, and they believe, from generations of experience, that proper and lasting marriages are arranged by the families. The chosen partner is usually a stranger who fits the age, education and caste. A web of relatives and friends is involved in the choice, and family and personal histories and astrology charts are perused. Later, photographs are exchanged and then, if all parties agree, a meeting is arranged. The horoscopes are an escape hatch. Most Indians I have spoken to are not forced to marry if, at the first meeting, the proposed partner does not appeal. No one's feelings are hurt if elder members of the family or go-betweens explain that the horoscopes did not match. However, if the bride or groom is brought all the way from India, pressure to commit to the marriage would be extreme.

In traditional families, Indian girls are chaperoned everywhere and never see a suitor alone. If an Indian girl were to go out alone with a man before marriage, she would be condemned as no longer pure. Indian parents, then, fall into the mistaken belief that any young Australian woman who mixes socially with friends of both sexes is immoral. Indian parents find it difficult to understand that few Australian women would risk a marriage until they knew their prospective bridegroom fairly well, particularly when there are great cultural differences to understand and overcome.

Young Indian people who have grown up in Australia and work with colleagues of the opposite sex are also beginning to demand freedom of choice, but newspapers circulating in Indian and Sri Lankan communities in Australia today still carry columns of advertisements for marriage partners. These are put in by parents who are quite specific about the educational qualifications, earning capacity, even height and colour of skin they require in a partner for their son or daughter. But arranging a marriage for one's child, even after all details including horoscopes have been matched, is no guarantee of success. Rasheel Kaur, a lawyer specialising in family law in Australia, says her work brings her into daily contact with female victims of arranged marriages.[18]

Before Australia opened its doors to all migrants, many Indians and Chinese men came without their wives, only returning home to visit the family every few years. As each son grew old enough he would accompany his father back to Australia, until eventually grandsons replaced the original settler. This way of legally circumventing the strict immigration rules was popular, and the grandfathers and their descendants retained Australian citizenship, even though they may have been living back in their homeland for many years. In a leafy outer suburb of Sydney's north I spoke to Wilfred, one such Australian, and his teacher wife, Jenny.

WILFRED My grandparents came out to Australia, and my father was born here. They went back to China and stayed there throughout the war, but they, and therefore we, were Australian citizens, so my mother and we four children came to Sydney in the 1960s. We went straight into boarding schools, while our mother travelled between Sydney and Hong Kong, where my father was a successful architect.

At thirteen, I only had enough English to half-manage, so the first year here was very hard, but I played sport, and my language skills improved. Now, most of my friends and colleagues are Australian.

AUTHOR Do you think of yourself as Australian?

WILFRED Yes. Australian/Chinese. I feel comfortable here. After finishing engineering [studies] at Sydney University I got the ballot for national service and went into officer training. The Army made much of me being the first Chinese officer in the Australian

Army. It was like a holiday. When I left the Army I began a diploma in accounting in Bathurst. That's where I met Jenny. The racial difference wasn't a problem for my family. We had always thought of ourselves as Australians. It was harder for Jenny.

JENNY   My family is a close and loving family, but very inward-looking. When I was in year eleven, my school class went to Noumea, and afterwards one boy, a Melanesian, wrote to me. My parents were horrified and forbade me to write to him. I disobeyed. When I found his replies in the mailbox, I thought it was a miracle, because I knew my mother always checked the mailbox. Of course, it wasn't a miracle. It was just that my mother's feeling of aversion was so great that she couldn't bear to touch his letters.

At Bathurst Teachers College I met a Chinese boy and my parents wouldn't even speak to him. Lots of nasty things were said and done, such as my sister shuddering her whole body and saying, 'How could you let him touch you?'.

That Chinese boy and I were good friends for a couple of years, but it was never going to last; we were both too immature. After that experience, my parents felt more comfortable with safe, conventional, respectable Wilfred.

AUTHOR   Do you ever have misunderstandings because your surname need not be Chinese?

JENNY   Yes, and it's difficult to know whether to explain. At one school, people were fairly racist — the conversation, the tone. For a whole year in the teachers' staff room, no one asked anything about me. What should I have done? Do I interrupt their racist-tinged conversation and say, 'By the way, my husband is Chinese'?

WILFRED   Deep down you always wonder about racism. I work for a Swiss firm, and there, I'm no worse than any Australian — I'm not Swiss. But perhaps I'm more different than most. One of my colleagues is a Fijian Indian, and our workmates' comment to him was 'At least you can be considered a Caucasian'.

Our children are both very quick to deny their mixed race. 'I'm not Chinese', they'll say. So they see it as something they want to disown.

JENNY   I think they see themselves as ordinary Australians, like their friends. People choose friends who are like themselves. Interracial friendships are still rare. I watch people at the shopping centre, and I enjoy seeing interracial couples, but I don't see many women — or men for that matter — in a racially-mixed group.

We're very close to Cherrybrook, with its enormous Chinese population. Cherrybrook is known locally as Chellyblook. I think everyone sees it as a joke, not thinking it racist at all. In a local coffee shop, I heard a group of women laughing about their Chinese neighbours. I felt like interrupting, but I didn't. Perhaps I should have.

AUTHOR   It's risky. You have to be prepared to embarrass people. I've done it. Once, I remember, when I felt I couldn't honourably avoid it. At a combined schools' concert to watch my son perform, the woman sitting next to me was watching her daughter. She was pleasant, and we chatted, and soon discovered we lived in the same street, a long street. She described where her house was, and in order to be sure I'd got it right I said, 'Oh, you mean next to that square, white two-storey house on the corner? I think it's just been sold'.

'Yes', she said, 'that's the one'.

'So you've got new neighbours', I continued chattily. 'I hope they're nice.'

'Nice?' she rasped. 'They're Indians! How would you like to live next door to a family of Indians?'

I gave it a few moments' thought, but in the end I felt constrained to answer, 'I wouldn't mind. I married one'.

'You what?' And the look she turned on me was one of distaste and horror.

JENNY So I was right to be wary of being upfront!

AUTHOR Her discomfort made me feel uncomfortable too. But she had asked me a question that had to be answered.

WILFRED Racism is everywhere — all races have it. I don't think Pauline Hanson changed anything. The undercurrent of prejudice hasn't changed in thirty years. The key to handling it is to learn acceptance. Travel and multiculturalism both help, and I think interracial marriage will help most of all.

3

INTERRACIAL MARRIAGES
FROM 1901 TO 1950

(W)e wish to see Australia the home of a great homogenous Caucasian
race, entirely free from the racial problems which have plunged the
United States into civil war

The *Age*, 1898

One of the first Bills passed by the new Federal Parliament in 1901 was the Immigration Restriction Act. It was acclaimed from all sides — Australia was the bastion of European civilisation in the southern hemisphere and in need of protection from being overrun. 'I don't think', said Australia's first Prime Minister, Edmund Barton, 'that the doctrine of the equality of man was really ever intended to include racial equality'.[1]

The leader of the Labor Party, JC Watson, added that his objection 'to the mixing of the coloured people with the white people of Australia ... lies in the main in the possibility and probability of racial contamination'.

The Brisbane Worker hailed the legislation as saving Australia from the coloured curse, and *The Bulletin* used typically graphic imagery to express its views on the matter of preserving the purity of the white race:

> [Australia] doesn't care whether he is black, or brown or bright green with red feet and a blue stripe down his back. So far from excluding the Asiatic solely on account of his colour, neither his race nor his colour have anything to do with the matter ... [Australia] objects to them ... because they intermarry with white women, and thereby lower the white type ...[2]

The Immigration Restriction Act of 1901 was the major discriminatory legislation underpinning the so-called White Australia Policy, and it remained in force until the Migration Act replaced it in 1959. The 1901 Act was an expression of the thinking of the times, in which Australia was not alone in trying to secure homogeneity within its borders. Nearly twenty years earlier the United States had passed the Immigration Exclusion Act to 'keep the nation pure', and other countries also enacted policies aimed at keeping their populations homogeneous.

The main means by which the Immigration Restriction Act enforced the so-called White Australia Policy was a dictation test, borrowed from Natal, in which officials could ask intending immigrants to translate a passage from any European language. Early legislators considered this test less openly offensive than an outright ban on the citizens of China, Japan and India — each a friend, trading partner or colony of Britain. Since any European language could be chosen, no matter how obscure — even Gaelic in one famous case — the dictation test was no less effective than a total ban. It did, however, allow for discretion in the admission of Maoris, some Indian wives and their foreign-born children, as well as sons and other assistants to work with Chinese businessmen.

From the beginning, the idea of an exclusively white European Australia was not supported by all Australians. In 1903 Edward Foxall used Biblical references to pour scorn on Australia's fears of being swamped by hordes of coloured aliens:

> Calmly viewed, the prejudice against a man's color is about the silliest emotion which a sentient being could cherish. There is more sense in religious bigotry than in Colorophobia. For, to a certain extent, at least, a man is responsible for his religion ... if he chooses he can change it. But he can no more help his color than he can help his height — Can any man, by taking much thought, add one cubit to his measure?[3]

In 1905 the Australian Labor Party expressed its policy as 'the cultivation of an Australian sentiment based upon the maintenance of racial purity'.

In 1901 there were about 47 000 non-Europeans in Australia — 1.25 per cent of the population — but in the next forty years that number declined steadily as many of the Afghan, Pacific Islander, Sri Lankan, Indian, Malay, Japanese and Chinese men who had not married returned home or died, and the families of those who had married Australians were absorbed into the white or Aboriginal communities and thus were no longer counted as non-European residents. Of course, there were other non-Europeans in Australia who had a prior claim to rightful residence, but it was not possible to count them. In addition, there were many uncounted, mixed-race people.

Douglas Lockwood gives a vivid picture of the plight of the increasing number of European/Aboriginal people in the Northern Territory prior to 1967:

> For the most part they had been educated and lived in the European community or on the fringes of it. They belonged to no tribe and were Aboriginal only to the extent that their veins carried varying quantities of Aboriginal blood. Yet for seventy years they were outcasts from the European community, stigmatised and controlled. Those who passed arbitrary tests in living standards, behaviour and education might apply for a licence to be free ... of the restrictive laws applying to Aborigines. This was known as the Dog Tag. Those who did not apply were legally classed as Aborigines. Alcohol was forbidden to them. They could not vote. They lived in a half-world of their own, belonging neither to the Aboriginal tribes nor the European society.[4]

Lockwood writes of the white Australian fathers who cared for their part-Aboriginal children, to emphasise the point that, in most cases, it was the unwillingness of white settlers, drovers, miners and others to take responsibility for their offspring that made the lives of the deserted Aboriginal women and their children so difficult, and led to many of the children being taken by government welfare agencies to be brought up and educated in missions and government children's homes.

In 1908 Stephen McGuiness went to mine tin sixty kilometres from Darwin and took his Aboriginal wife, Lucy, and their children with him. There he educated the children himself, after long hours underground. When the eldest son, Jack, was twelve, McGuiness died suddenly. Lucy had forsaken her tribe, so she could not return to her family. She went, with the younger children, to live in the Native Affairs' Kahlin Compound and worked as a cook, while Jack got a job as a stockman. In 1950 Jack McGuiness became the first president of the Half-Caste Progressive Association, which worked to remove all restrictions from part-Aboriginal people.

In the Gippsland forest country of Victoria in the early 1940s sawmiller Daryl Tonkin did what hundreds of other white Australian men did across the country: he set up house with the Aboriginal woman he loved. Daryl's brother and sister disapproved so violently that they kidnapped the woman, but Daryl rescued her and took her to a new camp, deep in the forest, where they could live safely and where they raised a large family. Much later, Daryl Tonkin wrote *Jackson's Track*, a book about how his beloved, forest-dwelling Aboriginals were dispossessed, and their way of life destroyed, by him and his fellow sawmillers.

Despite the Immigration Restriction Act some non-white immigrants did manage to enter Australia. One, a young Japanese art student, Moshi Inagaki, entered Australia and married Rose Caroline Allkins in December 1907. He painted and taught Japanese and refused to register as an alien until 1916, when wartime regulations forced him to do so. Rose, when she learned that, by virtue of her marriage to an alien, she too had become an alien, defiantly put 'British' in answer to the question about her nationality on the form she was required to fill in. Between the wars Rose continued to protest the loss of her citizenship, while Moshi taught Japanese language at Melbourne University extension classes. We know nothing of Rose's family or their attitude to her marriage, but making friends was probably difficult for the couple. Writing of Moshi's colleagues at the university, Rose recalled, 'Once back in 1934 or 1935 I thought it would be very nice if we did gather them around us but they all refused, so I did not try again'.

During World War 2 Moshi Inagaki was interned and Rose gave in and applied for naturalisation. At last this Australian-born, Australian woman was an Australian citizen again.[5]

To Melbourne in 1910 came a young man from China, probably as an assistant to a Chinese businessman or market gardener already resident here. Nearly forty years later the young immigrant was followed by his son, his daughter-in-law and their four sons. Two more sons were born to them in Australia. Paul, the second son, was the first to marry.

PAUL My mother was a progressive Chinese woman: it was she who encouraged Dad to migrate. I was nine when we landed in Melbourne and I became the only Chinese in a class of eighty-five kids! It was the late 1940s and in that big classroom there was only one Chinese and maybe two Italians, so yes, we were teased until they got to know us. Kids are cruel; they pick on kids with glasses, kids with red hair and kids who look different — as I did. Initially I hit back. Fisticuffs. Sometimes I won; sometimes I didn't. We forget how cruel kids are.

Several of the sons of mixed-race marriages whom I interviewed told a similar story, and during the race debate in the Senate in 1997, the people of Australia were reminded very publicly of how cruel children can be. Senator O'Chee, who is part-Chinese, told the Senate of children who dread playtime because with it they lose the safety of the classroom and are exposed to the terrors of the schoolyard. 'I was one of those children', he said.[6]

In Melbourne, while still remembering childhood taunts, Paul is philosophical about any discrimination he meets now.

PAUL I'm a physiotherapist and I do a lot of work for a football club. When I began twenty years ago, I'd occasionally get abuse from opposition teams and supporters — everyone does. If it wasn't my Chinese face it would have been something else. That's the nature of football.

I have never perceived prejudice from my colleagues, and rarely from patients. They depend upon me. If I strike trouble, it's usually from children. They're in a strange place and frightened, and I look strange to them.

AUTHOR Do you think of yourself as an Australian?

PAUL My thinking is Australian; my values perhaps a mix of both. If you want to be negative, you can say I don't belong anywhere. But I'm positive; I belong in both places. Yes, I'm Australian. This is where I belong. I wouldn't choose to live in Hong Kong.

AUTHOR How did your parents feel about your marriage to Paul, Bernadette?

BERNADETTE I'm a physio too, and when I met Paul at work I just liked him. I probably didn't mention to my family that he was Chinese, and when I brought him home, they almost died of shock.
     I've never felt discrimination or anything like that. Our marriage has been enriching for me. I embrace the Chinese culture, even though I cannot speak Chinese and we live like any Australian family.

PAUL When we are together, I notice odd looks from other Chinese. Bern is always surprised that Chinese people are prejudiced against our mixed marriage, but it is Chinese, in particular, who discriminate against us as a couple, both here in Australia and in Hong Kong.

BERNADETTE Chinese have always been regarded as very intelligent, and Chinese parents want the best education for their children. It must be a Chinese characteristic.

PAUL No, it's a characteristic of the underdog. It's a characteristic of people from countries that have never enjoyed high universal education. We Chinese do push our children.
     'Learn the facts, pass the exams, learn the facts, pass the exams.' That's the litany of Chinese parents. But people who are spoon fed in their facts don't necessarily learn to think. I like the Australian attitude to education better. Here there is less pressure and more encouragement to question things.

Paul's younger brother, Joe, was born in Australia and is now a doctor. He met Joy, his Anglo-Saxon Australian wife, while they worked together in Wangaratta Hospital.

JOY Once when Joe was the only doctor on duty, a fellow came in for a tetanus shot and, seeing Joe there, he just walked out again. He wouldn't be treated by a Chinese doctor.
     I forgot to mention to my family that Joe was Chinese, because only his face was different. In all other respects, his voice, his language and use of idiom, his behaviour, everything — he was so dinky-di Australian.
     When Joe called to pick me up the first time, he never made it into my parents' house. As he was crossing the front lawn my father saw him through the window and leapt out of his chair, yelping 'Bloody Chinese!'.
     I went out to meet Joe and we went on our outing. I didn't introduce Joe to my parents until his next visit, when they'd had time to get used to the idea.

Frederick Nell, a Sinhalese, brought his family from Ceylon in 1912. By 1928 his son had abandoned Buddhism to become an Anglican priest and married Margaret Turner of Inverell. 'I managed to get accepted by her father, an old-fashioned Englishman', he explained, 'by first giving aid to his beloved sheepdog'.[7]

Nineteen twenty-eight was also the year that Sydney and Melbourne newspapers splashed lurid headlines about a visiting black American band. Despite the popularity of their music, the musicians were evicted from their hotel and moved to a rented flat where they committed the horrible crime of dancing with white Australian girls. *Truth* breathlessly reported: 'The blinds were up ... the niggers and girls partly discarded their clothes and glistening black arms wound around white shoulders'.

Police raided the flat and charged the girls with vagrancy. On finding that they were shop assistants and milliners in paid work, this charge had to be dropped. However, before long the theatre cancelled the musicians' contract, while Ezra Norton, *Truth*'s owner, pushed for legislation making it an offence for a white woman to associate with 'Chinamen, Greeks and Asiatics'.[8] As late as the 1930s a custody case could be brought against an Australian woman for 'associating' with a Chinese man.[9]

Japan's entry into World War 2 re-awakened Australians' fears of the 'yellow hordes', but also introduced thousands of servicemen to other cultures. Until this time, geographic isolation meant that most Australians knew other peoples only through books and films. Face-to-face contact brought understanding and casual acceptance of other cultures and races, but the social taboo on mixed-race marriages remained. Australians felt very much at home with the philosophy of the American musical show *South Pacific* — a love story based on James Michener's tales set in World War 2's Pacific battle arena. The juvenile lovers are doomed because she is an islander; suicide is the only possible solution to their 'problem'. When the male romantic lead — an exotic European — admits to having had children with a 'native', this shocks the true-blue American female lead but doesn't ruin their romance, because the 'native' is now dead — i.e. she has been punished for her transgression.

In the early 1940s, too, Australia was facing up to the first marriages between black American servicemen and white Australian women with shock and dismay, and there was a general feeling of relief when most of the women followed their husbands back to the United States to live after the war ended.

In 1943 a Melbourne woman married Lorenzo Gamboa, a Filipino in MacArthur's American forces. Gamboa served with the Army of Occupation in Japan and became an American citizen. When he was demobilised in 1948, Australia's refusal to allow him re-entry to visit his Australian wife tarnished its reputation through-out south-east Asia. The Philippines threatened to sever diplomatic ties and the opprobrium was still bitter eight years later when one of Australia's first female diplomats, posted to our embassy in Manila, fell in love with another Filipino patriot.

Elizabeth and Tony told me how the trials of the Gamboas affected their own story, in their Canberra home forty years later.

TONY   When the Philippines was rebelling against Spain, we turned to the US for help, but instead of helping us, they took us over. The Philippines had become an autonomous commonwealth in 1935 but Japanese bombs rained down on the Philippines on the same day that Pearl Harbour was bombed. So we had to fight. In the jungle there were never enough guns, never enough ammunition, but in 1945 we raised our own flag. However, our country was still under America's thumb even when Elizabeth arrived in 1956 on a posting to the Australian Embassy.

AUTHOR   Elizabeth, you must have been among the first of Australia's women career diplomats.

ELIZABETH   One of the first.

TONY   And the prettiest. I was in love with her right from the beginning, but it took us seven long years. We couldn't marry until 1963.

ELIZABETH   The reason was partly financial. I was reluctant to give up my job, for in those days women were automatically retired from the Australian public service on marriage.

TONY   And I was not in a position to marry. I had a good job, but you know the kind of thing. The expats worked in air-conditioned offices, while we worked in the heat for half their salary and none of their perks.

ELIZABETH   At the end of my Philippines tour I came home and told my mother about Tony. She was not happy; she thought the change of lifestyle would be too difficult for me.

TONY   My father was not over-enthusiastic either, but I was 39 years old.

AUTHOR   He was probably glad to see you getting married at last!

ELIZABETH   I think that's right. When I returned to Manila to get married in 1963, Tony met me on the airport tarmac. His father was waiting to greet me halfway up the passenger concourse. I put out my hand and said, 'How do you do?' and met a blank stare.
Tony said, 'You may kiss him and call him Papa'.
I recall feeling most uncomfortable and not really welcome. However, most of Tony's relatives and friends were very kind.
I stayed with our Australian ambassador and his wife, Bill and Maidie Cutts, who gave us a magnificent wedding. The memory of the Gamboa case still rankled strongly in both official and private circles within the Philippines, so from a diplomatic point of view our wedding was valuable representation indicating, in a very public way, that not all Australians were racist.

AUTHOR   If you'd come back here to live in 1963, it may have been as difficult for you as it was for us. How was it in the Philippines?

ELIZABETH Very difficult. I think cross-cultural marriages are generally very difficult, but ours has certainly had worthwhile compensations.

TONY Affection for each other transcends everything else, and the children are so beautiful. We didn't have many friends, though I believe it helped that Elizabeth became a Catholic.

AUTHOR Perhaps it made it easier for the Filipinos to accept you, Elizabeth, once the church did.

ELIZABETH I suppose we were a difficult social mix. I often felt out of place. I didn't come back to visit Australia in all the years I lived in the Philippines — nearly thirty years. We set up our own export business and worked terribly hard because we wanted to be relatively affluent when we finally came to Australia.

Looking back, maybe I should have encouraged Tony to accept one of the overseas offers he had. But in those days well-brought up Australian wives followed and supported their husbands in whatever it was they wanted to do, and Tony was a passionate nationalist and wanted above all to contribute to his own country. So I helped him in that.

Both of us were involved politically. We were concerned about the poverty all around us and we thought at first that President Marcos's regime might introduce positive change, but conditions became disturbingly worse and worse, as Ferdinand and Imelda Marcos squeezed the economy for their own benefit and used graft, subterfuge and physical force to stay in power.

We took part in the final three-day demonstration on Epifanio Delos Santos (a six-lane thoroughfare) in support of the military coup that brought Cory Aquino into power. On that last night we camped out on the road at the point where it ran between the main entrance to Camp Aguinaldo (the Philippine Army headquarters) and the main entrance to Camp Cramer (the headquarters of the Philippines constabulary). Tony was worried about the possible use of mortars, but I was more concerned at how we would cope if armed troops came over the wall of Camp Aguinaldo just two or three metres from us.

Our children came out to go to university here and I followed in 1990. Tony was unable to join us until 1993, because the Australian health authorities declined to endorse his application for a visa, maintaining he had TB, which he did not. The effect of nearly two years' impasse over Tony's family reunion visa took its toll on all of us. But now we are all together again and enjoying living in Australia.

Sadly, Tony died not long after I met him, in July 1998. When Elizabeth told me of Tony's death she also told me a little of how he had fared during the few years he spent in Australia.

ELIZABETH It took Tony some time to move about with confidence after having a discriminatory experience when he arrived at Melbourne airport. However, the large number of Asians he met here, and the friendly associations in our church, as well as the warm acceptance by my family — who found him enchanting — served to erase the hurt of the inevitable negative experiences he occasionally encountered.

In 1947 Arthur Calwell, the Labor Government's Minister for Immigration, instigated the great immigration wave that changed

Australia's population. He provided berths on ships for war-weary migrants from Britain and northern Europe. These were the 'new Australians' of first choice, and among them was Eileen, one of the young Britons who responded to Australia's invitation for women to train as nurses. I spoke with Eileen and her husband, Herbert, an Australian-born Chinese who told part of his story in Chapter 1.

EILEEN My mother arranged my emigration in 1948. I never asked her why. I just did what I was told. As an ex-servicewoman my passage was free; others paid ten pounds. I was twenty-three, and on my first day as a trainee nurse in a tuberculosis sanatorium I met Herb. He was a patient and he was playing the piano. I liked him immediately. The fact that he was Chinese didn't worry me at all.

Herb was cured of TB and went home. Then I caught it. When I decided to marry Herb, I knew that my parents would be furious, but they were 12 000 miles away.

HERB My mother thought I could do better, too. Eileen was sick and she had no money.

AUTHOR Have you been aware of any prejudice shown you, as a mixed-race couple?

EILEEN Only once, years ago, while holidaying at Mt Kosciuszko. An English family from Malaysia would not speak to me. We were standing in a group and they were both chatting to Herb. I asked a question and the man just looked through me, deliberately indicating that he would not deign to answer a creature who had so demeaned herself as to marry an Asian. Yet they were perfectly happy to chat to Herb!

HERB I've met very little prejudice in my life. I got on well in business. I've had to confront very aggressive people at meetings, so I pretend to be naïve, malleable, as if I am unsure of myself. If I couldn't get what I wanted straight away, I'd delay a decision, suggesting we leave it on the table. In the end I usually got what I wanted.

EILEEN Herb, you're building up a stereotype of the wily Oriental!

HERB The Jews and the Chinese in Australia have made a lot of money because we're very clever at business. That causes resentment, even hate, but it really has nothing to do with race.

EILEEN Over the years a few people have asked me things like, 'Couldn't you find an Australian to marry?'. I've learnt to reply: 'I married an Australian'.

As well as the British and northern European migrants of first choice, Australia received shiploads of 'displaced persons', refugees from war-ravaged countries throughout Europe. These people were accepted 'without discrimination of race or religion' and immediately had equality in law, just as all former immigrants had had. These refugees from post-war Europe qualified for Australian citizenship after five years. At the same time, the Chifley Government was moving to deport other war-time refugees: those who had escaped to Australia during the Japanese conquest of south-east Asia. Some had already married Australians, but they and their families were deported despite the public protests. Arthur Calwell must have believed that he was expressing public opinion when he vowed that the 'flag of White Australia will not be lowered'.

A Queensland woman who had married an Indonesian refugee during the war years, and thus, according to the laws of the day, was no longer an Australian citizen herself, accompanied her Indonesian husband back to Indonesia when he was deported. There she found that as a Christian Australian, neither she nor her English-speaking children were welcome in her husband's village. With return to Australia impossible, she circumvented the wrath of the villagers around her by 'becoming Indonesian'. She discarded every trace of her former ways of thinking, worship, manners, language, clothing and hairstyle; everything that might distinguish her and her children as white foreigners. The transformation was so complete that her younger children never learned to speak English, and when she returned to Australia after her husband's death forty years later, her own English was rusty and unreliable.

Another Indonesian refugee, Mrs O'Keefe — who married and was then widowed in Australia — refused to leave when deported and appealed to the High Court, which ruled that since Mrs O'Keefe had not been issued with a temporary permit (and most refugees had not) it could not be cancelled. The Labor Government's response was to pass special legislation to allow the expulsion of what Arthur Calwell called 'this recalcitrant minority'. The War-time Refugee Removal Act of 1949 was directed at repatriating all non-European refugees, irrespective of whether they were aliens or British subjects, and irrespective of whether they had married Australian spouses and already had Australian-born children.

From the SBS television series 'Tales from a Suitcase', I learned that one of Calwell's recalcitrant minority, a refugee who had British Crown Colony citizenship, had been deported. After fighting in the courts to beat a second deportation order, he now lived in a Sydney beachside suburb with his Australian wife of fifty-five years. When I visited them, Samad and Mavis showed me the video of the television episode highlighting details of their lives, and told me their love story.

SAMAD I was born in a village near Malacca, when it was a British Crown Colony. My mother was a teacher in a Malay school, but I went to an English-language school. Later I served as a Royal Naval Cadet. In late 1941 I was working on a minesweeper when the Japanese bombed us in Singapore Harbour. I was lucky to get another ship — to Batavia — but by the time we arrived Japanese bombs were falling there too.

Japanese submarines were sinking ships travelling in convoy so we sailed very close to the coast, always heading south. We didn't go ashore at Broome; we didn't know that the Japs were not there too. We followed the Australian coast down to Fremantle.

I had just the shirt and trousers I wore, because we had thrown everything over-board to lighten the ship's load. On Fremantle wharf the Red Cross and the Salvation Army gave us everything we needed — food and clothes and many things. Some people invited us to their homes. Everyone was very kind. It was a wonderful welcome to Australia.

We learned that the Japanese had taken Singapore, and we had nowhere to go. The Australian Government took us over and we sailed around the coast to Sydney where I joined a troop ship to Milne Bay.

On the second trip Japanese bombers began falling as we unloaded the troops. Many were killed — blood and broken bodies were everywhere. I woke up in the hospital — a US hospital, because they thought I was Filipino. After three months they sent me to Townsville Hospital, and then to Brisbane. As soon as I was fit enough I came to Sydney and stayed at the Sailors Home in Millers Point. That's where I met Mavis.

MAVIS   I worked in a shop, and Samad came in and asked me to go to the pictures with him. Some people looked at us funny. In a tram once people were rude to Samad, and some of my friends turned up their noses and said, 'Fancy going out with a Chinaman!'. But I didn't care.

I was only seventeen, so I had to get my mother's permission before we could marry.

AUTHOR   Your mother must have been a very liberal-minded woman. For at that time, in war-time, when the country was threatened by Japan, racism was probably at its strongest in Australia.

MAVIS   Some people disapproved. People were very critical in 1943, but really it was only between Samad and I. I knew it might be difficult, but it is important to marry who you want, and we were sure. Three months later we were married.

SAMAD   I didn't go back to the war. It took me months to recover my strength; my injuries were huge. So after Mavis and I were married, I worked on ships around the coast until the Manpower Office sent me to a textile company in Botany.

Our first baby, Merriam, died, and then Omar, our eldest son, was born. When the war ended I was deported. It was the White Australia Policy and I was a non-European alien. The textile company where I worked offered to put up a 100-pound bond so I could stay, but the Immigration people wouldn't accept it.

MAVIS   They came and took Samad away as if he was a criminal. He was in his pyjamas, and they didn't even want to let him put his clothes on. They locked him up. I could never understand it. Samad was a British subject, born in a British colony. He'd been wounded by the Japanese while carrying Australian troops. Yet he was called an alien.

They said they'd pay my way to Malacca, too. They told me I wasn't a citizen anymore. Not an Australian because I'd married Samad! I couldn't vote or anything. I'd lost all my rights. I still find it hard to believe.

SAMAD   After the Japanese Occupation things were too bad to take Mavis back to Malacca. I went back alone, but I soon joined a ship coming back to Australia. When it got to Sydney I just left the ship and came home. I got a job, and we were happy for a while, until someone reported me. The Immigration Department had to follow it up and deport me again. It was the law.

MAVIS   They took him straight away, and said I had to pay 200 pounds for him to get bail. I didn't have 200 pounds, hardly 200 pennies, and no way of getting it unless I sold the goodwill on our rented house. You could do that in those early post-war days when housing was so scarce. I was working in a kindergarten at the time, and one of the fathers belonged to the RSL. He said he would help. They saved the house for me, and put up the money for the bail, so Samad could come home.

The RSL and the Ironworkers' Union and the World Council of Churches decided to fight Samad's case in court. They raised money. People everywhere held concerts and all sorts of fundraising functions, as well as the money they gave.

AUTHOR Yet the trade unions were strong supporters of the White Australia Policy ... not to mention the RSL.

SAMAD By that time I belonged to a trade union and the RSL recognised that I had been wounded by the Japs at Milne Bay, so they — and the churches — put up money to pay the lawyers.

MAVIS We won the court case in August 1949 and I was given back my rights. Suddenly I was an Australian again, and so was Samad.

The inflexibility of the Chifley Government in the matter of deporting war-time refugees is only understandable if one remembers how soon it followed the very real danger of Japanese invasion and the anti-Asian propaganda of the war years (combined with the average Australian's tendency to lump all 'Asians' together).

In December 1949, only four months after Samad and Mavis won their court action, the Liberal Party won government and honoured an election promise not to implement the Refugees Removals Act. All 800 Asian refugees who were still in Australia were granted permanent residence.

Omar was the eldest of five surviving children of Mavis and Samad. I spoke to the youngest daughter, Carol, who grew up in the 1950s and 1960s amid the white Anglo-Australian population of a Sydney Housing Commission area. Married with children of her own, Carol is now the head teacher of an Intensive English Centre.

CAROL I started out teaching steelworkers' children in Wollongong, most of them from non-English-speaking backgrounds. Their problems interested me because I've seen how Dad's life has been made so much harder because his English is not perfect.

AUTHOR When you were small there must have been very few mixed-race children. Did you suffer because of this?

CAROL Never. My older brother, who grew up in Palmer Lane, experienced prejudice, but we moved to Chifley when I was three, and I cannot remember being the butt of any discrimination, not even teasing. We were just one family among others struggling to set up house in a Housing Commission area. Had Mum been Malay as well, things might have been harder, but Mum was a good neighbour and a good manager, so people came to her for help.

Mum's decision to accept the Muslim faith must have been very hard. She was a Presbyterian, but for Dad's sake she gave up that and became a Muslim. She adopted the Muslim name of Mina and made sure we kids knew the rules of Islam — she felt she owed Dad that. But she sent us children to Sunday school at the Presbyterian church.

At high school the playground had a pecking order. The Aboriginal children from the settlement at La Perouse were on the bottom, then the Greek children from Bunnerong, then the Italians, then the Anglo-Saxons. So I just fitted in at the edges and was hardly noticed. Dad didn't teach us Malay, because he wanted us to be Australians. All my playmates and schoolmates were white Australians. We spent our days at the beach. I didn't see Dad's Malay heritage as being part of my life until very recently.

The only blatant prejudice I came across was to do with Dad. When I was about fifteen, I worked in a delicatessen after school, and one day my dad came in. When the owners of the place saw that he was Asian, I was sacked. They told me they didn't like Asians because of the war. I don't think I ever told my parents why I left that job. Even then I felt that Dad had been hurt enough.

AUTHOR   You noticed your father hurting, even though you felt no discrimination yourself?

CAROL   Oh, yes. Dad worked at the same place for years and years, yet they never called him by his name. They called all Asians 'Peter'. When my brother, Omar, went to work at the factory with Dad, they called him 'Little Peter'. Omar didn't mind; he was very entrenched in Australian culture and glad to have an Australian-sounding name because it fitted who he was.

My mother gave the boys Malay names to honour Dad's heritage, but Dad gave the girls Australian names because he wanted to minimise any difference. Dad was right. My brother Rahman is called Ray; he's much more comfortable with the Australian part of his heritage. So am I. I'm glad people just call their children a pretty name these days. It's a little step towards removing barriers between people.

I guess you could say we are all very definitely Australian, which is exactly what Dad wanted. All except Margaret, who married a Malay, became a Muslim and now lives in Malaysia. She adopted a Muslim name for her life in Malaysia, but when she comes for a visit, she's still Margaret.

Dad worked six or seven days a week for all the years we were growing up; he wanted so badly to give us a good life. Mum and Dad did a good job. We are okay. Although geographically split, we're still a close family. How many ordinary Australian families can say that?

4

INTERRACIAL MARRIAGES IN THE 1950s

We must marry them to enrich our gene pool.

<u>Sir Macfarlane Burnet, 1959[1]</u>

When the Liberal/Country Party Coalition won government in late 1949 it adopted a more liberal stance towards Asians in Australia and also eased the restrictions on Asian immigration. At the 1950 Citizenship Convention the new Prime Minister, Robert Menzies, said: 'We must strike down at its very conception the rather insular tendency ... to object to a man because of his race or his religion — to raise matters of sectarianism or racialism ...'. 'If I do not want a man to come to my country to live, then I must keep him out. If I let him in, then he must be a member of my national family.'[2]

When viewed from fifty years on, the Menzies era is seen by many Australians as somewhat rigid and race-conscious, but it was Menzies' Coalition Government that began to whittle away at the edges of the White Australia Policy. After his government's decision not to implement the previous Labor Government's Refugees Removal Act, the External Affairs Minister, Percy Spender, spoke in Singapore of Australia as a bridge between Asia and the West. Australia's immigration policy was then relaxed to allow the entry of 'highly qualified and distinguished Asians'. Many diplomats posted to Australia, and businessmen with interests here, took advantage of this provision to stay in Australia and make it their home.

In relation to mixed-race marriages, there were three other policy changes that were even more significant:

- The introduction of the Colombo Plan, which provided for the entry of large numbers of Asian students into Australia.

- The decision to allow part-Europeans from India (Anglo-Indians) and Sri Lanka (Burghers) to immigrate when their countries became independent after Britain's withdrawal.

- The special legislation that allowed the entry of Japanese wives of Australians serving with the British Commonwealth Occupation Force in Japan.

The Australian Army authorities serving with the British Commonwealth Occupation Force in Japan did everything possible to discourage personnel from engaging in romantic relationships, enforcing strict non-fraternisation rules and warning soldiers that they would possibly not be permitted to take their fiancées back to Australia. There was no provision for either the Australian Consul or Australian Army chaplains to conduct marriages between Australians and foreigners. From 1945 to 1952, no marriages conducted under Japanese law were recognised as legal in Australia, thus the only authority able to perform a marriage ceremony between an Australian soldier and a Japanese woman — a marriage that would be legally recognised in Australia — was the British Consul, and he often seemed unwilling to do so.[3]

Despite these hurdles, from the beginning of the Occupation there were clandestine romances and liaisons, for these men had already experienced months or years of wholly male company in battle or in camp. When the fighting was over, they sought female company. Several men, in love with Japanese women, returned to Australia, obtained a discharge, then applied for their Japanese fiancées to join them; others went to Canada where their Japanese fiancées could join them and be married there.

In Tokyo, when Army sergeant Bill fell in love with Pat, the Japanese clerk who delivered his mail, military officials sent him back to Australia to consult his parents in Mildura. Unless they confirmed, by letter, that they approved of their son's marriage and would provide accommodation for him and his Japanese wife, there would be no marriage. Bill's parents were not enthusiastic, but his powers of persuasion triumphed. He returned to Japan with the all-important letter.

Back in Japan, negotiations proceeded with Pat's family. Pat's mother had been killed during the war, in the bombing of Yokohama when their house and everything in it was destroyed. Her father did not exactly welcome Bill as a husband for his daughter, but her sister and grandmother did, so Bill and Pat decided to take the matter into their own hands. They married three times — first in a Japanese registry office; then they stood before the British consul in Kobe to get the marriage certificate that was registered in England

and legally recognised in Australia; then Bill insisted on a church wedding, 'because that's what really makes a marriage'.

After receiving many requests from families of soldiers wanting to marry and bring their Japanese wives home to Australia, the government put up the Validation of Marriages Bill giving approval for Army chaplains to perform marriages for Australian service personnel on foreign soil, and on 9 May 1952 the embassy in Tokyo advised that the Australian Government had approved the admission of Japanese wives of Australian servicemen into the country, provided all enquiries confirmed that the soldier was of good character, that he could support his wife and family, and that the Japanese wife 'was of a type that would be readily accepted by the community in general'. The Kure Municipal Police were to screen the women and 'submit a report on whether she had been a communist, a prostitute, had a criminal record, and whether there was any sign of insanity in her family'. In addition, the wife needed to have a very thorough medical examination and obtain a statement that she was of good character.[4]

After learning Japanese at school in Canberra, Ted had served as an officer interrogating captured Japanese soldiers in the islands, and then after the war joined the Department of Foreign Affairs and was sent to serve in Japan. Ted told me his story.

TED   When I was consular officer, it was thought in Australia that no foreigner could meet a Japanese girl except in a bar or some other sleazy place. That impression was quite wrong. Many of the young fellows had met some very nice girls. When they came to see me about getting married, I found many of the chaps didn't speak Japanese, and many of the girls did not speak English.

AUTHOR   Could one have a courtship without language?

TED   With Japanese you can. They have obligations in a fixed fashion. The parents were often glad for their daughters to marry foreigners — happy to be relieved of the worry of marrying off a daughter, without cost. The chaps knew the problems about taking their wives back to Australia.

Ted has lived in Japan or been closely connected with it ever since. He has served as Trade Commissioner in Tokyo, and later ran his own business there. In 1985 Ted married Taeko; they live in Canberra now, but as Taeko says, she remains very much a Japanese person.

In the 1950s Australians still reeled from revelations of the atrocities suffered by their sons and husbands and brothers in Japanese prison camps. Dame Enid Lyons, widow of a former Prime Minister and one of the very few female members of Parliament, wrote an article in *Australian Woman's Day* in which she posed the question: 'Do you think it fair that Australians should be expected to accept Japanese wives of Australian soldiers?'. And she gave her answer. She believed that women on both sides of the battle had taken part in the war, and that all Japanese could not be blamed for the horrific behaviour of the prison camp guards.

She then addressed the general problem of mixed-race marriage: 'Whether or not it is wise for people of different races to marry is a question that may well be argued … [but] the number of Australian soldiers contracting such marriages are very few, and the number of half-castes resulting will be so small as to be negligible in the general population'. She went on: 'Life for them, either in Australia or Japan will not be easy, especially while feeling still runs high'.

It was not easy for Cherry Parker. Cherry married Gordon Parker early in the Occupation of Japan and she was the first Japanese bride to arrive in Australia, early in 1952. Following her arrival, she and her husband were subjected to six months of abusive letters and telephone calls. But Cherry proved to be a good ambassador for the brides who were to follow her. When Bill and Pat arrived, later in 1952 with most of the other 300 or so Japanese brides, they met no abuse, and very little unpleasaness.

PAT All the time I have been here, I haven't met any unpleasantness. At first I was lonely, staying home with the children when they were small. Then, later I started teaching at Melbourne University temporarily, and stayed twenty-five years. I've had a great deal of companionship, satisfaction and happiness there.

AUTHOR Did your children have any difficulties?

PAT Yes. I think the eldest, the boy, did. Teasing. He looked different and he felt different. He was clever, and perhaps he was shy. But he had a lot of friends. They're all grown up and doing well now.

BILL Mum had not been keen when I told her I wanted to marry a Japanese girl. 'It's your problem, son', she said. But then, when I brought Pat home, they treated her like a daughter. Once I left some clothes lying around and Mum tore into me. 'Pat's not your housemaid here', she said.

PAT Bill's family were very good to me.

AUTHOR I am pleased, but surprised, Bill, that your parents welcomed Pat so warmly, for there was a lot of ill feeling against the Japanese brides among country people. Only twenty miles away from your home, and four years later, my parents used every ounce of parental pressure trying to dissuade me from marrying Joshua.

BILL It's because I'm a bloke. Sons are seen as responsible for their own lives, 'specially in the country. Daughters aren't — or weren't. It's easier to welcome a small pretty girl, too, than to welcome a big foreign-looking bloke.

In the 1950s some parents did find it difficult to welcome a 'big, for-eign-looking bloke' into their families, but forty years later time had softened what can only be called racist antagonism. In the early 1990s Jeannie, a social worker who took her family to the Northern Territory because she 'didn't want to live and die in a small Victorian town', accepted the challenge.

JEANNIE   Leila brought him home when she was eighteen — a big Torres Strait Islander with a history of alcoholism and violence. We were apprehensive because, of course, people had let us know his history. But despite his past, he was most polite and respectful towards us, and we liked him. After a few months Leila asked us if he could move in. Well, our house was quite small, and with the two of us, two teenage sons and Leila, it was already crowded. But in the end we decided that we'd rather have her with us so we'd be around for support if she needed it.

They stayed with us for about two years, and all that time he has been a pleasure to have in the house. He has given up alcohol and wants to marry Leila now that she is twenty-one. She seems reluctant to commit herself, and in the end she decided to visit him on his home island for three months to see if she can fit in there. She's there now, helping him and his family build a church.

Later, Jeannie wrote that Leila was back home, alone. She had learned a lot, particularly about how difficult it is to be the outsider in a close-knit community.

Allan and Teri came to Australia on the Japanese bride ship with Bill and Pat in 1952.

ALLAN   My mother's brother was killed by the Japanese in a prison camp in Java, so when I wrote to my mother to tell her I was thinking of marrying a Japanese girl, there was hell to pay. The last thing she wanted was a Japanese daughter-in-law.

I could understand how she felt but I wasn't going to give up on marrying Teri, so I considered joining the American Army. Weren't we lucky not to walk into that situation? They're far more racist than anything we know here.

We were all told we had to go home before the election, for if Labor got in with Calwell as Immigration Minister, our wives might never be able to go to Australia. So nearly everyone was married in 1952 and the Army arranged to get us all home before the election. As it happened, the Liberals got in again, with Harold Holt as Immigration Minister, so it needn't have been such a rush. But I'd been in Japan seven years. It was long enough.

I needn't have worried about how my mother and Teri would get on, either. 'Oh you poor little thing', my mother greeted her, 'you must be starving'. And Mum started to teach Teri how to cook and do housework and that sort of thing. And Dad was fantastic. Teri learned more about my dad and his exploits in France in the First World War than he'd ever told me — or anyone.

After four years Teri applied for naturalisation. I was working the day of the cere-mony, but my father bought her a new hat and dress, and off they went to the city hall, and she became an Australian citizen with my father — an old World War 1 digger — there to cheer her through it.

AUTHOR What about you, Teri, were your parents happy about your marriage?

TERI My father was dead. He'd lived in America and later he ran an American-type restaurant in Japan, so we were Westernised. My mother was happy, because I'd already refused to let her arrange a Japanese marriage for me. I didn't want to be a slave to my husband. That's what women in Japan are — third-class citizens.

ALLAN I was turned off Australian girls, too, after the one I had ditched me. In the middle of the New Guinea campaign she sent my ring back with a 'Dear John' letter.

In Japan I was pretty lonely, till a friend took me to Teri's mother's beer shop. She was a great lady. After her husband died she'd set up the shop to earn a living with the beer ration from her husband's restaurant. Anyway, I met Teri there, and soon we began to live together.

When we came back here, there were never any problems of discrimination or anything like that. There were already a lot of European migrants in the area. We were all too busy to worry about race. Everyone was trying to build or buy a house. Dad had started building this house on the block next door to his, so when I arrived home, he sold it to me. This house and shed became the centre of the neighbourhood kids' activities, just as my father's house had been the centre for their parents.

When my son was just a kid, I'd said, we're going to settle in Australia as Australians, and to hell with Japanese culture, so he was brought up totally Australian. I was wrong, and when he was about twenty we sent him to Japan on a work permit, and he learned to speak Japanese there. He's so big, he was called a sumo, so whether here or in Japan, no one would say anything rude to him!

While Australians were accepting the Japanese wives of their former fighting men rather better than Dame Enid Lyons had expected, other interracial couples were finding faces turned against them.

In a *Sydney Morning Herald* interview Aboriginal arts administrator Rhoda Roberts spoke of how small-town Australia in the 1950s was not ready for a marriage between her mother, a Sunday school teacher from solid Anglo-Celtic stock and her father, the Church of Christ pastor from the local Bandjalong people. In the eyes of Lismore's white community, her mother's status changed overnight, from respectable young lady to cheap trash when she married an Aborigine. The significance of her parents' brave but unconventional match did not dawn on Rhoda until a visiting minister lectured the congregation about the evils of mixed-race marriages. Teenage Rhoda heard the man of God proclaim that children of such marriages were the spawn of the devil.[5]

Another Australian couple who entered a mixed-race marriage in the 1950s was more fortunate than Rhoda's parents. Unlike Lismore on the lush New South Wales north coast, Bendigo, the Victorian mining town, has seen and accommodated mixed-race marriages for over a hundred years.

Russell Jack — an Australian-born Chinese who had a white Australian great-grandmother — is the instigator, fundraiser, creator and director of Bendigo's famed Golden Dragon Museum, while his wife, Joan — descended from Anglo-Celtic convicts of the second fleet — is the award-winning curator of the museum that has taken over their lives. Joan embraced her husband's culture and lifestyle, though she learned that it was not easy to be accepted by the Chinese community if one had a white face.

JOAN When I told my mother I was going to a dance with Russell Jack, she said, yes, she had known the family since before I was born — though Russell and I had not met earlier. There was no problem.

AUTHOR Was it usual in the 1950s for a 16-year-old Australian girl to go to a dance with a Chinese boy?

JOAN In Bendigo, we all knew a Chinese family or two. Russell's being Chinese didn't worry me. Actually, I never liked Australian men. They were always in a pub, drinking. I wanted more out of life than a man coming home half-drunk and demanding a meal.

RUSSELL The Chinese integrated into the mainstream white population early here in Bendigo. Way back in 1865 Australians and Chinese got together to raise money for charity. Many of us married Australian girls, and my family in particular played a lot of sport, which breaks down barriers.

AUTHOR What about your children?

JOAN Our son was nicknamed Hop Sing at school because 'Bonanza' was on TV. He didn't mind. Sometimes nicknames can be cruel but not always. A little boy named Kong stayed with us and at school he was called King Kong. He loved it!

Here in Bendigo many people of mixed ancestry try to hide it. One of Russell's relations did that, and when their daughter was about ten she came home from school, crying, 'Why didn't you tell me you were Chinese? I hate you being Chinese'.

RUSSELL Australian kids soon won't care what shape or colour their faces are. We grew up speaking only English, but now Chinese language is taught at school here. That's an improvement.

JOAN But English is even more important, because you speak real Australian English, and that's why you fit in so well with everyone here. It's one of the reasons you and I communicate so well, too.

Our house is a Chinese house, though. My daughter's English boyfriend finds it very hard to adapt to our noisy way of life. They come up from Melbourne for the weekend and there'll be lots of shouting and calling one another strange names, because we address one another in the Chinese equivalent of grandmother, sister, etcetera. He says he can't tell them apart and he finds it all so noisy.

AUTHOR Yet you adapted to this, after an ordinary Australian childhood.

JOAN It just happened step by step, though I did throw myself into it, rather. I learned to cook Chinese, shop in Chinese shops, and we always eat with chopsticks. When the children were born, the elders of the Chinese community named them, and when we built our house, it was built according to Chinese ideas. Yes, I adopted Russell's culture completely.

AUTHOR Did the Chinese welcome you into their community?

JOAN No, they did not. As a European woman, it was very hard to break into the Chinese circle, even though I was happy to fit in and change over to the Chinese way of doing things.

Our son died in an accident when he was twenty and I had him buried with all Chinese rites. I'm going to be buried in the Chinese style too. I've told all my Chinese friends not to let me be buried the Christian way.

RUSSELL Most Chinese say that Joan is more Chinese than the ones with Chinese faces. But no matter how we live our private lives, we're still part of this town, part of the Australian culture. I think that's important.

AUTHOR Are the Chinese of Bendigo all Australian-born Chinese of generations ago? Or have some of the recent migrants come here to live in this town where the races mix so easily?

JOAN The local churches got houses for Vietnamese refugees and fixed them up. We did everything we could to welcome them into the town, but they wouldn't stay. They missed the bright lights of the city. They went straight back to Melbourne. People who come here to Australia to live don't always feel they should adjust to our way of doing things, yet when I travel overseas I fit in with whatever they do. If they sleep on the floor, then I sleep on the floor too.

AUTHOR Sometimes it's Australians who can't adjust. An Australian/Chinese man living in the poshest part of town got on well with his wealthy neighbours, and was surprised to find that when visitors to the house next door, seeing him in the garden, remarked on the Chinese neighbour, their host explained his presence by saying, 'Yes, he's the gardener; a good chap, he does our garden too'.

JOAN That happens to me! Sometimes people coming to see me, say, 'Your gardener does a good job', or 'We've just been talking to the gardener'. And I say, 'That is my husband'.

AUTHOR So there's stereotyping, even here?

RUSSELL I've got too much Aussie grit in me to let them get away with real insults, though. At the service station down the road where we always bought our petrol the man grizzled about going to the hospital and having to see a Chinese doctor — to me! We never bought our petrol there again.

Following the post-World War 2 abandonment of colonies by the European powers, countries to our north became independent nations, and some part-European citizens of India and Sri Lanka sought asylum in Commonwealth countries. Australia agreed to accept some Anglo-Indians and also Dutch Burghers — the part-Dutch, part-Portuguese or part-English citizens of Sri Lanka — under very stringent conditions that included written documentation that applicants were of more than 50 per cent European blood. The Australian High Commissioner in Colombo was also charged with ensuring the Burghers looked substantially white — i.e., that their skin colour was fair enough to allow them to blend into Australian society of the 1950s.

At least one official at the Australian High Commission in Colombo was colourblind, for Keith, who came with his Burgher family, would much more easily pass as 100 per cent Sri Lankan. He told me his father's skin colour is even darker, but it has not hindered their integration into Australia.

KEITH   I was six or seven when we came to Australia; we were the only coloured kids in the school. School started at 9.00 am, and at 10.30 I got into my first fight. We were hauled in front of the head teacher. The other guy got the strap, and by lunchtime we were all friends again. In 1967 we had a novelty value, and if you were prepared to establish yourself, you never had to fight again.

Although I know my skin is very dark, I have never thought of myself as black. Sometimes, when I was in my teens, people gave me a hard time by putting on an Indian accent, but for many years now I have thought of myself as an Australian, and have been treated as such.

AMY (KEITH'S AUSTRALIAN WIFE)   I met Keith at school. My parents lived in a very multicultural area and didn't object to our marriage at all; it was not an issue for them as long as I was happy. Some funny things happened, though. One marriage celebrant we saw spoke only to me, then he'd turn to Keith and raise his eyebrows, and ask, 'Okay?' slowly.

When our first child was born, one of Keith's relatives took my dad aside and said, 'Well, at least the baby's not too dark'. My dad was upset to think my baby's skin colour was an issue. But we have never been offended by things like that. We don't really think about it much at all.

KEITH   My parents expected me to marry an Australian, I think. They brought us here to be Australians, and that's what we are — my brothers and I.

AUTHOR   Are your parents still pleased they came to Australia?

KEITH   Oh yes. Mum went back for a holiday and we offered to pay for Dad to go too. He said, 'No. Australia is my home'.

Over there Mum did nothing but manage nannies and housekeepers and gardeners. Here she had to learn about cooking and cleaning in a little flat with three kids and no money. It was a very brave thing to do, but my mother has never regretted coming.

Any person coming to Australia has to learn to adjust to cultural differences. But that can often be a positive thing, leading to new experiences. I have lived here most of my life so it is not an issue in our marriage.

From the late 1940s Australia recognised a duty to assist in the development of the newly-independent former colonies, particularly with education. Under the Colombo Plan, students from Asian countries were encouraged, and in some cases were funded, to study at Australia's schools and universities. In putting out the welcome mat for a prolonged visit by young Asians, the bureaucrats understood that they were bringing young people, mostly men, to our shores just when they were of an age to marry. It must have come as no surprise when so many of them did.

The government policy in the early 1950s was not to grant registration to British subjects of non-European origin, nor to non-European spouses of Australian women, although Australian wives were now able to retain their citizenship. In 1956 these provisions were modified and in 1957 non-Europeans who had been in Australia for fifteen years could become citizens (the waiting time for immigrants of European origin was, at that time, five years). Between 1955 and 1965 nearly 3500 non-Europeans were naturalised and 1500 British subjects of non-European origin were registered. The government went as far and as fast in the direction of liberalising racial restrictions on immigration as it felt the electorate would accept. The historic 1901 Immigration Restriction Act was superseded by the 1959 Migration Act. The dictation test was abolished, along with all reference to race or nationality. Instead, an entry permit was granted at the Immigration Minister's discretion.

Meanwhile, the Colombo Plan students who married young Australian women in the early 1950s were still foreigners who had to return to their own country when their course of study was complete, though it was not long before changes were made to remove these restrictions. Soon after our marriage in 1956, when my husband went along to have his student permit extended for three months to allow him to complete the last few months of practical experience following his degree, he was offered permanent residency, 'because your wife is Australian'. At that time, my husband was not interested in staying in Australia; he planned to return home to Singapore. He refused the offer of permanent residence.

Perhaps the government of the day moved faster than many citizens could accept, for in the same year that my husband was offered permanent resident status, the staff common room of the school where I taught regularly resonated with groans of concern about 'yellow hordes advancing from the north', from an Italian Australian. In that same common room, I was drawn reluctantly into an argument with another teacher, a middle-aged English migrant who had lived much of her life in Jamaica and spoke scathingly of the various non-European peoples she had lived among while there. 'They're of a lower breed. They're everywhere over there now, even in high positions, but you don't actually mix with them. You don't invite them to your home!'

I protested mildly about her blanket prejudice against whole groups of people simply because they had different coloured skin, until she said in haughty, plummy tones, 'You don't know what it's like. You know nothing about what these people are like'.

'I do', I said. 'I married one of them ...'

What followed was quite a battle, and I felt somewhat guilty because I knew her position, whereas she had not been aware of mine. My status in the common room rose significantly after I trounced her, but I have never known whether my arguments convinced the rest of the staff to be colourblind, or whether they were just glad to see one of their own discomfit the pompous Britisher.

We went to live in Singapore just at the time when that country was moving from British-appointed legislators to its own fully-elected parliament. My husband was excited and proud to be involved in Singapore's emergence as a democracy. When our first two children were born there, I, as their Australian mother, could not register them as Australian citizens at the Australian High Commission; only Australian fathers had that right. We soon realised, too, that democracy had not taken root in Singapore, and came to believe that a place with such a dominant non-Christian Chinese culture was not the place we would choose to bring up Christian Australian/Sinhalese-Indian children, even though they were born in Singapore.

We began to think about where in the world we would fit in. Another couple, an English woman and her husband, a Ceylonese/Malaysian doctor who had studied in Australia, joined us in poring nightly over atlases, histories and current affairs journals, seeking some place in the world where all races were treated equally and with dignity. Three of us knew Australia intimately, and we all considered that Australia in 1959 did not fit the guidelines. The two men had been subjected to gross racism during their years in Australia as students and I, a fourth-generation Anglo-Celtic Australian, had been the surprised victim of bigotry for the year I had lived in Adelaide after my marriage. I vividly recalled seeking in vain for a flat, when we were about to be married, and being rebuffed time after time with, 'No, I don't want those sorts of people living on my property!' when landlords learned that my husband-to-be was an Asian student. The pain of my father's refusal to come to my wedding, and the hurt caused by friends' refusal to visit me after I married, was still very fresh.

The country we decided upon was Brazil. We set ourselves to learn Portuguese and save the capital to emigrate there, but long before we reached either goal, my husband was offered a job in Melbourne by a visiting Australian. He insisted that Australia had changed and that Melbourne had always been a more cosmopolitan city than parochial Adelaide. As far as legislation and officialdom were concerned, he was right. I returned to Australia almost immediately with the children properly and legally included on my original Australian passport, and my husband's application for permanent residence was granted at once. We had never thought it would be otherwise; it was not official Australia that had humiliated and insulted us, but Australians.

Not all Australians who married Colombo Plan students in the late 1950s struck prejudice. Two Australian women who married Chinese students told me that they met no discrimination at all. Both couples lived in Singapore for the first several years of their marriage, then returned to Perth in order to provide a better lifestyle for their children.

ADELE ONG   Never had a problem — not with family, not with friends. Neither did our children.

BEVERLEY (WHO HAS SINCE DIVORCED)   My parents were okay too. No obstacles. My in-laws in Singapore were very welcoming. I did lose touch with some of my friends. It may have been that they were opposed to my marriage.

AUTHOR   If you'd married a Chinese girl, Thomas, would your life have been different?

THOMAS ONG   Yes. I think my outlook on life changed. Most Caucasians in Malaya and Singapore thought they were superior beings. But Australians are not like that. Adele is a good manager, too. In Singapore when our salary was cut by half, maybe a Chinese wife would have left.

Another odd thing: when I go for a walk in the mornings, just around the suburbs near my home, Australians always greet me, just 'good morning' or 'lovely day', something like that. But the Chinese look straight into my face, my Chinese face, and ignore me. Chinese will not greet me.

They are suspicious. If it's a woman you might be trying to chat her up, but even men are suspicious. I think they were just not brought up to say hello.

AUTHOR   Were you?

THOMAS   I'm not sure. I can't remember, but I think whatever outgoing friendliness I have, I picked up at university here, and from Adele.

ADELE   Our children are as Australian as meat pies.

BEVERLEY   Our children think of themselves as Australians — not as Europeans, Chinese, Eurasians or anything else, just as Australians.

THOMAS   That's good. I don't believe in joining any of those Chinese clubs or Malaysian clubs. Everyone should be Australian.

If you want to marry someone from another country, it helps if you live in that country for a while. That's why it was easier for me — and for Josh too. We were here as students before we married and went home. None of you girls had that advantage.

I think integration is important. If you decide to settle in a country you have to assimilate, otherwise why didn't you stay at home? A lot of people from Asia, including Chinese, come and settle down here and maintain their own culture. They refuse to assimilate. Yet they came for the better life here — we all did — but you can't pick and choose. Australia offers a better life partly because of its freedoms, the attitudes and the lifestyle, and even the manners and the habits of its people.

Even though Prime Minister Menzies and his Minister for Immigration were much more tolerant towards Asian immigration than the Labor opposition, they were probably somewhat surprised when Sir Macfarlane Burnet, Director of the Walter and Eliza Hall Institute of Medical Research, opened the 1959 Citizenship Convention with a speech urging the Australian people to take the Colombo Plan students into their families. 'We must marry them', he said, 'to enrich our gene pool', explaining that a steady flow of foreign genetic material would help maintain the vigour and diversity of the population.[6]

Sir Macfarlane's views on such matters had to be taken seriously. His field of study was genetics, and the following year he was awarded the Nobel prize for his work in biotechnology and genetic engineering. Children born of a mixed-race marriage, he told the Convention, often showed greater physical health and mental ability than either of the parents. In fact, serious attempts had been made to show that genius was most likely to be found where different racial groups mingled. He told us that we should allow into the country as much non-European genetic material as the community could safely assimilate, and we should not only expect, but welcome, new combinations of body build, skin colour and even personality. He suggested that such a course might also improve our relationships with Asian countries.

The closing session of that 1959 Convention developed into a general debate about Asian immigration. A Church of England canon appealed for migrant quotas for Asians and a representative of the Methodist Church said there could no longer be any genetic objections to Australians marrying Asians. But AE Monk, president of the ACTU, 'questioned the motives of the Immigration Department in asking Sir Macfarlane to prepare a paper on the genetic aspects of intermarriage without reference to the social problems involved ...' and added that 'Asians were more prejudiced about intermarriage than Australians' and that 'economically and socially, Australia could not allow complete intermingling of races'. The RSL representative said his organisation strongly opposed intermarriage with Asians, and Mrs M Watts of the Good Neighbour Council of New South Wales stated that 'intermarriage with Asians will lead to difficulties'.

Sir Macfarlane repeated his claim that genetic diversity brought advantages, but added cautiously:

> That does not mean that I am urging at this time the introduction of large, or even small, quotas of Asians into Australia. But where mutual choice tends to marriage it should not be regarded as a disgrace, but ... with the utmost charity and goodwill.

We have the task of building up our population to the numbers suffi-
cient to justify our monopoly of this continent. We must aim ... at
doing everything we can to ensure enough interracial marriages so
that eventually we can regard the whole Australian population as a vast
pool of genes from which nature can select the multiple combinations
which are needed for a vigorously diversified population.[7]

In the press, particularly the letters pages, Sir Macfarlane's speech
created a furore. It turned upside down former images of contamination of the pure white blood. Among all the outpourings of wrath,
the voice of Dr HI Higbin, reader in Anthropology at Sydney
University, added a measure of scientific calm, but it is doubtful
whether readers remembered that he wrote:

From the social point of view, racial intermarriage would be a very
good thing for Australia. But from a biological point of view I do not
think it makes any difference. Australians, as Europeans, are already
racially mongrels. This has done us no harm in the past and there is
no earthly reason why we should not be more mongrelised by intermarriage with Asians.[8]

5
INTERRACIAL MARRIAGES IN THE 1960s

At the personal level intermarriage has both enriched
and complicated family life.

Janet Penny & Siew-Ean Khoo, *Intermarriage*[1]

When Donald Horne, as the new editor of *The Bulletin*, dropped its
long-time slogan of 'Australia for the white man' in 1961, there
were some surprising consequences, which Horne recounted in a
newspaper article in 1996:

> I received bucketsfull of abuse from racists, and more than the usual
> quota of threats. And a large house brick was thrown through our
> windows.

> This was followed by an abusive telephone call to my wife that if I didn't
> shut up they would blow my brains out — delivered in broken English
> — of continental European background. This is worth remembering
> when the current 'racist' discussion is blamed on Anglo-Celts.[2]

In 1964 Western Australian researcher Mary Hodgkins found that in
marriages between overseas students and Australians, life was easier, and
the marriage more likely to be happier, if the couple lived in the wife's
homeland. This meant that if an Australian woman should marry, say, a
Colombo Plan student, she would adjust better in Australia, although at
that time the husband may not have gained a position as well-paid as
that of a comparable Australian male graduate. The researcher found
that if the Australian wife journeyed back to her husband's homeland,
she, or even the couple, was likely to be marginalised.[3]

Among interracial couples we knew, this conclusion was not

widely applicable, even in the 1960s, though it may have been applied, more credibly, to the many students who returned home without graduating, to take low-paid jobs in countries where the difference in payment for unskilled work and professional work is vast. An example is Pauline, who did not like living in Jamaica — this was a reflection of the poor salary her husband was able to command.

My husband and I and the two other couples whose interviews appear in Chapter 4 all lived happily and comfortably in Singapore, with all the husbands and one wife (myself) in well-paid professional work. We all returned for reasons related to political freedoms — freedom of the press, freedom of expression and a better future for the children in a less monoculturally Chinese environment.

For a magazine article some years ago, I also interviewed three other Australian women who each married in the 1960s and went to live in Singapore — their husband's homeland — and stayed there. All of the husbands were successful and able to provide well, even handsomely, for their families. All the Australian wives had adjusted happily despite the fact that by that time, they could not work at their professions in Singapore without giving up their Australian citizenship, which none of them would do.

These examples are all of Singapore, and perhaps Australian wives would not be as happy in a less Westernised culture. Research for this book centred on mixed-race couples living in Australia, though Elizabeth lived in Manila with her Filipino husband for nearly thirty years. She had to make serious and difficult adjustments and she did not find it easy to make female friends among the Filipinas. But Elizabeth and her husband did operate a successful business and were politically active; this does not suggest marginalisation.

Margaret and her Sierra Leonean husband lived in his homeland for eight years after he finished his specialist training. Their fourth child was born there, and Margaret fitted into its cosmopolitan society as well as her husband, because Western education had already isolated Nuli from the tribe he was born into. They returned to Australia only because political unrest degenerated into civil war.

Establishing a home in a country where both partners feel comfortable is a difficulty that might need to be overcome in many interracial marriages. Of the many wives from other countries I interviewed, I remember only one who said she would prefer to live in her homeland. Most quite actively preferred to live in Australia, and many had decided to stay even before they met the men who became their husbands. Rashda, the Englishwoman with a Pakistani tan, explained how she and her Irish husband came to choose Australia as their home after marrying in the United States in the 1990s, and the importance they placed on their perception of Sydney society's attitude towards interracial couples.

RASHDA   We'd made a list of what we wanted in the place where we'd live, and Australia came out on top. We could have lived in Ireland, but it was just coming out of a recession; or the US — we both knew that well and had relatives there, and Michael had a green card ... but ... there were too many things we didn't like, such as the racism towards mixed-race families. Then there was Britain, but we'd both grown out of that, and our families hadn't been that pleased about our marriage.

We took into account such things as the weather, and whether we could contemplate bringing up children here. We considered the racial mix and attitudes towards us and towards any children we might have, and also education and the general structure of society. As far as we could tell, there were a lot of children of mixed background here. In fact, in that first year when we met, we had also met a few interracial couples who were about to have children — or were themselves children of interracial marriages. We both liked what we saw here. So it was Australia for us.

MICHAEL   We already had become friends with educated Australians who had lived here all their lives, and we thought it would be lovely if our children could be just like them. The education system and the structure of society was a way of life we liked. And the food is wonderful.

As Rashda's and Michael's 'mix' is similar to my husband's and mine — though reversed — their whole-hearted choice of Australia contrasts with our hesitancy thirty-five years earlier and vividly reflects the changes that have taken place in Australian society.

Just a couple of years after we left Adelaide for Singapore, a young Chinese woman, Bernice, came from Singapore to Adelaide to study medicine, married an Australian fellow student, and after nearly thirty years of working as a general medical practitioner, was elected as a Liberal member of the South Australian Legislative Council. As one of Australia's few Asian-born parliamentarians, she had an opportunity to speak for Australians who come from a different background than that of the Adelaide establishment.

BERNICE   When John and I married, my people would not accept John. His people didn't think it marvellous either, but they were more accepting of me than my people were of John. Within our marriage race is not a problem. The only real cultural difference John and I have is with the children. I want to give them as much as possible — everything. After all we can't take it with us. John thinks they can manage themselves. He had to do it himself and they can too.

AUTHOR   Have you been discriminated against?

BERNICE   I see very little, I never did. But I may have a skewed view because of my marriage.

AUTHOR   I asked because of the job you do. In politics, particularly in South Australia, politics is a white male club.

BERNICE   Well, yes. First I am a woman, then I'm an ethnic, then I am in my fifties, whereas Australia worships the young and blond and blue-eyed. Politics is dominated by men, dominated by the establishment and dominated by the right way to do things. I am not even fully aware of these things.

In Singapore we were the majority group, and racism was against the Malays and the Indians. I've been on both sides, you see, and know how it feels. When you're the mainstream, you feel very secure, you feel very superior.

Here in Australia it's not a huge wave against us, just small pricks. I feel that the mainstream in Australia is all for the underdog. Australia has a history of welcoming minorities. All those bedraggled refugees and migrants from Europe who came in the 1940s and 1950s have not only fitted in but they've become part of the mainstream. Even better, they've enriched the mainstream culture. Eventually, the Asian migrants will do that too.

Most white Australians have already been generous in reaching out to we overseas-born people; white Australians have gone three-quarters of the way. I think now it is the time for us to reach out and go the rest of the way. We are equipped with English language, and we know where you're coming from; now we should embrace multiculturalism. I'm sorry to say that many ethnics want to remain separate. You see, it's not only the mainstream that sees us as different. We see you as different too. I see you as white. It will take the next generation before my children or my grandchildren see you as just Australian.

In the cool quiet of Adelaide's legislative chamber, where the ghosts of South Australia's history wander the corridors, Bernice's statement shocked me. I firmly believe we should all see one another as Australians — just Australians. By writing this book I was hoping to encourage what I call ordinary Australians, like me, to see Bernice and other Asians not as Asian Australians, but just as Australians too. I also hoped that Chinese Australians like Bernice would see, say, Indian Australians and African Australians and Lebanese Australians as just Australians. What I never dreamed was that Bernice, highly intelligent and community-conscious, thirty years an Australian resident and, at that time an elected representative of a slice of Adelaide, would see me as a 'white person', not as the ordinary Australian I am. For I am a very typical representative of the Australia she came to in the 1960s.

Shocked, I recognised in myself the disorientation her statement thrust me into — the same confusion felt by many mixed-race children, including my son (and perhaps Bernice's son too) when he realised that, at his new school, the other boys did not recognise him as the Australian he knew himself to be, but saw him as a 'wog'. The experience was salutary; I walked in another's shoes, if only for a moment.

While listening to interviews I learned that, contrary to what may be thought of as established opinion, racial prejudice was often found among the most highly educated and scholarly in our cities. Dominic, an academic at a Queensland university, already had a strong interest in Asian culture when he met Robyn, the Chinese-Malaysian girl who became his wife.

DOMINIC Robyn's parents opposed our marriage at first, but later they were accepting. We didn't have any really bad experiences based on race, except from among my colleagues at the university. One day I said something, which provoked the radical feminist in our department to snap back across the common room, 'Not only are you a miscegenist, you're also a misogynist'.

Once there was a comment about my Chinese wife, and a senior member of the department, unaware that I could hear him, said, 'He doesn't have a screwed up mind — so why on earth did he marry a Chinese woman?'.

Our daughter had a few bad experiences, too. On her first day at school — and she had been so looking forward to it — she came home before the day was over, sobbing, 'They won't play with me because I'm different'.

We found another school in the next suburb where there were several Chinese and mixed-race children, and she loved it there. Our son spent his primary years there too, and neither of them had any problems after that.

Fabia, an Australian teacher, is original, different, perhaps even eccentric. We sat in the garden of her home where the trees looked more ancient than they could possibly have been, and drank tea amid an array of Balinese artefacts.

Fabia's first husband was a Chinese accountant, whom she thought already quite Australianised when they met and married in the late 1960s. They had two sons, and after that marriage broke down Fabia travelled, and fell in love with a Thai, but though they had a daughter, they never married, and the relationship collapsed after two years. She met her present husband in Lombok, after working for four years in Indonesia.

FABIA You're living proof that a mixed-race marriage can work long term.

AUTHOR I'd not deny the difficulties, though. It's harder than if I had married the boy next door.

FABIA I sometimes think I would never have been happy with an ordinary Australian husband — too boring — and I am too far removed from the Australian 'girl next door' norm. But there's no denying that those of us who marry out have to work harder at making the marriage a success. I know I do. I still have a lot of sadness that I failed with the boys' father.

My mother didn't approve of him at first. She didn't want me to marry him. But later, we all lived together here in her house, and she became very fond of him and loved having my boys grow up in her house. Other people didn't approve though. It's an Australian attitude that every couple needs their own space. In an Asian family, it's okay to live with relatives — three or even four generations. Our elder son benefited tremendously from having three educated adults sharing his home. The second boy suffered a bit, because his important years coincided with when we all suffered, towards the end.

My husband became very authoritarian about the children's lives and about household management; every day he criticised my cooking. Every day of my married life! Food is so important to Chinese; it dominates their thinking in a way we find hard to understand. He'd come home from work … lift the saucepan lid and pronounce judgment. 'This is overcooked', he'd say, or 'Not enough soy'.

AUTHOR It's a wonder you didn't flee back to Australian roast lamb and three vegetables, because with that, you'd be the expert.

FABIA Even with that, he'd do the same. It was cultural. For Chinese, food is the most important thing in their lives. He didn't try to fit in with Australian conventions, either, but did outrageous things, such as going to a wedding or a formal party in shorts and sandals. He used to embarrass me. He had a biting tongue, and often yelled at me or at anyone else. He was not restrained by any sense of good manners. It was that kind of thing which turned my friends against him, rather than that he was Chinese.

In the end, all his anger and unpleasant behaviour and constant criticism, and my rebellion, turned our marriage into a monster, and we were both glad to end it.

Ten years later I met my second husband in Lombok, on the beach. I had already lived in Indonesia for four years, teaching English there, and just before I was due to come home, he strolled up the beach and announced that he was going to marry me. I was very wary, for one is approached by many odd men on the beach, and I'm not in the habit of taking up their offers. I did a lot of checking up on him.

We are getting on very well, even though there are a lot of cultural differences. I'm forty-nine now and I'm fairly secure in my personality. I don't need to rebel, as I did in my twenties, and though my husband doesn't speak perfect English, I speak Indonesian.

AUTHOR Have you met criticism, discrimination in this marriage?

FABIA Absolutely! From all sources. Perhaps they worry for me, fearing that he is a 'gold-digger' or a 'fanatical Muslim'. One of my friends won't speak to me.

It was, and still is, a big gamble, I know. But I did marry him, and I did bring him to Australia. I think it is working, though there are problems I never dreamed of. For example, when he is upset or we disagree, he sulks — the great Indonesian sensitivity! But I find the sulking much easier to cope with than the ranting and shouting of my first husband.

My second husband left his children in Lombok, and he misses them; he would like us to return and live there. It's a lovely Sleepy Hollow sort of place. My sons are grown up now and don't need me, but I don't know whether my daughter should be educated in a sleepy Lombok school. At the moment we accept that we will spend periods of time apart.

I met Olivia at a library function and she told me about her marriage to a Hong Kong Chinese man.

OLIVIA I married him in 1963. Mixed-race marriages were not so common then, and people said, 'Will the children be all right?'.

When the marriage broke up in 1969 the boys were five and six. We were living at Dulwich Hill, and the first Arabs had moved into the area. The Italians, Yugoslavs and old Aussies didn't like it, and I was concerned about having two rather slightly built, half-Chinese boys in a school where there was not a happy racial mix.

I sought professional advice and was advised to choose a place which had no racial threats at all. So we moved to Chatswood. It was a good move. The boys grew up where they were no threat to anyone. However, they have little sense of Chineseness; they feel Australian. The differences my former husband and I had were not cultural; they were personality problems. He was much too harsh with the children and incredibly inflexible.

Ironically, since the 1980s Chatswood — a busy shopping and business centre north of Sydney Harbour — has become the heartland of white-collar and professional migrants from Hong Kong, Taiwan and Korea, while many Japanese executives have made their Australian home in nearby Northbridge.

Susan was twenty-one when she met Dayal, a Sri Lankan, in Melbourne in 1967. Both were students, Dayal doing a PhD in electronic engineering, and Susan researching for an honours degree in history.

SUSAN   When we married I took Dayal's name without hesitating. He offered to change it because Australians weren't very good at 'Abeyasekere', but I didn't want him to give up his name.

AUTHOR   What did your parents think about your marriage?

SUSAN   My mother thought I was jumping in too fast. Dayal didn't tell his parents until after the wedding. Religion was never a source of tension, rather the opposite. It was the religious discussions that drew me to him, and we went to the Buddhist temple together. I wouldn't have thought racial difference was important in our marriage, either, but in the end, perhaps that is what led to its breakdown.

Dayal had enough self-confidence not to notice racist pinpricks, but at the end, the lack of promotion got to him, and he believed that he was being discriminated against because of his race. Dayal began to feel that if he hadn't married me, things would have been better. He certainly would have gone back home, so he had a feeling of being trapped, and then he began romanticising his homeland. After we separated, he struck up a relationship with a Sri Lankan woman in Brisbane, and died not so long after.

I don't regret the marriage. We were together for twenty-two years, and most of those years were very happy.

People who have already been displaced from their cultural base mention few differences encountered within an interracial marriage, or only favourable ones. Perhaps the adaptability that comes from growing up in a culture not completely one's own enables one to continually adapt.

At fourteen, Zareena, an Indian from Fiji, went to Hobart to finish school because her father had enjoyed his years of study there. While studying science at the university, she met Gideon, now an academic at Melbourne's Latrobe University and a talented artist. Gideon's father and uncle had fled Hungary in 1939, and Gideon's family in Europe disguised their Jewishness by joining the Catholic church. This did not work. Whatever remained of Gideon's family in Europe disappeared; only his father and uncle in Australia escaped.

GIDEON   Apart from the cross-cultural interest, one good thing about our marriage is that I gained a large family, which I had missed all my life. First-generation Australians, with a small pool of relatives, are limited to a narrow slice of society. My uncle and three cousins can't provide many links, but I now share Zareena's hordes of relatives who have an abundance of talents, professions, interests and personalities here and in New Zealand and Fiji — a wide and deep cross-section of society. I love it.

ZAREENA   A cross-section of religions too! When I moved from my Hindu–Muslim family to Hobart, I became a Christian. I was about fifteen. Gideon's Jewish father became a Catholic and then an agnostic, and Gideon's path has been similar.

After I finished my degree, I went back to work in Fiji, while Gideon went to Adelaide to do his PhD, and after a year I came to Adelaide to marry him. My father had just had a stroke, so although they were happy about my marriage, none of my family came from Fiji for the wedding. Gideon's father was not happy about it — more worried than disapproving, I think.

GIDEON   The worst part of the whole thing was at the Immigration Office when I went to get Zareena's entry papers stamped. The gentleman behind the desk asked, 'Is your fiancée a prostitute?'.

There was no point in making a fuss. I just wanted to get the thing stamped so she could come and marry me, so I said, 'No, sir, she is not'.

AUTHOR   So you were a young mixed-race couple in Adelaide in 1966, just as we were ten years earlier. Did you have any trouble?

GIDEON   By 1966 things had changed. Don Dunstan had come in. Also, I was a white man married to a black woman, and this is more acceptable in Australia than the reverse.

ZAREENA   It didn't take long for me to get used to Australia, and in all the years that I was teaching in Adelaide, I was the only black person in the school. But I didn't think of myself as any different from anyone else, because the students treated me as they treated all teachers — with respect. I think at that time children, or perhaps all Adelaide people, were more polite.

But ten years ago when I returned to teaching here in Melbourne, the kids in the classroom started putting on Indian accents to mock me. All of a sudden, I saw things differently. I'd never struck racism before, but I struck it here, teaching the children of migrant families.

AUTHOR   Have your children struck any racism?

ZAREENA   They are conscious of it, but I don't think they've been hurt. Dan, our eldest, was good at sport, and that helps. He was confident enough to wear a sulu and bare feet to a school party. He's finished medicine now, and has worked for short stints in several of the South Pacific Island nations. Susie has no trouble either. Michael perhaps does, because he is isolated; he has spina bifida and is on crutches. He does not identify with the Indian part of himself at all.

Cornel and Hiroe live serenely in their hilltop studio-cum-gallery-cum-home, which Cornel built outside Queanbeyan. Both are artists. Cornel now paints full-time after spending his early years as a successful designer and illustrator. Hiroe is one of Australia's most widely admired potters.

CORNEL I came to Australia in 1952. The good old days! Australians were casual in a nice sense; people are more materialistic now. I had my mid-life crisis in 1965 and became very disillusioned with my work. I travelled overseas, and fell in love with Japan, with Kyoto. Then I met Hiroe. After three months my visa expired, so I went to work in Singapore, but Hiroe wouldn't accept my proposal by letter, so I went back to Japan.

AUTHOR Hiroe, what did your family think of your marriage to a non-Japanese?

HIROE They accepted it. I wouldn't have married if they hadn't because I have a strong obligation to my parents, and I knew if I married Cornel, I would have to leave Japan. Now, my parents are here in Australia too.

At first it was very hard for me to adapt to Australia. The atmosphere is so different; so bright, and the colourful housing — everything is so garish. Kyoto is very subdued; browns and greys and black. I missed Japanese culture and I was homesick, too, but Cornel made me see that I had closed my mind.

He said, 'Of course you miss your home because you stay by yourself. Why don't you go out? Get to know Australia and Australians. If you don't like it, after trying, then we'll go back to Japan'.

So I went out to look at Sydney, and I liked what I saw. Soon I felt more relaxed, and I began to understand Australians.

I teach at the School of Art here in Canberra, and I fit in well. Japan is well known for ceramics. I spend most of my time working alone here in my studio, though. If you want to achieve something you must be serious about it. If you're serious, you'll want to work all the time. It takes everything you have.

AUTHOR Your friends? Speaking to interracial couples, I sometimes find that all their friends are actually of the one race — the other incoming race, not old Australians.

CORNEL Yes, until the life they lead is like living in a ghetto. Why don't they seek people related to their current life? My first and best friend in Australia is a Chinese Australian. It didn't happen because he was Chinese, but because we met and liked one another. I worked with him, and I never looked at racial difference. I told Hiroe years ago: don't seek out Japanese, and don't become friends with Japanese you meet simply because they are Japanese. Look for people you like, and it doesn't matter where they come from.

Today everyone is told to cling to their backgrounds. How can they ever be Australian if they cling to what they were before they came here? I see the merit in using what they brought here, capitalising on their skills to improve Australia. But to hang onto their old cultural stuff here, their languages and customs and all the rest is just rubbish. If they wanted that, why didn't they stay where they were?

HIROE Migrants can help Australia and Australians if they care to. A few years ago I was in Cairns to give a workshop. I was able to help the local potters benefit from the Japanese tourists. Shopkeepers were happy to have many Japanese tourists, but other Cairns residents were not so happy. So I went to a local Japanese restaurant and asked them where they got their pottery plates and bowls for serving Japanese meals.

They said, 'From Japan, because we can't buy them here'.

I told them, 'You tell Australian potters what you want, they will produce a sample for you — and then a series. They can produce your pottery right here'.

CORNEL I always tell people that I came to Australia to become an Australian.

Holland is only accidental. I came from there, that's all. I am now, and have been for many years, an Australian. The idea of racial purity is nonsense.

AUTHOR   Hiroe, your culture in Japan differs much more from Australia's than that of the Netherlands. How do you feel about distancing yourself from your Japanese culture?

HIROE   The same as Cornel. Very much so. I say to my students: my race is Japanese, but I am Australian. I'll stay here 'til I die.

6

1960s MARRIAGES WITH MIXED-RACE CHILDREN

I cannot understand people who go to church on Sundays to worship a
man with coloured skin and then for the rest of the week practice the
intolerance of the colour bar.

Mahomet Allum[1]

In 1965 the official government policy on immigration was relaxed
to admit many classes of non-European migrants, though it was not
until 1966 that the Prime Minister, Harold Holt, announced the
abandonment of the so-called White Australia Policy. Between
March 1966 and September 1970, 15 000 non-European migrants
settled in Australia.

The Coalition Government had put an end to all institutionalised
racial discrimination; a change supported by all major political parties after the Labor Party finally dropped its policy of racially-based
exclusion. Politicians from government and opposition alike were
unsure whether the electorate supported such historic changes in
population policy. The Immigration Minister reassured Parliament
in March 1966 that the aim of retaining homogeneity and compat-
ibility would be kept in mind with regard to immigration, even while
the government was opening Australia's doors to immigration without racial restraints. Politicians may have misjudged the Australian
people, for only one year later the 1967 referendum was passed by a
massive 90.8 per cent of Australians, who voted to remove all restrictions on Aboriginals and to admit them to the full rights and respon-
sibilities of citizenship.

International educator Lawrie, an Australian of English/Dutch extraction, and Pat, a Malaysian-born Chinese woman, have been married for over thirty years. Lawrie believes that the way two people from two different cultures come to learn to live together within one of those cultures is far more important than any friction the couple might meet in the wider Australian society.

It is possible there were more hurdles to overcome, more adjustments to be made within their marriage than many others, due to Pat's Chinese education and continuing cultural orientation and Lawrie's heavy involvement in sport, of which Pat had little understanding. It is also likely that Lawrie encountered less overt disapproval from other Australians of his choice of bride — petite and beautiful Pat — than the discrimination, sometimes ostracism, that others suffered during the 1950s and 1960s.

LAWRIE I remember the first day of the 1963 school year. I walked into the lecture room at Swinburne and saw this most incredibly beautiful Asian woman. I was twenty-three and I'd never really spoken to anyone from a different culture. I was bowled over. I said to myself, 'I'm going to have her'. I did not know then that I would have to marry her first.

Since our marriage I have come to understand that in any mixed marriage there will inevitably be a lack of shorthand communication — where one sentence can conjure up a great deal more than is actually said, because that one sentence is based on a shared Australian heritage. That lack can be frustrating. I cannot really talk about meanings behind the things in my past life — such things as football, cricket, Australian folklore, and the continuing influence they can have in one's life.

Within the family context I feel isolated, as the children do not relate to that past either. When they were young, I was working hard, so Pat really brought the children up, told them Chinese stories, etcetera. I'm glad she did that, of course, but they missed hearing Australian stories from me, and now I realise they did not get them at school either. Of course, our marriage has many plusses that more than make up the lack I've described — but I do miss that shared connection with Pat and with the children.

AUTHOR Did your parents approve your pursuit of Pat, and your marriage?

LAWRIE My mother took it quite well. She was a farmer's daughter and remembered being fascinated by the Indian vendors who used to visit their farm regularly. My father was brought up in a goldmining town where the Chinese had a reputation of being honest and hardworking. Maybe they saw Pat as an honest, hardworking daughter-in-law. Anyway, they were very good about it and we had few problems.

PAT At first I had no idea that Lawrie was interested in me. We Malaysian students stuck together in those days and didn't mix much outside our own group. Even when Lawrie became our friend I thought he was a friend to all of us. We Chinese never thought we would marry outside our race. My English was not good because I went to a Chinese school.

Early on, Lawrie took me to watch him play football. I took my knitting and my portable radio, and after a while there was a break and I realised it was three-quarter time and I didn't know how Lawrie's team was going. I looked around the football field, and — no Lawrie!

LAWRIE   I'd been carted off unconscious and she hadn't even noticed. It brought home to me how different our backgrounds were — even at this lower level of cultural activity. Pat did not mix in this type of sporting scene; drinking at the bar after the game was not her style. Although in those days, if you remember, decent women didn't go to bars anyway. Inevitably, when I finished playing sport I left those friends and way of life behind, and my life took another turn. I began to study again. So you might say as a result of marrying Pat a total reassessment of my former lifestyle took place.

AUTHOR   Was your family happy about your marriage, Pat?

PAT   They were not happy; they were concerned for me. My mother would have liked me to stop seeing Lawrie, but by that stage I had finished my studies and got a job. I told them I could support myself if necessary.
   I think it's hard for a mother to accept a foreign husband for her daughter. In those days in Malaysia people thought any girl who married a white man was a tart. My parents did accept our marriage later, and we have tried to visit them in Sarawak for a month or so every couple of years — so the children know that culture too.
   We thought the children might have trouble, and of course there was some.

LAWRIE   Our son, Leon, was an average kid, and in primary school a much bigger boy taunted him and they had a showdown behind the service station. The big kid came out with his fists up, and Leon shaped up like a Kung Fu fighter. The other kid was so startled that he backed down. At that age, boys' business is all about shove and push, then you settle down and become friends.

PAT   I feel I've lived all my married life according to Australian ways. As a family, we are 50 per cent Australian and 50 per cent Chinese, yet we celebrate Christmas, Easter and all other festive occasions but the only Chinese festival we celebrate is Chinese New Year.

LAWRIE   But we live in Australia. How can you expect my parents and sister to embrace all the Chinese celebrations? That they even know it's Chinese New Year puts them ahead of most Australians.

Lian, Lawrie and Pat's 27-year-old daughter, is working towards her Masters degree in psychology, and deciding who she is.

LIAN   At school my brother and I were seen as Chinese and we were teased. I'm not a natural fighter, so I ignored it. In high school I wasn't teased but I felt I was an outsider. Until I went to university I never even realised that my mum has an accent. Now I see that she is still very Chinese.
   I've struck more curiosity than racism. In Malaysia people always stare, but in Australia people are more discreet.

AUTHOR   What do feel yourself to be now? Would you answer instantly — an Australian?

LIAN   No, I don't identify myself as an Australian at all. I'm an Australian citizen, but I am not an Australian. I'm neither fully of the white culture, nor fully of the other. I don't have a cultural structure for my inner self nor guidelines as to behaviour; I flounder a bit.
   The easiest way to describe it is like having a religion or not. My dad is Anglican and my mum is Buddhist, and they decided to let us choose, so I have no religious or

other code of conduct. I have to create my own guidelines. It's not always a negative thing. I'm freer; I can choose.

I was brought up in Australia, amongst Australian children, with Australian grand-parents nearby, yet my upbringing didn't give me an Australian identity. And though we always had Chinese things around us, and food, and Chinese visitors who lived with us for years, always speaking Chinese with my mother, and all those trips to Sarawak — despite all that, I did not get a Chinese identity either, although now perhaps I lean that way — towards Eastern culture more than towards Australian. But I do question who I am still. Other half-halfs must also be questioning themselves.

The 1960s was a time of increasing prosperity and confidence in Australia, and like thousands of other young Australians, 21-year-old Pauline set off to see the world.

PAULINE Starting in England, as one did in those days, I dated boys in every coun-try in Europe. Then I crossed the Atlantic, and how I loved the buzz of New York. I found a job and got a cheap apartment and met a group of West Indian students living in the apartment below mine. Soon I was very smitten by one of them — the man who later became my husband. At first, though, it was just part of my love affair with America.

Peter had more free time than I did and he made himself indispensable cooking for me; a lot of chicken actually, and the next year when I was in Jamaica, my brother-in-law asked, 'How did Peter win your heart? Did he cook a lot of chicken?'. And when I said yes, my brother-in-law said, 'He put a Voodoo spell in the chicken to win you'.

After a year in New York I decided to see the rest of the US and South America, while Peter finished his studies. Six weeks later, in Washington, I found I was pregnant. I couldn't just have this child by myself in a country where there were no medical ben-efits, so I returned to New York. I realise now that I put a heavy load on this 25-year-old student who still depended on his father for pocket money, but because I had worked and kept myself for years, I didn't realise how immature he still was. We both got jobs and worked right up until the baby was almost due.

It was going to cost $500 to have the baby, so I said, 'Let's spend this $500 flying to Jamaica and I'll have the baby there'.

We flew off to Jamaica and caught a bus to Peter's village. I was left sitting in a grotty Chinese coffee shop made of bamboo and wire netting while Peter borrowed a bike from the shop owner, and went to break the news of our arrival to his father. There I was, perched like a pregnant penguin until Peter returned and dinked me through the village to his father's house.

Peter's father was well-off and we stayed in his house, which was large and pleas-ant. The maids did all the work, so after I'd read every book in the library and walked everywhere around the village, I commandeered the yard-boy's bike to explore further. It was quite safe, but I shocked the locals. A very pregnant white lady in shorts and shirt riding a bike with bare feet was a rare sight in Jamaica. My mother-in-law was mortified. She was always saying, 'Put your shoes on!'.

Peter's father always knew where I was. If I had a puncture, a truck would be there to give me a lift. I used to tease him about listening to the drums, but actually he cared about me. I heard him telling my husband, 'You can't leave this woman alone all the time'. Because that was the problem; I was terribly lonely, for Peter wasn't interested in coming with me on these excursions.

AUTHOR Why did he stop being the charming, attentive man who won your heart in New York?

PAULINE   He became a Jamaican again, he just enjoyed his leisure. Peter is well read, quotes Shakespeare and Omar Kyam, knows all the cultural things which in my snobby way, I value. But he could do nothing else. Peter not only didn't work, he didn't do anything. As a fiercely independent Aussie, I couldn't understand that.

AUTHOR   Where was the baby born?

PAULINE   In the village hospital. The doctor was a Greek Jamaican who smoked a huge cigar and charged $5. The mosquitos ate me alive and after twenty-four hours of pain and screaming, my daughter, Marcia, was born.

I planned to take her to the Salvation Army Chapel to be blessed, but the family were disgusted at that — so low class — and arranged an Anglican christening. Although Peter and I were not married at that time, everyone assumed we were.

Peter finally got a job and we rented an apartment, but the pay was so poor there, his wages barely covered the rent, so though I hated him gambling, he had to play poker to keep us going.

I wanted to show the baby to my mother and the only place we could earn enough money for the fare home was in the US. We flew to Miami, had a one-night honeymoon, then set off on a Greyhound bus to Cleveland. This was 1964. People threw acid at mixed-race couples then. If shopkeepers saw the baby they wouldn't sell me any food for her, so I'd leave Marcia with Peter while I shopped. We got out of the southern states as fast as we could and in Cleveland we stayed with Peter's aunt and uncle, and we both got jobs. It was a black town built around automobile manufacturing, and black people frightened me too; they would stop me in the street and demand, 'Is that baby yours?'.

Black/white marriages were still unlawful in nineteen US states until 1967, when miscegenation laws were abolished throughout the United States. The abolition was not universally popular — 72 per cent of whites in the southern states and 42 per cent in the northern states wanted to keep interracial marriage outlawed.[2]

Things change. Tiger Woods, the son of a black/Asian marriage, is now a star in the golfing world, with fans across all races. Recent high-profile mixed-race couples have also woken the American public to the fact that there is probably no more racially-mixed population than theirs, because of their history of slavery when records were not kept, or true ancestry was deliberately hidden.

PAULINE   I hated Cleveland. I wanted to see my mum. So I hopped on a mail boat in Seattle, with my baby and a crate full of baby food. There were fourteen passengers, all Americans except for an elderly Japanese couple, and all prejudiced. A month is a very long time on a ship when no one will speak to you.

At last we arrived home. Everyone thought Marcia was gorgeous — just like a Topsy doll. My mother adored her. People stopped me in the street to admire her. The contrast with America and Americans was startling. It was wonderful!

All my family loved my baby, except my father. My parents had been separated for some time, and he came down from the country to see me. One day he was in the garden, and when I took him afternoon tea, he said, 'If you put that little mongrel in an orphanage, I'll buy you a business, or finance you through university'. I picked up the teapot and emptied it over his head. I never saw him again.

After six months I felt Marcia should be with her father, who had gone back home to Jamaica. I didn't want to live in Jamaica again, so I went to England, arranging to meet up with Peter there. We were going to stay with a very old friend of mine. She was very proper, and her daughter rang me up and said, 'Mum's got a problem with the idea of you two sharing the same bed'. So we got married.

I thought the whole thing was a bad idea. I don't remember the ceremony. I hated what I wore. We had no money, so Peter didn't even buy me a bunch of flowers. He borrowed a car but didn't put any petrol in it, so we ran out of petrol on our way home. For our big celebration we went to a film, *My Fair Lady*. I've hated that film ever since.

We got jobs and a flat but all we could afford at first was a tiny dingy room with ghastly floral wallpaper. Nevertheless, I believed that the sky was the limit for Peter, but he had no ambition. I had plenty of ambition and I wanted a better future for Marcia.

When I became pregnant again, my mother came over, but almost immediately she found she had cancer, so she returned to Australia and waited, desperately ill and in terrible pain, for her longed-for grandson to be born. Anxious to release her from pain, my aunt sent her a telegram saying that I'd had my son. My mother died in peace, and then a few weeks later I had my second daughter, Lola, whom I swear my mother jumped into the skin of.

Then one day my husband said he wanted to go to Australia. At first I protested, 'You didn't want to go when my mother was alive. Now, she's dead, and I have a really good job, and I don't want to go'.

It was 1970 and at a Commonwealth Conference in London an Australian Minister had said there was no colour prejudice and that anyone with a British passport could go to Australia. So we went to Australia House and after much argument they told us Peter could immigrate if he had a job. He left five days later, travelling overland with a busload of Aussies. Peter loved Australia and Australians. They were always inviting him to drink with them. My husband doesn't drink, but right from the beginning he loved their friendliness.

I had travelled halfway around the world to be with Peter, so I knew I had to give up my good job in London and follow him.

AUTHOR How did you find it after you got here?

PAULINE We never had a problem, even though Peter's job involved moving from one small Victorian country town to another, while living in an SEC caravan. I remember big burly Aussies knocking on the caravan door and asking 'Wanta go rabbitin?'. Peter had never held a spotlight in his life, let alone wrung a rabbit's neck, but he went off with them and they taught him all the essentials.

After three years I decided that I didn't want to live in any more country towns in a caravan. I wanted to come back to Melbourne. Some years later I had Saul, my longed-for son, and it was just after Saul's tenth birthday that Peter and I split up. Ever since returning to live in Melbourne, for maybe fifteen years, I had made a lot of money as an artist. I paid all the bills, the ballet classes, all fees, food, clothes and everything else, while Peter just paid the mortgage on the house.

Then my paintings stopped selling and Peter had to support me and the kids. He didn't want to do that. I told him I'd need his support for a year while I learned to make a living at writing, because I still had two children at school. When Peter wouldn't support us even for one year, I told him to go.

It was always a stormy marriage.

He's re-married now and he seems to be very happy. He meets no prejudice whatsoever; he never has. Australian men have this tremendous affinity with Jamaicans because of cricket. It's almost a brotherhood. And he strikes another chord of brotherhood with Aborigines, triggered by what they have in common — their dark skin.

AUTHOR Do your children have problems fitting in?

PAULINE Not really. Marcia the Mighty is a fixer, too. Lola, my younger daughter, is a fighter. She was coming home from school in her school uniform one day when a woman rolled up to the tram stop and said, 'So now they let boongs into my old school, do they?'.

Lola tried to ignore her, but the woman kept repeating the jibes. Finally Lola gave her a mighty whack and knocked her down. Another time when we were at a barbecue for my son's footy club, Lola and Saul went up to get a sausage and the man serving the food said to Saul, 'Why don't you get back into the trees where you belong?'.

Lola kicked his barbecue over. Sausages and meat flew everywhere. We've only had those two nasty things happen and both times Lola dealt with the unpleasantness magnificently.

When Pauline's daughter Marcia came to my house, I saw at once why her mother called this young woman 'Marcia the Mighty'. She carried herself like a queen, totally and happily sure of her place in Australia and the world.

MARCIA In England we lived in a poor working-class area, and there was lots of racism from black people. I remember black bus drivers saying, 'There's something wrong there', with winks and nods at me and my blonde, blue-eyed mother.

In Australia when we came everyone was white. I went to more than a dozen primary schools in country towns. Sometimes I'd get a nickname about blackberries or something. It was not upsetting; others were teased because they were fat or wore glasses. I was aware that other people didn't have a black father and I had a vague sense of not fitting in, but I never related it to my colour.

Maybe it was my attitude, because I remember thinking, 'It's funny how many people are wrong about things'. I didn't have many friends, but a lot of the children did shoplifting and I wouldn't. I don't think any of my problems had to do with having brown skin.

When I was seventeen or eighteen, two girls attacked me at a party. I left quickly, and so did everyone else who was a bit different. Then a few years ago my sister and I and a couple of friends were at a pub when a man started punching Lola, then others joined in. When the police came they just sent the offending ones home, and treated us as if we were drunk. Next day, I put on a business suit and lodged a complaint. The treatment I got then was quite different. Taxi drivers are very free with racist comments, too, but in ordinary jobs, in offices, meeting clients, I am not aware of any colour problems. In fact, I think Australia is changing colour. The kids' faces at school now seem darker, more varied than when I went to school.

AUTHOR Are you Australian?

MARCIA Yes, I'm Australian. If people can identify themselves as Aboriginal with only a minute amount of Aboriginal blood, then my 50 per cent Australian blood certainly allows me to identify as an Australian. Actually my husband has a tiny proportion of Aboriginal blood but he considers himself to be Australian, and so do his sisters, though their mother claims Aboriginality.

I think all Aborigines, in fact everyone who lives here as an Australian should think of themselves as Australians.

AUTHOR Does your father think of himself as an Australian?

MARCIA It depends upon who's winning at cricket.

Nuli and Margaret met at university in 1967. Nuli had come from Sierra Leone to study medicine, with plans to return as a specialist paediatrician.

NULI When I arrived in 1962 people greeted me in corridors, invited me to drink with them. At the same time, I also remember being stared at, rather as if I were an animal in a zoo, when I travelled by bus. Two years later, travelling on the same bus, I noticed nothing. Had I become less sensitive, or had people become used to Africans?

In 1969 I graduated and started work. Margaret and I got married just before I did my residency in a country hospital, and in 1971 our only son was born. However, I did strike discrimination here where I least expected it — in my university examiner — when I was going for my College membership. The chief examiner, I was told, almost always failed non-whites. His second in command thought I deserved a pass, and gave me a very good reference to get me to London.

AUTHOR You had to go to London to get the specialist qualifications that this man's prejudice caused you to fail?

NULI Yes, and in London I got it, too, but to this day I don't know whether he failed me because I was African or because I spoke out against his management style.

AUTHOR How much it cost you, in money and years of your life! We are brought up with the idea of universities being a meeting place of minds, where petty, personal judgments aren't made. That's not true, is it? Not in Australia, anyway.

NULI But it is still better than in England. In England the cold way that people received us contrasted with Australians' happy way of including everyone in their activities — old Anglo-Saxon Australians, anyway.

They greet you in the corridor, invite you into their home for a cup of tea. That would never happen in England, and this is one of the differences between white Australians and English people. Those old Aussies have changed since their ancestors came out from England.

AUTHOR Yes, we have changed. We have become Australians.

NULI In 1962 I found everyone was friendly, and only later found discrimination among academics. Since I came back as a consultant paediatrician I've found colleagues in the hospital system are much friendlier than those in private practice because it doesn't cost them anything. So I think sometimes discrimination or unfriendliness, in the professional world anyway, is as much about economics as it is about racism.

MARGARET My father did not like my marriage one bit. He'd travelled a lot and seen mixed-race couples in bars; he'd seen mixed-race children begging, selling themselves, making a living any way they could. He said, 'I won't take you to the church'.

NULI My mother disapproved too. I told her that if I didn't marry Margaret I would not marry anyone, so she gave her blessing. My eldest brother is the head of the family. He disapproved too. In a tribe, personal rights don't count, but I had already grown away from the tribe.

To Margaret's father I also said, 'In my tradition the marriage may not work if parents don't give their blessing'. Eventually it was okay.

AUTHOR What about racism generally?

NULI It's a reality, but often it's best to ignore it.

MARGARET People seem to think that unusual couples give them license to ask personal questions. People try to work out why you're together; they are curious. A neighbour and I used to go to P&C meetings together, and one evening he said, 'I can't figure out why you married a black man'.

I said, 'I married Nuli. The colour of his skin wasn't the issue'.

AUTHOR Maybe we should say, in answer to that question, 'To protect my children from skin cancer'. When my first grandchild was born, the country doctor attending my daughter, referring to the cancer-resistant skin she had inherited, told her, 'The best thing your mother ever did for you and your children was to marry your father'.

MARGARET After my children were born, people wanted to know how I came to have a curly-haired, dark-skinned baby. That was just curiosity. The only hostility I encountered was in London. Here, people are friendly; our neighbours are always dropping in. We've never had trouble with neighbours. Have you?

AUTHOR For many years, and in many cities, no. Most of our former neighbours remain friends. But recently, in Point Piper, it was unpleasant. Nearly all the neighbours, who happened to be Jewish, would not speak to Josh. It shocked me because one would think Jews, rather more than most people, would be conscious of the evils that come from ideas of racial superiority.

When you were in Sierra Leone, how was it?

MARGARET The first time we stayed a month, and I felt that people were on their best behaviour. In 1981 we went there to live and it was much better. Our last child was born there. I did not engage as much as I had hoped with Nuli's mother. Perhaps I didn't do all the ceremonial present-giving that is part of the culture. But we got on well enough.

NULI I was already set apart, a loner in my family. In some ways Margaret had a privileged position there, a hangover from colonialism. She was regarded as the prime person for official contact.

My mother concerned herself with Margaret's welfare, too. She said to me one day, 'You know Margaret has no father or mother here, no sisters or brothers. You must always look after her, never allow her to feel alone'. My mother wanted my assurance that I wouldn't compromise my marriage by becoming involved with local girls.

Sometimes people would refer to the children as white people, too, although I believe black communities accept children no matter what their skin colour. Australia's white community seems less ready to accept mixed-race children.

MARGARET Yet on my way to Sierra Leone with the children — for Nuli had gone ahead — it was an African man who came up to me and said, 'Do you really think it a good idea to have children of mixed race? They won't belong to either race'.

I told him, 'Our children belong to both'.

In fact, in Sierra Leone the children were well accepted, and the positive experiences there stood them in good stead back here. Our son and eldest daughter came back to finish school in Hobart when they were fifteen and sixteen.

AUTHOR Why did you come back?

NULI We went there for keeps, but after twenty years of independence, things had begun to break down and were getting worse. Since we left, there has been civil war. And I must say that despite the odd pinprick of racism, Australia is a much better place to live.

Among Africans here, from different parts of Africa, there is not much talk of discrimination. Most have jobs and are getting on with life, though it does seem harder for an African woman to find work.

Margaret and Nuli's only son, Chris, is also a doctor. He opened our discussion with a question of his own: 'Where did you get the idea for this book?'.

AUTHOR The spur was Mayor Peter Davis' remark that the children of mixed marriages were mongrels, which reminded me that a hundred years ago mixed-race children were commonly referred to as 'mongrels' and worse in stories, cartoons and newspapers of the day. I was suddenly conscious that some of us have not learned to be more loving, more accepting of one another's differences, even in a hundred years.

CHRIS Davis is stupid. As if there's any pure race, anyway. I first noticed racial differences and racial abuse between West Indian boys and white boys when I was very small, while we were living in England. The first time I was aware of racial discrimination directed at me was in Tasmania when I was about eight. I'd never heard the word 'nigger' before. I had to ask Mum what it meant. There was quite a lot of racial abuse in the playground directed at me and also at a Yugoslav boy.

It was so bad that I was looking forward to going back to Sierra Leone, but when we got there, it was all just very difficult in terms of ordinary living. Our relatives were very nice to us, but there were so many of them. Dad has an enormous family there, and I didn't understand what they were saying at first. I was there from when I was eleven until I was sixteen. I got teased at school there, just as in Australia, but their threshold of violence is much lower than here; they fight very quickly.

AUTHOR So you got knocked about a bit?

CHRIS Yes, I did. Boys there learned to fight as soon as they could walk, so they were experts. I always came off the worst of it. I wasn't harassed exactly, but I was fairly solitary.

Because I was Dad's son, I was Sierra Leonean, and there were many kinds of people, many colours. It was a lot less monocultural than the Tasmania I had left, and returned to.

AUTHOR What did you find at Friend's School at sixteen?

CHRIS I found that people were very ignorant of other cultures, but had no real hostility. University was something else. Six of us shared a house, and one man was a maniac. He'd go on about black people who are never any good at anything except music and politics. Then he'd go on about Asians, because a Filipina girl lived there too.

Apart from that, uni was no problem. But Tasmanians were pretty narrow anyway. They couldn't get away from stereotyping; to them any black man was a sexual animal and good at sport.

AUTHOR Do you feel yourself to be an Australian?

CHRIS Yep! Born here, feel Australian. No problem, I'm Australian.

AUTHOR If you could wave a wand?

CHRIS I'd leave things pretty much the same. Australia is more or less as I'd wish it. Our standard of living here is about the highest anywhere. Not money, but space, comfort, variety. Australia's great!

I haven't come across much racism, though there was a tendency in the hospital in Launceston where I was doing my internship for patients to yell, 'Bring me a white doctor'. And people ask me where I come from.

AUTHOR That's only curiosity.

CHRIS Yes. So I ask where they're from too. It's interesting to know. The best thing about having parents from different backgrounds is simply that it's given me an open attitude about people's differences; not the fact that I've got some cultural heritage from my father and some from my mother — just the fact that I can look at what's around me and appreciate it for the differences as well as the similarities.

The only bad thing I can think about mixed heritage is that you don't have the same sense of certainty as you would if you could say: I am so-and-so from such-and-such a place and my forbears have always lived here, and we do this and we've always done this, and we will always do this. I think that having that unshakeable certainty of your identity and your heritage and your future must give you great strength. At the same time I would never want to be like that, because inflexibility is a weakness.

Though their personalities and their experiences are very different, Chris and Marcia and my daughter, Charmaine, all responded in very similar ways to being the eldest child in a mixed-race Australian family with an Australian mother. Their confidence in their identity was unshakeable and they all saw their mixed heritage as a positive in their lives.

I asked Charmaine what she thought of mixed-race marriage.

CHARMAINE For me it's perfectly normal, with no problems specifically related to nationality or race. There was no enormous decision you had to make, because Dad is a Christian, and has always spoken English. If he was Muslim, or Buddhist, that would have been a bigger difference — or if English had not been his main language.

If there were differences between you and Dad, they were sorted out and decided before I knew anything about them.

Of course, I noticed the physical differences, but I was always proud of who Dad was. I never tried to hide it. Never. Other kids at school, Italians and Greeks and others, often tried to hide who they were, and pretended to be ordinary Australians. I never did. I was glad Daddy was different. I was glad he wasn't like all the other fathers. I was even glad that our family had friends who were different — the Manochas, the Stocks, the Pisciottas — all different races as I see now.

AUTHOR Were you proud, or happy, to be different too?

CHARMAINE Yes, I guess I am. I was always happy about that. Everyone knows I'm different, but they never pick the Indian or Sinhalese bit. It has always been a positive thing as far as I'm concerned. Tasmania was the only bad time, partly because I started in the middle of a school year. But, even then, I was picked on less for my mixed heritage than kids with glasses or kids with braces, or any other differences. It never bothered me.

Maybe Ashley (the oldest of her three brothers and only a year younger than Charmaine) might have had more trouble than I did; he's the most Indian-looking in the family. But I don't think he did, unless there was name-calling that I never heard about. He always mixed in well. On the other hand, you get picked on if you're exceptionally brainy, too. And Ashley is that. He was always tall, too, and good at sports. That surely helped him fit in.

I can't think of anything negative at all. I always was so proud of you when you were all dressed up in a sari. They're so beautiful — far better than any Western dress.

We grew up Australian because your influence was greater, because you were always there. If you had been a Sri Lankan/Indian mother, then your different way of doing things around the house would have influenced us as children.

I remember your efforts to mix us into the Indian Cultural Society in Tasmania. We didn't fit, because we were already Australians. I'm sure you tried because you thought it the right thing to do, but you must have realised that it wasn't quite us, because we only went twice. I knew it would have been your idea. Dad was always busy, working so hard — perhaps because he always had to be twice as good to get rewards such as promotions, and also becoming as Australian as possible. He was right, anyway. If you live in Australia, I think it's important to live as an Australian, be an Australian, though it's okay to keep an interest in one's heritage.

AUTHOR What about your children? How do you explain that one of their four grandparents looks very different?

CHARMAINE Well, one of them came in, covered in mud, at two or three years of age, saying, 'Look, now I'm like Grandpa!'. Not so different from what you tell me I did at about the same age.

They're aware of Dad's difference; they know his skin colour has affected theirs, even if only marginally. They know his family came from where the tea grows. We talk about it; it's part of their heritage too.

7

INTERRACIAL MARRIAGES IN THE 1970s

We want Australia to provide the world with the first truly multi-racial society, with no tensions of any kind possible between any of the races within it.

Prime Minister John Gorton, 1971[1]

Coalition governments led by Prime Ministers Menzies, Holt and Gorton steadily opened Australia up to multi-racial immigration. In 1971 Prime Minister John Gorton announced in Singapore that the Australian Government was determined to work towards a balanced multi-racial society. Many mixed-race immigrants had come to Australia from India and Sri Lanka, and many students, mostly from south-east Asia, had decided to stay here after finishing their education. There were already 23 000 Chinese permanent residents, less than half of whom were Australian-born. Just as in the 1890s, they were as vehemently opposed to intermarriage as other Australians. Lee Siew-eng, in a study of Sydney Chinese, found 64 per cent of them opposed mixed-race marriage, compared to 69 per cent of the general population identified in a similar study.[2]

By November 1971 the Liberal Prime Minister, William McMahon, had withdrawn the last of Australia's troops from the conflict in Vietnam, and in 1973 Gough Whitlam's Labor Government adopted a policy of non-discrimination on racial grounds in applications for citizenship. The Australian Citizenship Act enabled all immigrants to apply for citizenship after three years' residence in Australia. For the first time non-Europeans in Australia faced no extra hurdles.

As in all wars, Australian soldiers fell in love with young women in the countries where they fought, and Vietnamese brides of Australian soldiers slipped into the country with much less antagonism than that faced by Cherry Parker — the first Japanese bride — twenty years earlier. Saigon fell in April 1975, and thousands of refugees fled Vietnam. During the same period East Timorese sought hasty refuge from Indonesia's invading forces. By the end of 1975, when Malcolm Fraser's Liberal Government took office, over 1000 Vietnamese and nearly 2000 Timorese had been accepted for resettlement. Within one year, boats overloaded with refugees fleeing either war or economic hardship began arriving on our northern coastline. Australia became a port of first arrival after officials in Singapore, Malaysia and Indonesia refused to let Vietnamese refugees land, and sent the boats back out to sea. For the first time, Australians felt they had lost control of who could enter their country, and by 1978 it was established that ethnic Chinese made up the greatest number of refugees. These included those fleeing Vietnam, and also refugees from Indonesia's invasion of Timor, such as Betsy's family.

BETSY My family came here from Dili when the Indonesians came. I was fourteen, and I went to school here in Darwin for two years, but did not learn very much English. I met Daniel when I was twenty, but my father wanted me to marry a Chinese man.

DANIEL I was born in Mount Gambier in 1962, and I'm fifth-generation Australian — actually more than that on my father's side, because his mother was half-Aboriginal. My grandmother's family lived as ordinary white Australians, though. They didn't hide their Aboriginal ancestor, but mentioned it only as a matter of interest.

I met Betsy here in Darwin in 1982 when I was twenty and travelling around Australia, so though I liked her I didn't stay, but kept on travelling. When I got back to Mount Gambier, I felt like settling down and I married the wrong girl. When our marriage broke up, I thought of Betsy, and wrote to her. She said, 'Come and visit me'.

I should have married Betsy when we first met, for her first marriage — to a Hong Kong businessman to please her father — was disastrous too. Her family is very patriarchal. The father demands obedience, and all that big family, twelve of them, have followed his wishes and disowned Betsy. Because of her divorce, Betsy is dead to them.

AUTHOR It must be an uncomfortable situation for Betsy here in Darwin.

DANIEL Yes, but her former husband has shared custody of their son. If we left Darwin now we'd have to leave him here with his father. We're working hard with the plan of leaving in a few years. We have a coffee shop with snacks and light meals. Betsy is a good cook and I work every daylight hour. There is a lot of money in Darwin and in ten years we'll be able to retire and live wherever we like.

Except for the problems with Betsy's family, we have no difficulties at all. In Darwin, everyone marries anybody. Just go to Casuarina Shopping Centre if you want to see mixed marriages!

Do you know Betsy's family has never seen our little Benjamin?

AUTHOR   I can hardly believe that anyone is willing to give up a daughter and a grandson.

BETSY   It's not the first time. When I was one month old, I was sick so they gave me away. Then, when I was five or six years old my foster mother died so my first family had to take me back. My auntie was given away too.

DANIEL   It's hard to understand people who'll give away their children, then years later demand a say in their lives, isn't it? At the moment there are vast differences in understanding between people. Asians can't understand that Australians like to discuss the ins and outs of things, even though they don't necessarily agree with them. And we can't understand their habit of giving their children away.

I think even here in Australia, or perhaps especially here where there are so many different people, discussion of this race or that will die out. It doesn't matter whether we ever come to look alike, but for the future of Australia we will all have to learn to do things the same way, to think alike, and to understand one another.

From the early 1970s there was another, more orderly, trickle of refugees, this time from south Asia. Unlike the turmoil in Vietnam and East Timor, the introduction of socialism in Sri Lanka under Mrs Bandaranaike's Government was not bloody, but it was disturbing enough for many professional, English-educated Sri Lankans to seek a democratic haven in Australia.

Bandhu, a former senior government engineer, brought his English wife, Joan, and their three children to Australia in 1973.

BANDHU   We were not allowed to bring much capital out of Sri Lanka. One hundred and fifty pounds for each adult and seventy-five pounds for each child was sent by bank draft. In cash, we were allowed only two pounds, ten shillings each.

We arrived on Saturday and on Monday I started looking for a job. I was interviewed the next day, and on Thursday I started work on the construction of a pipeline across the Hawkesbury. At that time there were many jobs for experienced engineers.

I applied for citizenship three months after I came because I was nearly forty-five and, with no capital here except my skills, I needed to get into the public service, and onto their superannuation scheme. For that I had to be an Australian citizen. I had no qualms about applying for citizenship as soon as possible, and have never regretted it.

I didn't encounter any discrimination at work, but I can't count the slurs, the racist gestures, the condescending tones I have met in daily life. When people ask what my nationality is, I say Australian. And yet, after all these years, while fully aware of how good Australia has been to me, I don't feel at home here, especially now after the recent racialist headlines. I think such feelings were there all the time, but now it's out in the open.

I'm retired now, and the children are all independent, so twice a year I go back to Sri Lanka. There, I feel at home immediately. But I'm not complaining. We got what we came for. Our children are all 100 per cent Australian; they and our seven grandchildren have a good future here.

JOAN   I like it here. Had we not fitted in comfortably we would have gone to England. But I'm happy here. Our friends are mostly Sri Lankans and other mixed couples, and I've made a lot of women friends, too.

BANDHU Women seem to make friends more easily. Even coloured women are better able to assimilate here than coloured men. When I meet the neighbourhood women while walking they don't speak to me, but if I'm with Joan, it's always a 'Good morning!'.

AUTHOR That's because women fear men; it doesn't make any difference what ethnic origin they are.

JOAN You're right. Women in Australia — well, here in Sydney — are very wary of men; all men. We have had no problems living here. We've had lovely neighbours throughout, and there's never been even the faintest suggestion of any sort of racism or them not wanting us here, or anything like that.

Many of our behaviours, reactions to situations and perceptions are imprinted by the culture of our childhood, maybe even past generations. In the 1970s Alison, a young Australian nurse, met and fell in love with a handsome Egyptian Muslim scholar whose different perceptions of marriage and family changed her life.

ALISON I was twenty-one when I met Hamdi, who was doing post-doctoral research here. He was charming, well-travelled, and well-educated. He spoke seven languages. He was brilliant. He quite dazzled me. He was my first lover.

I was just this quiet little girl from the country who'd gone to boarding school and then into nursing. Living in the nurses' home, doors locked at 10 o'clock, and you never got married during your training — never! When I wanted to marry Hamdi, I had to see the Matron, then the priest at the church attached to the hospital. They did not like an interracial marriage one bit — and even worse, a Muslim!

Hamdi had to see them too. He was so charming, such a man of the world. After an hour with him, they probably wondered what he saw in me! He won them over.

My family hated my marriage. The more they said, 'You're not going to do it', the more determined I became. They wouldn't attend the wedding, nor finance any part of it. I was even cut out of their wills. No Muslim was going to benefit from any of the family money!

I put together a few pennies for a suitable dress, and my girlfriend let me have her house for the reception. I did all the catering the night before, and we were married in a local church because the father of one of my nursing friends was the vicar. Later we had an Islamic ceremony.

AUTHOR Did they forgive you after a while?

ALISON They never forgave me. I had no support from anyone all through our marriage, which lasted for five years.

AUTHOR Was the split anything to do with the racial difference, or religious incompatibility?

ALISON Everything to do with it. At the wedding I was so in love! I was married to this wonderful man — my dream come true. I danced on air!

The morning after the wedding my husband told me he didn't love me. He told me he married me so he could stay in Australia. He was here on a student visa; he had to return after finishing his studies. Marriage to me — or some other Australian girl — was his way of circumventing that.

I was so shocked I was numb for weeks. It didn't matter, he said, because we got on well, and he quite liked me. In his culture he was accustomed to arranged marriages. He said, 'People grow to love one another after marriage'.

I began to think I didn't know what love was, because it was my first relationship. I wondered if what I felt was more hero-worship than love. We were good friends, and I thought maybe he would grow to love me, so I did my best to sustain the marriage. Throughout our time together Hamdi was very good company, but it was not the marriage that most Australian girls dream of.

While we were studying, working, living an ordinary sort of life in my beloved Melbourne, I could cope, and I thought we were getting on well. But Hamdi pined for his own people and his own culture. He became a leader of his community, and thrived on their accolades, becoming more and more involved. I would come home and find the house full of people speaking Arabic. I determined to do everything I could to become a part of his life, so I went to classes in Arabic and French, because they spoke French too.

From time to time we would go to Canberra for a weekend. I'd live in a Muslim community where the women spoke only Arabic, and spent all the weekend preparing and cooking food. I was with them day and night, and as well as helping me with my Arabic studies, they taught me how to cook their Arabic dishes.

We fed the men first, and they'd go to the sitting-room; then we'd feed the children. Then, the women would eat whatever was left, even though it was cold and scrappy. It really opened my mind, but I wasn't hurt or angry, I was too busy learning about how these people lived. They were good people, and I wasn't sorry to have that experience.

Then for a year or so, my husband was very busy with a special research project at the university, spending most nights and weekends there. I helped him in this, and it became very important to me. I had been feeling so insignificant — just a little nurse who had never even been on a university campus. Gradually, Hamdi gave me more and more things to do, and soon I was marking students' assignments, checking papers and keeping notes for him, and naturally reading all the books for the course and more, because I was so nervous about making a mistake.

Then one Saturday morning, we went into the lab, and he was looking at the apparatus, puzzled, for he could not see why the nitrate was not refining to the degree he wanted. I'd been staring at that apparatus for the last month of nights, so I explained how a plug of cottonwool would create suction, etcetera, etcetera. He wrote the paper and got the reward, but I got an even bigger reward. I realised I could think. I began to concentrate on my language studies for hours every night after work.

By this time we had been married over four years and I wanted a child. I was busy saving up the deposit for a house, making plans, but not yet pregnant, when my husband said, 'Six weeks after the baby is born, we'll take it back to my parents. It will be good for you to meet them, and we'll leave the child there with them. I want the child raised in Egypt as a Muslim'.

From then on my legs were crossed! There was no way I was going to have a child, only to give it up! That was really the end of the marriage. All my traditional dreams of a loving husband and home and family were gone. I told my husband that our marriage was over, and slept in the loungeroom for six months before I actually left him.

One day, I gathered my strength and told Hamdi I was leaving that day; it was a Sunday. After he'd gone out I sat on the bed and my knees shook so much I couldn't move! I knew I had to leave him, but I couldn't actually do it!

I rang my family, and they came and bundled up my clothes as fast as they could and whisked me away.

Then I went into my academic career full of excitement and energy. I went to university and graduated and went onto the university staff and actually before long I outstripped Hamdi! It's what I have done, and loved for nearly thirty years. I have no regrets.

On the eve of our divorce all those years ago, Hamdi came to me and said, 'Will you please come back? I've made a mistake. Since you left I've realised that you really are the woman I want to be with. It happened like I said it would. I did grow to love you'.

'You're too late', I told him. 'I've already paid the solicitor for my divorce, and I'd never get my money back.'

Between interviews in Perth I went to a hairdresser, who was curious about the notebooks and tape recorder I carried. When I explained what I was doing, Charlotte offered to tell me her story while she did my hair.

CHARLOTTE I was born in 1948 and brought up as a Catholic. I learned all about the evils of racism, but when I married my Chinese husband, I found out that Asians are far more racist than we are. Asians — well, Chinese, anyway — are completely different. Their totally different culture includes different values, a different thinking system altogether, and I don't think Australians have realised this yet; they haven't realised what these changes are doing to our society.

When I first met my husband, though, I found him extremely interesting; so different, so exciting.

AUTHOR He fascinated you with the differences that later became a worry?

CHARLOTTE Exactly. From the beginning my father felt that the man I loved was unknowable. I respected my father's judgment, so I didn't marry until after we'd lived together for three years in Manila. We married just before we returned home to Australia. By then it was 1975 and we both knew what we were doing.

It's ironic, but now I know that that is exactly the time that our marriage began to break down. Over the years that followed, our relationship became more and more difficult, but I didn't know why, and I struggled on. We had three children.

My husband had spent the most important years of his life in Australia, but he was still very Asian. I didn't know it then, but he had been going to prostitutes regularly — probably since he left school, and for the past seven years ... since shortly after our marriage and our return to Australia, he had been seeing just one prostitute, and he had fallen in love with her. He was besotted with her, so I took the children and moved out.

I didn't know him until I left him. Christians will never understand how Chinese think. What we do in kindness, they see as weakness. Chinese think they're better than anyone else, and they will never understand the idea of actually considering some one else's feelings. I know how to get his respect now. I speak to him roughly. I show him no kindness. I am deliberately hard; harder than I'd ever dream of behaving towards anyone else. It works. It's the only thing he understands, and he respects me now, because it matches the way he and other Chinese behave — completely to please themselves.

We keep in contact only because of the children — three beautiful, spectacular Australian children. They were the bonus I got from my marriage. Otherwise it was a disaster for me. I can no longer relate to men, or indeed to anyone.

Grace and her brother and sisters came from east Malaysia to Australia thirty years ago as students, temporarily under the care and guidance of a Sydney couple. The children's Chinese parents had asked a long-time pen-friend to become the guardian of their children while they completed their education in Australia. It was a demanding, even onerous, task. The boy soon fell ill and returned to Malaysia, but the Australian couple were responsible for Grace and her two sisters for seven years, while they finished school and grew up. Only then did Grace's parents and the rest of her family migrate here.

Grace became a successful dress designer, achieving fame when she designed the uniforms for Australia's participants in the 1998 Commonwealth Games.

GRACE I've often thought that Auntie Chris and Uncle Jack took on a big job, supervising three teenagers from another culture, another part of the world. We were very lucky to have such guardians. I've been lucky in other ways, too. Racism is around, I suppose, but I've lived in Australia for thirty years and I haven't noticed anything. Perhaps it is just here. In a Double Bay cafe you can count the true-blue Australians on one hand. Everyone is a ring-in. So who would cast the first stone?

I married my first boss. George is a Greek Cypriot, so he is not fair-skinned. We blended well together. We were married in his Greek Orthodox church, because that was important to him, but eventually our marriage failed because of racial difference. Although George came here when he was three years old, he was still very much a Greek Cypriot husband, and he wanted a meek, demure wife who would be content to stay at home and manage the household. But I am modern and strong; I didn't want to stay at home. I'm a good designer, and I wanted to work.

AUTHOR But you'd worked together. He knew how important designing was to you.

GRACE Yes, he did, but when our second boy was born, he wanted all my time to be spent raising the boys. So I stayed home for six years and did just that. Then, when I wanted to stretch my wings again, we separated. My husband was happy to leave the boys with me because he knew I was a good mother. They're sixteen and nineteen now, growing up; they live their own lives.

Some Chinese cling to their culture but I don't, and my kids act like and feel like Australians. I love Sydney — we all do. I travel a lot, and every time I go away, when I come back, I'm so glad that I live in Sydney. My sons and I are happy here, comfortable. We feel Australian. We are Australian.

Cynthia, an Australian nurse, had a troubled marriage after an idyllic romance.

CYNTHIA My husband is Sinhalese. I met him in 1973, and I didn't know how my parents would take it, but they were wonderful. We married within five months, but my husband didn't tell his family until after we were married.

Adjusting to different cultural attitudes within a marriage is tiring, even though Buddhism is fairly compatible with Christianity. Our marriage is not really the best, and my husband works in another city now. He visits as often as he can, and the boys go and stay with him every chance they get.

There are all kinds of cultural things that make mixed-race marriages difficult. For example my husband doesn't like me to even talk to other men, and the most public of social kisses evokes extreme jealousy. Then, there are different family expectations, particularly different behaviours and courtesies with family members, particularly when they come to stay as guests in your house. Sinhalese, or perhaps Asians generally, expect to live in your house for ... well, for as long as they want. But Australians are used to a fair bit of privacy. We both found adjusting to different expectations very difficult.

Ben and Nirmala also had to undertake vast adjustments to their different cultural behaviours and expectations. Ben came as a migrant to Adelaide with his parents when he was a child, and traces of his north England accent remain. He met Nirmala, the daughter of a Hindu Tamil family, at the home of a mutual friend in Singapore.

BEN   When I go out with Nirmala, I don't notice any prejudice, except sometimes when we meet people for the first time. They look at Nirmala up and down, slowly, and then look at me. I'm aware that they're thinking, 'This is an odd couple'.

No one has ever been rude. I've never met any form of discrimination here in Australia. Sometimes, when we are shopping, Nirmala and I become separated, and I go looking for her up and down the aisles, and then I'll see her, this dark woman! And I'm reminded that, indeed, she is dark! Otherwise I just don't see it.

NIRMALA   When we were first married, people here in Australia would look at me and say, 'Nice and brown', or something like that. Not unpleasantly, just observing that I was unusual.

AUTHOR   What did your family feel about you marrying Ben?

NIRMALA   My mother was devastated because it meant going so far away. But my family gets on well with Ben. They like him.

BEN   My family welcomed Nirmala. When my Uncle George — a typical uneducated north-of-England man — said something racist to my mother, she told him off. In England there is a lot of racism. I notice it in the streets when I go there.

Young people at work have asked me for advice on interracial marriage. I tell them that if they want it to work, they have to give in 90 per cent of the time, because different backgrounds do add stress.

NIRMALA   One major difference is: Australians have an argument and five minutes later it's all over. Asians, particularly Indian women like me, hold a grudge. We have such a strong pride — so strong it makes us behave stupidly sometimes.

BEN   Many times Nirmala has not spoken to me for a week. I know she's nursing a grudge, though I don't often know what it's about. This is why I want to help young people who are considering marrying someone from a different race or background. There must be tremendous adjustments — a deep understanding that other people do things differently. You have to be prepared to learn what you can about them, about their beliefs, upbringing, all the things that will affect the marriage, and even if you can't understand, if the marriage is going to work, you've just got to accept the differences. I've had to make an effort to understand Hinduism, too. I've really studied it.

AUTHOR   This willingness to bend, to adapt, to undertake serious study towards understanding your wife's culture possibly played a big part in the happiness, even in the survival of your marriage.

BEN   Yes, I believe it has. At difficult times I saw that it was necessary for me to give way, or, if you like, move towards Nirmala's perceptions of the situation or problem. As I tell the youngsters considering marriages like ours, we, the Australians, have to be prepared to give in 90 per cent of the time.

It seems, from among the couples to whom I've spoken, that many more of the 'ordinary Australians' — like Ben — have taken pains to study the culture of their 'other' spouses and make changes to more fully adapt to their needs, than the reverse. Perhaps, though, the partner coming into Australia's culture has been making more subtle, more constant ongoing changes as he or she learns to fit into the wider Australian society.

8

1970s MARRIAGES WITH MIXED-RACE CHILDREN

> I'd like Australia to be a place where everyone
> can be whatever they are,
> and be comfortable, and nice to one another.

A 14-year-old Australian schoolgirl of Celtic/African parentage

Many couples spoke of their pre-marital concern for any children they might have, and this was also an oft-mentioned worry of the couple's parents, but after the children were born most parents of mixed-race children felt comfortable that in Australia, the children probably suffered less than if they were brought up elsewhere. A Japanese mother said of her Japanese/Spanish Australian son: 'Australia is a much better place (than Japan) for a boy like him to grow up'.

Ian, now a successful lawyer running his own practice, and his Chinese wife, Claudia, have lived and worked in New Zealand, Sydney and Adelaide, and now make Wollongong their home. They have noticed that within each of these communities, attitudes to their marriage vary widely.

IAN I met Claudia when she nursed me during a stay in hospital when I was a student. We began going out and I suddenly found myself in an Asian environment. It was a novelty for me, exotic.

CLAUDIA I came from Malaysia to Australia for nursing training in 1969. I've had very little trouble. Elderly patients sometimes ask for an Australian nurse to look after them and once a very dark Lebanese patient, much darker than I am, said he didn't come all the way to Australia to be looked after by someone like me. So even though we were both migrants, he perceived himself to be superior.

IAN   Visible difference is an issue, particularly with European migrants. Our daughter has suffered from slurs all her life.

AUTHOR   What about your families? Were they happy about your marriage?

CLAUDIA   I never asked them. My family was poor and needed my financial help, so I sent every alternate pay home.

IAN   My family objected. I was only twenty-one, so they would have objected to me marrying anyone, but Claudia being Chinese didn't help. My grandmother didn't speak to us for three years.

When my mother (an Anglican) married my father (a Catholic), my grandmother reacted in much the same way. Yet when my father died, my grandmother took us into her home, helped us financially and in every other way. My mother and sister and I have every reason to be grateful to her. She got over her anger about my marriage to Claudia, too, but it took time.

Claudia and I have met very little racism here in Wollongong. When we're in Sydney we notice it much more. In big cities there are many derogatory terms used for Asians, such as 'slanty eyes' or 'power-points' or 'slopes'. Once, in Sydney, I was congratulated on the amount of international work I was getting for the firm. 'It's recognition', I was told, 'that Sydney is now an international city'.

I was pleased and said, 'Yes, it is. Twenty-five per cent of the north shore is Asian already'.

Someone said, abruptly, 'You don't have to remind me. I live in Chatswood'. Then he remembered Claudia. In Sydney, little things like that happen a lot. There, when I walk down the street with Claudia, I'm conscious of walking with an Asian. Here in Wollongong and in other places, I'm not.

I think there should be more control of racism. A lot of people criticise Mahathir, but in Malaysia and Indonesia and Singapore, the leaders know that you have to control the press while you preach racial tolerance. Racial tension is there, but you never hear anyone say it. Mahathir rules over institutionalised racism in Malaysia, but he will never verbalise anything but racial tolerance. And the media in Malaysia is terrific.

AUTHOR   But in Malaysia the media is censored, controlled by the government.

IAN   If the choice is freedom of speech or racial division, I'd give up freedom of speech, like Mahathir and Lee Kuan Yew have done.

At our farewell from Sydney, for the first time in twenty-four years someone asked me, 'What's it like to be in a multicultural marriage?'. But we have a monocultural marriage — a culture we've built over twenty-five years — mostly Chinese, I suppose, but here in Australia with Australian value systems. It's right for us. Perhaps that's what multiculturalism is. I understand how everyone is confused about multiculturalism because here, in Australia, the cultures aren't mixed; there are several different cultures side by side.

CLAUDIA   My colleagues often say, 'It's difficult enough to keep a marriage together if you're both the same. How do you manage, being married to someone of a different race?'.

My answer is that it really isn't different; you're just working at different issues.

IAN   You go in knowing that you have to work at it.

CLAUDIA Every time I go out, every time I go into a shop, I'm ignored, or not served in turn. Is it racism or is it because I'm a woman? Sometimes I've said, 'Am I invisible … ?'.

IAN It's more than that. Asians have body language that Australians mis-read. For example, Claudia never maintains eye contact when she pays over money — Australians do. Claudia and her family don't maintain eye contact with a waiter or waitress in a restaurant — Australians do. Australians feel that Chinese deliberately distance themselves.

CLAUDIA There's something else we, as Chinese, do that upsets Australians. Our loudness upsets people, and after thirty years, I've just realised it. I am now conscious of how a group of Chinese speaking Chinese in public are perceived. When my mother and father and aunt come out here to Australia, they speak Chinese loudly — talking and laughing, really loud belly laughs. If they argue it gets very noisy.
　　People are offended, just because of the noise. Australians are quieter. It took me a long time to realise that it's just the loudness, just the noisiness of Chinese talking that Australians find offensive.
　　I find myself seeing some things from the Australian point of view now, and I find myself criticising some immigrants, too. A few will be genuine, but the criminals will be the ones with money to get here. And, I know that Asians are cheating with this family reunion scheme.

IAN It's difficult to say that, in the present climate in Australia. But perhaps Claudia can say it.

Ian's view that the way to combat racism is to hide it is shared by many journalists who over the years have written admiringly about the lack of public racism in countries such as Malaysia, Singapore and Indonesia. Journalist Louise Williams, more perceptive than most, wrote in 1996 that discussion of racism in Indonesia is taboo simply because the honesty of bringing it out in the open would be too violent to bear.[1] But things do not go away just because we do not talk about them, at least not in a country with a tradition of open public discussion, such as Australia.

　　Though only very few of my interviewees approved of anything Pauline Hanson said or did, many said they were glad that her contributions ensured open discussion of race differences. In race riots in Indonesia during recent years many Indonesians were killed, and hundreds fled for their lives. Who can say that open discussion among all Indonesians about their commonly-held nationality, and the many beliefs that Muslims and Christians share might not have made the mobs more reasonable? Talking about differences may have sufficed to air grudges, and perhaps violence may have been avoided, or lessened. Whether or not this is true for Malaysia or Indonesia, I am sure that Australians like to bring concerns and differences of any kind out for open discussion and possible resolution.

　　Katy, Ian and Claudia's daughter, followed her father into law and is currently working in a big city law firm.

KATY   Children of mixed-race families learn quite young that our identity is going to be questioned. Other people are not sure, just by looking at us, who we are, but they know we are different.

I've always identified with my white Australian family. I've never really known my mother's family. Yet, at the age of five or six, when I started school, the other children didn't see me as an Australian. They didn't know who or what I was, but they thought I was different. The problem was that I didn't feel different. I was called a 'Ching Chong', 'slanty-eyed', those sorts of things. The biggest shock wasn't the names they called me, but that they called me names at all, because I felt myself to be just like them.

Mixed-race children who feel themselves to be Australian, but are not recognised as such, have a peculiar barrier thrown up between them and their peers. I'm sure all mixed-parentage children feel this. When I was growing up there were years when I tried not to have Chinese friends, because I didn't want to be seen as Chinese, because I wasn't Chinese. I spent a lot of time telling children that I was just like them — I read the same books, knew the same stories, had the same friends, not Chinese friends.

AUTHOR   The way you're telling it, you saw your Chineseness as a negative, whereas your parents see it as a plus.

KATY   It all comes back to a question of identity. My mother is Chinese, and is easily recognised as an Asian woman who has been in Australia for some time. My father is quite clearly a white Australian. With me, some people assume I'm a white Australian; some think I'm a full-blood Chinese; others don't know what I am.

AUTHOR   Could you have done anything different? Anything that may have helped you cope with what seems to have been a continual battle ever since you were very small?

KATY   I could have learned an Asian language, for a start. I refused to do that. I was determined that I wouldn't learn Chinese when my mother tried to teach me. That was one of my big trump cards: 'I don't speak Chinese, only English, therefore I'm Australian'.

I remember finding some white make-up when I was a child, I put it on to make myself up to look white. My skin is fair enough so that I buy a pale make-up now, but it doesn't matter, I still **feel** dark.

I'm not sure I'll have children. All my life, I've had to prove that I am whiter than white. I identify myself as white European, to strengthen me when I'm told go back to where I came from.

AUTHOR   You're still told that?

KATY   Oh yes. Countless times. Not every day, but many times every year. The worst occasion was at a railway station. Some men walked behind me, talking in an odd way. Then I turned and saw they were two neo-Nazis — the tight jeans, the big belt buckles, the tattoos, jackboots, tight white T-shirt and no hair — and I realised they were saying particularly unpleasant things. They were saying, 'I give you dog, you suck my cock' — that sort of thing — in a terrible mock Asian accent. They spat at me and told me to go back to where I came from, that I wasn't wanted in this country.

That was the worst experience I've had. I couldn't catch a train for about twelve months after that. But what upsets me still is the realisation that my first thought was not outrage at their disgusting behaviour, but outrage that they thought I was Chinese. They thought I was Chinese, and that's not who I am. I am Australian.

I was already adult then, yet I was too busy, and am still too busy, fighting my own identity battle to jump quickly to the front-line of the general racism battle. I'll always be too busy asserting, 'That's not who I am. I am Australian'.

AUTHOR There's an answer to this. You're the face of Australia's future. That's what this book is really about, I hope: saying that these boundaries between Asian migrants, white Australians, Aboriginals and whatever else are useless boundaries, they shouldn't be there. You are an Australian and need not worry about whether you're a mix of this or that, for everyone is a mix of something; there's no pure race in the world.

What I'm hoping is that you and others who are worried by a lost sense of who they are will say, 'My father is Indian or my mother is Chinese or whatever, but I am Australian'.

KATY Maybe that will be the future. At the moment, mixed-race people are still forced to find themselves, particularly if we look different. Even some of my friends still say things which remind me that to them I don't belong here. The other day we were discussing whether 'Celtic' was pronounced with a soft or a hard C. I said it was pronounced with the soft C, and now I realise I was probably wrong, but it was only a gentle argument for the sake of argument. I felt I had a particularly cogent argument — that if it came from the German and Latin, then it would be a hard C, but if it came from the French and Latin, it would be a soft C, and as we have no way of knowing which, I plumped for it coming to England via France.

My friend put me in my place very neatly by saying, 'What would you know? This is my racial history, not yours'.

AUTHOR But, Katy, you had a marvellous answer — two marvellous answers. Firstly, it is your heritage. From your father you're up to 50 per cent Celtic, and secondly, there is your knowledge of Latin and other European languages.

KATY I can't fight back. To be told I don't belong here still shocks me. My father has some difficulties too. If people say things when Mum and I aren't present, he has to choose to nail his colours to the wall, or sit quietly and say nothing. Unless things change fast, and dramatically, my fiancé will have to tolerate that too.

AUTHOR What can be done to change this situation?

KATY Too many migrants live, and their children grow up, in their own cultural community pockets and never know anyone from another culture well. Most Chinese and Greeks and Italians, in particular, don't even know the mainstream Australian majority culture, let alone anything about one another. The father I remember as a child was extremely Aussie, but he loves my mother, so he began to value and learn about Chinese culture, and he taught me. Most of my love and appreciation of things Chinese — Chinese gardens, Chinese cooking — comes from my father.

AUTHOR You're saying that the people who immigrate here will stay separate until they immerse themselves in the mainstream culture, and at the same time we should all try to do what your father has done: learn as much as we can about another culture — perhaps many. That sounds difficult, but easier if one is married to someone of another culture; at least there's more motivation.

KATY We are, all of us, a mixture of an incredible number of influences, but when anyone meets me, what they notice is the colour of my skin.

It disturbed me that any young Australian should feel so displaced here, in the country where she was born. What is the Australian norm today? Most of the mixed-race young adults I met were relaxedly and happily Australian. What was notable in the interviews, too, was the number of 'other' partners, such as Nirmala (a Tamil), Grace (a Malaysian Chinese) and Saemi (a Japanese) who now feel happily, almost fiercely Australian, but there are many who, even after twenty years here with an Australian spouse and Australian children, still regard Australians as foreigners.

Malcolm, an Australian academic, met Nilanthi, his Sinhalese wife, when they were both students. They get on well despite the vast differences in culture and religion, for Nilanthi's Buddhism is very important to her. For over twenty years they have adapted and adjusted their lives and only now, perhaps because they now know each other so well, they find there are many areas where they thoughts and feelings diverge. Perhaps it is just because they are so happily settled one with the other that they now feel confident enough to address the differences.

NILANTHI I came from a homogenous society where a white man sticks out like a sore thumb. When I first came from Sri Lanka to Australia, I used to think I would stick out like that too, but no one took any notice of me. No one cared that I looked a bit different; there were lots of people who looked a bit different.

AUTHOR Did your parents approve of your marriage?

NILANTHI No. In Sri Lanka you don't marry out, you marry into a caste, into a family. People talked.
    When we brought my parents out here for the wedding, we put them into International House, and married three days after they arrived. They had just enough time to listen to all the students saying how wonderful Malcolm was.
    When I first married Malcolm, I used to feel self-conscious about taking him into Sri Lankan groups, but when they get to know him, they like him better than me. So now I think it's a plus to be an odd couple.

AUTHOR Has your marriage disadvantaged you in any way?

MALCOLM Advantaged, rather. I have very few characteristics that mark me out from the mob, but going in to a dinner or a party, with Nilanthi in a sari on my arm, does reinforce her, and thus my difference. The only negatives are in our particular characters.

NILANTHI That's what I'm beginning to feel. I would like Malcolm to learn Sinhalese, but he's hopeless with languages.

MALCOLM It doesn't concern me that I can't speak or understand Sinhalese. I've never had the time to learn, but also, language is a way of distancing myself. I need that distance; it's a way of coping.

NILANTHI Malcolm is agnostic, but allows me my religion, and I take the children to

Buddhist classes. I feel very sad that Malcolm is not into all this spiritual stuff, because he's very wise and would get a lot from it — more than me. In day-to-day life Malcolm is more like a Buddhist than I am.

AUTHOR You mentioned different attitudes — to what? To bringing up children?

MALCOLM There have been great differences, but it would be hard to put it down to differences between Australian and Sri Lankan attitudes. We're noticing them more now, but that is probably because as the years go by we get to know and understand one another better.

NILANTHI We've not had much conflict until now. Malcolm is very perceptive, aware of many subtle things. Sri Lankans are some of the greatest racists, I think. They think nothing of making racist statements. If you people spoke like that to us, you'd be sued, and quartered at dawn! Ethnic groups refer to Australians in dreadfully scathing terms. One European migrant I know won't let her children play with Australian children.

Australians are a very tolerant race. I think we're very lucky. If you went to Sri Lanka you would not be treated so well.

AUTHOR Do you think of yourself as Australian, Nilanthi?

NILANTHI After twenty years? Not really. I'm Buddhist, I think ...

MALCOLM Nilanthi is very much a Sri Lankan. She has a very strong identification as Sri Lankan. She is like most Sri Lankans here; they retain a very strong connection with their former homeland. I've rarely heard Sri Lankans discuss an Australian problem, such as the plight of the Aborigines or the deteriorating environment.

It's very easy to say that differences a couple might have stem from racial differences, but I believe they're often personality or character differences.

Sharmila — Malcolm and Nilanthi's 17-year-old daughter — is a first-year Arts/Law student. She has a younger sister, Rani, and a brother.

AUTHOR Do you feel that your life differs from those of your friends?

SHARMILA We have two cultures in our home, whereas most other kids don't. We have restrictions put on us that other kids don't have. We know it's Mum's culture, but it has nothing to do with us, here and now. I have a lot of friends who are Sri Lankan, and they face the same problems.

AUTHOR Do you feel yourself to be ... what? Australian? Sri Lankan? A mixture?

SHARMILA I'd probably say Australian, with a little bit of Sri Lankan. Because I look Australian, I'm treated differently by the Sri Lankans, until they realise I have a Sri Lankan mother, and when I'm with Australians, they think I'm Australian. When I was younger, my Sri Lankan friends were called 'dog poo' and nasty things like that. I didn't cop it, because I'm not dark-skinned. My brother is called 'curry man'. He hates it.

AUTHOR (TO THE YOUNGER DAUGHTER, RANI) Did I hear you refer to yourself as a 'half-kid'?

RANI Yes. There are a lot of us at school. We call ourselves that or 'halfies', 'mongrels'. The Indians and Pakistanis call themselves 'curries', the Greeks and Italians call themselves 'wogs'. They're just names we call ourselves, affectionately.

AUTHOR   I think you're the lucky ones. You're sure enough of your identity to turn cruel nicknames into jokey pet-names. I've spoken to young people who've felt very unsure, and are hurt by such names. Even Sharmila only remembers the nasty names, not the acceptance, and turning them into a joke. Perhaps there are more mixed-race children at your school now.

RANI   Yes. There are quite a few. The only thing I don't like is having to do things differently because Mum wants us to do only what she did thirty years ago in Sri Lanka — nothing else, nothing modern, nothing Australian. Maybe they don't even live like that in Sri Lanka anymore. Things have changed everywhere, so why not there?

SHARMILA   Here in Australia it's the boy/girl thing. From thirteen or fourteen they get around together. But not in Sri Lanka, and not with us! I never wanted to do that at thirteen anyway. But even if I wanted to now, as a 17-year-old university student, Mum wouldn't let me.
      What happens with a lot of Sri Lankan kids is they just do it anyway and keep it secret. In a way I'm fortunate, because I've got one parent who sees life from the Australian point of view.

Hope and her husband, Marcus, a Eurasian from Malacca, have felt very little discrimination, and nothing that could be called racism. Yet their children suffered taunting and bullying at school and felt 'different', just as Katy did. Unlike Katy, however, they overcame these feelings of rejection in their teens, and became secure in their identity as Australians, albeit Australians with something extra.

HOPE   I grew up in a country town and went off to university to study town planning. After graduating, I took a year off to travel around Australia, doing odd jobs around the country, until I came to Perth. I loved Perth from the first day, and got a job in a town planning office, where I met Marcus.

MARCUS   I'd come from Malaysia to do engineering six years before, because my aunt and uncle already lived here. When Hope came into the office it was love at first sight for me.

AUTHOR   What did your parents think when you wanted to marry?

MARCUS   Marriage wasn't important in the seventies. I'd already left my uncle's house when I graduated, so Hope and I just moved in together. Later, when we decided to get married, we told both sets of parents.

HOPE   One of the things that has helped all through our marriage is that I fell headlong, blindly in love with Marcus. It did hit me eventually that other people were unaware of our great bond when time after time shop assistants treated us as if we were not together.

MARCUS   They ignore someone who looks different. It's the same when clients come into the office. Even though I'm sitting at what is obviously the senior table, customers will address my junior colleague, because he is the right colour. I don't worry about it. When they realise the situation, they come and talk to me.

HOPE   People do feel more comfortable with someone like themselves. After we'd been married a couple of years, when Anton was still a baby, we went to Malacca to live for two years to get to know Marcus's family. A few months after our arrival, they took me to play mah-jong, and I was immediately drawn to an Australian girl I met there, though I soon realised that we were poles apart in everything except our nationality.

A daughter, Maria — now eighteen — was born in Malacca during the family's stay there.

MARIA   As a small child I always felt a sense of alienation, which I thought must be my fault. Every so often I'd get a comment, patronising me or putting me down. Last January I moved to Melbourne and it's a different life there. Everyone just accepts me. It's just great. No one thinks of me as different, because everyone — or so many — are different. Everyone is just who they are.

ANTON (AGED TWENTY)   It was different for me. The first time I felt alienated was in year six. When we were organising a cricket game at lunchtime, it was: 'Aussies on this side, and wogs on that side'.
     I felt Aussie; I knew I wasn't a wog.

AUTHOR   Did you stay in the middle and say, 'I'll be referee'?

ANTON   No, I went to the Aussie side and everyone stared at me. Primary school was all right, but then I went to an all-boys' school, a Catholic college. That was very harsh. I didn't fit into any of the gangs or any of the racial groups. The Aussies wouldn't have a bar of me either. 'It's a bit Nippy around here', they'd say. I was a major target.
     On the bus, a bloke said, 'Do you know how to use chop-sticks?', and when I said 'yes', he went, 'Ha ha! You don't know how to use a fork!'.
     It sounds mild now, repeating it, but there was so much, all the time. It was incessant, and I got into so many blues, I hardly dared talk to anyone. The school had a counsellor, but going to see her was just a way of missing some classes.

Many mixed-race children spoke of being hurt by questions or comments from other children. It was the tone of voice, the implied racial criticism that hurt. One child, during a family visit, had to listen to her cousins saying 'all sorts of negative things about black people', while all the time pretending that they were making no reference to her or her African father.

HOPE   There was physical harassment, too. Someone walked on Anton's hands, and another time his fingers were slammed in the locker.

ANTON   That was in year seven or eight. I was innocent then, ignorant really. I woke up eventually in year nine or ten, and began to fight back. One day in class a guy kept pushing and pushing me, taunting me, gradually getting more and more nasty. Then his mate came and joined in. I walked away and they all thought I was going outside to cry — they were used to driving me to tears.
     'Have a sook! Have a sook!', they'd all yell. But that time I didn't go outside to cry. I picked up a block of wood the teacher kept near the blackboard and whacked the guy with it as hard as I could, till the footy-heads came and pulled me off.

Even then, while the teacher was sending me over to the Deputy Principal for disciplining, I was thinking, 'I've learned something. Fighting back has some effect, even if I am punished for it'.

AUTHOR Were you the only non-blue-eyed Aussie?

ANTON No. I was an odd Asian. I fitted nowhere. Italians or other darkish-skinned boys were in a group. They wouldn't have a bar of me. As for the Chinese boys — they pushed me out too. Come year ten I'd found out that I was a pretty fair musician, and I made a few friends then. Unfortunately, I had to get through a lot of fights first.

HOPE I remember Anton once being put upside down in a garbage bin. That was just cruel. We were brought into the school about that, and about the board incident too. They didn't blame Anton. On the contrary, it was as if they were patting Anton on the back, saying, 'If he's been driven to this point ... etcetera'.
Eventually we took him out of that Catholic college and sent him to a co-ed school.

ANTON And I was suddenly very popular. I was that exotic, foreign-looking guy.

My youngest son, Jeremy, also found his senior years in an all-boys' school to be the most traumatic of his life. We spoke of it years later.

JEREMY In primary school I felt pretty average. I mightn't have been aware that Dad was different. He had been in Australia so long that he's Australian anyway.
I don't think the way I felt had much to do with Dad. I was shy, and later, at Sydney High, maybe I was too sensitive, too insecure. It wouldn't have happened if we'd stayed in Tasmania, but at Sydney High you're either an Aussie or a wog. If you're playing any sort of game, be it a yard game, handball or a touch football match, it's the wogs versus the others.

AUTHOR And what side were you on?

JEREMY I was always on the wogs' side.

AUTHOR How did that make you feel?

JEREMY I knew it didn't really matter. The wogs were proud of being wogs. But it annoyed me. No, not annoyed, actually; it shocked me, because suddenly I realised others didn't recognise me for the person I knew myself to be. It was strange, because in Sydney High while I was there, the wogs were Greeks who always hung around together and talked in their own language. So how could anyone think I was one of them? They certainly didn't. But I didn't worry much. I was growing up, learning about life.

AUTHOR There were quite a few Chinese boys there, too. Did they fit in?

JEREMY No. They didn't fit in, not at all, but there was a group of them. Same with the Jews. There were also a few Australian-born Chinese, and the funny thing is, they were classed not as Chinese, but as wogs. They probably felt as shocked about that as I did.
It wasn't necessarily a bad thing. Some would have you believe that merely defining difference means that you don't like someone, that you hate them. But that's not so. It's just an Australianism, and it was not malicious.

In Darwin I haven't noticed the Aussie/wogs division at all. It's as if the divide between Aborigines and the rest is so great that everyone else becomes a dinkum Aussie as they arrive, and that includes me.

AUTHOR   What about prejudice?

JEREMY   Verbal abuse? Copping flack? Teasing? Only in high school. That was the bad time. Kids are really cruel. Somewhere you've got to draw the line, though, where you can't blame anyone else. There were taunts, and I could choose how I reacted. I withdrew. I didn't make friends, and I don't now.

AUTHOR   Anything physical? Any fighting? You never mentioned it.

JEREMY   No, nothing like that. There are other differences as well, though. I always feel that our family has been a little bit different from most mainstream Aussie families anyway. For one thing we were always church-going. And always moving. Those things, especially the constant moving, made us different, too.

I've noticed now I'm older, no one cares who my parents are or where I come from. I have sometimes been mistaken for an Arab or something.

AUTHOR   What are you? Are you Australian?

JEREMY   Oh yes. Of course I'm Australian. What else could I be? I assume you've been talking to people who belonged to an ethnic group, or have somehow re-found an ethnic group here. But we're not part of any other ethnic group, and never have been. I remember those Indian nights we went to in Hobart. I always love Indian food, but what else is there? Nothing for us, I believe. Nothing binds us to anywhere, except to this land, Australia.

Probably religion plays a part, and Dad and you are both Christians, not Islamic or Buddhist or Hindu. That sort of thing is very important.

I have a Chinese/Malaysian friend who has lived in Australia for years and years now, so when is she going to feel Australian? Not until she stops feeling Chinese or Malaysian, I believe. She comes from the same place Dad does, yet for as long as I've known Dad he's been Australian, definitely Australian.

We Australians, Anglo-Celtic Australians, don't value where we come from as much as the more recent immigrants do. I love Australia and I like being Australian, but in a way I'm also a citizen of the world.

Cynthia (mentioned in chapter 7), whose husband is Sinhalese, says both her sons experienced racial taunts and physical attacks from their peers at school.

CYNTHIA   We have two sons. Both boys have had a lot of problems about being different in appearance — or, more bluntly, their dark skin. Their difficulties began when they were quite small, at pre-school. Then Michael was viciously attacked and punched when he was about ten, by three boys, who were then suspended from school.

Our younger son, Pete, has had to put up with constant harassment too. A couple of years ago, I moved him to a Catholic college, but the problem has not gone away. He is still bullied and ostracised, but the teachers there don't seem to believe him, saying that these things don't happen in our society. But you and I know that they do!

9
_____

1970s — MARRIAGES AND PARENTAL DISAPPROVAL

Let us remember that the right to choose one's mate is almost
universally accepted and upheld by all civilised people.

Dame Enid Lyons, 1952

During the latter half of the 1970s many of Australia's immigrants
came from Asia and Oceania and were very different from those
who fitted the profile of acceptability thirty years earlier. Australians
met and became familiar with new and different customs, and many
of the immigrants had to adjust their lifestyles as well. In one interracial family the Chinese wife had to learn to cook Australian meals
exclusively because, even after twenty-five years of marriage, her
husband refused to eat with chopsticks. 'We live like Australians
because we are Australians', he said. While remaining on good
terms with his wife's family, he adamantly opposed his father-in-
law's plan to take the children back to Hong Kong to be brought
up as Chinese. 'I wouldn't allow it', he said. 'My children are
Australian, and we'll bring them up as Australians.'

Paul, from country New South Wales, met Bernie, a Chinese
woman from Fiji, in 1975, on her twentieth birthday. He was more
flexible, easily able to embrace the new and the strange, yet despite
that, a very Australian family life has evolved in their home too.

PAUL Education is important to my family. We lived in a small country town, with only
a primary school, and my father had two jobs all his life, so he could send us all — six
children — to good boarding schools. My parents worked hard, and went without so
much, just so we would have a good education.

There are a lot of similarities in the way my family and Bernie's viewed education. Bernie and I are both more relaxed about education, though; more relaxed about everything. We have only three children, and two jobs between us, and we couldn't possibly afford to send our children away to boarding school.

BERNIE   The difference between our families is that I wasn't going to be educated, because I was only a girl! I pushed on, supporting myself, until my mother realised how serious I was, then she helped me. I repeated the last year of school here in Australia, in a country boarding school, and I met Paul's sister there. All the girls were friendly, and invited me home for holidays. English wasn't a problem, but it took a while to get used to the slang. They'd say 'Come on, China', and I didn't realise that it was their way of saying, 'Mate' from 'China Plate'.

AUTHOR   Maybe there was a bit of irony, too. That rhyming slang comes from convict or Cockney speech and is used almost exclusively by men.

PAUL   That's right. It's not usually used by women, to women, or even in their presence. But the girls at that school were very ocker, so maybe it was just their way of integrating Bernie into their circle. When I met Bernie, it was love at first sight, and we've been together ever since. We married in 1978.

AUTHOR   What did your parents think about that?

PAUL   They are very tolerant. They welcomed Bernie.

BERNIE   All the country families, friends of Paul's family, welcomed me. At the bowling club, it was, 'Any friend of Frank's son is a friend of ours!'.
      They went out of their way to be friendly towards me. 'You're most welcome to Urana, and we hope you enjoy your stay here.' That's the sort of thing everyone said to me. There is a lot more racism in other countries, and by other people, including Chinese. Most Australians are inclined to take you as they find you.
      Sometimes a group of friends might talk about 'the bloody Chinese ...' and then realise that I'm Chinese and I'm sitting in front of them. It doesn't upset me.

AUTHOR   You're generous enough to say that it doesn't upset you, but what does it do? Anger you? Discomfort you?

BERNIE   None of those things. I really think of myself as an Australian now. Sometimes I get angry with the Chinese myself, particularly the newly arrived ones. Many of them are not doing the right thing.
      My father was always against mixed marriages. My oldest sister had married a Fijian. By the time I got married, my mother's attitude had relaxed and, as far as she was concerned, if I wouldn't marry a Chinese, marrying a white man was better than marrying a black man.

PAUL   I was surprised at the racism among the Chinese. I had thought racism was a European attitude.

BERNIE   Chinese have travelled everywhere, but they've always tried to keep their stock and their culture pure. With our marriage, Paul's family are not so Irish any more, nor is my family so Chinese.
      When Barney, our son, was born, my Australianness disturbed me. I realised how little a part Chinese culture played in my life and I felt then that if my mother would take

Barney for a few years, I would let him go, to be brought up in the Chinese way. So you see, I still retain a lot of the Chinese feeling for family. Of course, I knew if I had suggested it, Paul would have flipped!

AUTHOR The grandmother taking the children is fairly common in the Chinese family, isn't it?

BERNIE Not only grandmothers. My childless aunt wanted my mother's third child, her second son, in 1953. My mother would not give him away, but when, in 1955, I came along, my mother told her, 'You can have this girl'.
     My aunt didn't want this girl — me!

AUTHOR The meaning of 'close family' changes between societies, doesn't it? Australian families are not seen as particularly close, yet they never give their children away, and think of anyone who does as cruel, uncaring. As you immediately recognised, Paul would never have tolerated the idea of letting his son go, even for a year. Yet you say Chinese families are 'close'.
     It reminds me of when I began work as a social worker in the Singapore Children's Society, where adoptions and abandoned children were a big part of our work. Two other social workers gave me a quick lesson in local values. The Indian social worker said, 'Indians never give away their children. If an Indian family wants to adopt, there is never an Indian child available; they'll have to accept an unwanted Chinese child. Indians think Chinese are cruel and unloving for giving away their children'.
     Then the Chinese social worker told me, 'That's true. As you've already seen, there are always plenty of Chinese babies abandoned. The mothers of the abandoned babies are always hoping the baby will find a better parent. The Chinese think Indians are selfish because they will never give their children away, even if they can't afford to look after them properly'.

BERNIE Yes, that is the attitude. Also their attitude to education. Chinese regard education so highly, they push and push their children to study, even if it means driving them mad or losing them.

The open-hearted welcome that Bernie met among Paul's family and neighbours at Urana in the 1970s was not the universal response from country parents when introduced to a potential bride from another race.

DAVID My father was a country doctor in Red Cliffs. In 1968 I came to Melbourne to school, then university. My parents came down to see me when I was nineteen, and I took Belinda to meet them. Their reaction was very acrimonious. I knew at once, though I had not expected it. Nothing had warned me that they'd object. My family had travelled extensively. There had been no mention in my childhood of race or racism.
     As a young woman my mother had not been allowed to marry a Catholic. My father had also been prevented from marrying a Catholic. You'd think their own disappointments would have helped them understand, but it did not. From that day on, they cut off my financial support; they cut me out of their will. Immense pressure was placed on me. Under instructions from my parents, my sisters stopped writing to me or phoning me. My mother's expectations for me were not fulfilled. So, to her, I died. They even had my death notice put in the paper.

Belinda and I married, we graduated, and our children were born. There was still no contact with my parents.

BELINDA My parents also objected to our marriage at first. Only when we went to see them about two years after we were married, did they give in. Since my father died, my mother visits us, but not often, because she really is not comfortable with our way of life.

But deciding to marry David — well, it was different for me. Rightly or wrongly, I perceived Chinese men — all Asian men, really — to be very demanding. I didn't like my mother's role in our home. I had never wanted to marry a Chinese man; I had always wanted something different.

AUTHOR So you're living as an isolated nuclear family as so many Australians are.

DAVID After we learned that we would be cast out from our families, we had to ask ourselves whether insisting on being together was rebellion or real commitment to one another. When we decided that we'd stay together, we knew we had to be strong.

Our marriage made us extremely focussed and independent; we effectively became a separate family. Belinda graduated, and then worked and supported me while I finished. Then, while still at university, when I couldn't go home, we met the parents of a friend of mine, and it is they who have acted as grandparents for our children, and they have become very important to our whole family.

Many years later, I somehow learned that my father was sick. I knew I had to make the move. They wouldn't. I arrived at my parents' door at 7.00 p.m. precisely, when I knew they'd be watching the ABC news. My visit broke the ice. Six months later I took the children up there for my mother's seventieth birthday, in June 1995. That was the first time my parents saw their grandchildren.

There was no great reconciliation. We are still nibbling away, snatching at crumbs. I managed to get my father to visit me down here in Melbourne just once, and then last November he passed away, with all the issues between us still unresolved.

My mother's on the 'Oriana' now on her way to London, and we've just received our first ever letter from her. The envelope was addressed to 'Mr and Mrs'. That is a great triumph for us. We've been married twenty years, and you can't believe such a small thing could give us such pleasure.

AUTHOR You seem to live a very Australian way of life altogether, Belinda. Why did you choose that way?

BELINDA We are living in Australia; the children will stay here, so we are an Australian family. I was brought up in an English school and I find I can't write to Mum anymore in Chinese, even using an English/Chinese dictionary, so I ring her up. It's really the only time I speak Chinese, because nearly all our friends are Australian. Our boy, Tim, is learning Chinese, so soon I'll get some practise talking to him. Tim has a Chinese attitude to food, too — totally committed from one meal to the next. On the other hand I have dropped my Chinese attitude to food. Now I think of food as Australians do. I feel totally Australian, and so does Kathryn, our daughter.

I love living in Australia. The only thing I don't like now are the drugs that seem to have got worse since the Vietnamese came. The Vietnamese don't want to assimilate. They want to cling onto their culture, but they wanted to come here, so they should be prepared to change to fit into Australian culture, not expect Australians to do all the changing, or even accepting all the differences.

DAVID   I've never heard you express that before, Belinda.

BELINDA   There's nothing wrong with their culture, but they came here, so they should try to fit into this culture; they should be prepared to change. All the people who came when I did, young or old, were prepared to change to fit into Australian ways, and we're glad we did.

AUTHOR   It may be a matter of the group's size, Belinda. Perhaps when there's enough newcomers, they draw their strength and companionship totally from within that group; they see no need to fit into Australia culturally. Whereas there were so few of you when you came, for self-preservation you had to fit in. And because you were seen as trying to fit in, most Australians welcomed you.

BELINDA   Yes, we wanted to fit in. With the new migrants, even Chinese from Hong Kong, they don't want to. I don't have anything in common with them. I feel isolated from them. I might look Chinese, but I feel Australian. When I go into a Chinese restaurant they treat me rudely because I can't speak their language. I feel like a second-rate person.

AUTHOR   You mean they treat you like an ordinary Australian?

BELINDA (LAUGHING)   Yes.

DAVID   I've travelled to a lot of countries and I don't think there's any place where different races mix better than here in Australia. I'm not sure our planning is very good but I think that by accident we're heading in the right direction as long as we continue to take people of great diversity and from all walks of life.
   I think the diversity is important, but perhaps the intake should be slowed down so the earlier ones have time to adjust before more arrive. Country people, people out of the mainstream, haven't absorbed the second-last wave, let alone this most recent one. People need time to breathe. They need to have time to feel comfortable with one transition, before moving into another.

BELINDA   We appreciate Australia so much when we've been travelling and we come home. I value the freedom that I, as a Chinese, have here.
   I notice the children at school; there are so many different faces — Greek, Chinese, Eurasian — and they are all growing up comfortable with the mix that is now Australia. I don't know what an Australian is now, unless it is anyone who is born and bred here.

In 1972, 19-year-old Hannah came from Hong Kong to join her brothers, who were studying in Sydney. It was there she met Greg.

GREG   I was born and grew up in Sydney. Hannah and I met at university, and when we finished our undergraduate work, I started a job, but then I was offered a scholarship to Cambridge. We married just before we left, and spent our honeymoon travelling through China in 1979.
   We spent three years in Cambridge, and Hannah did further study in London. Then I had a fellowship at Harvard University, so we moved to Cambridge, Massachusetts, for two years. Our first son, David, was born in Boston just before we left the US. We returned to Canberra, where we stayed until nine years ago.

HANNAH   In Canberra our second son was born and died, and I finished my PhD after eight years. I was pregnant with our third child, Alex, when we came to Melbourne.

All I could get here was casual teaching and interpreting. Either that or filling in for people who took sabbatical or maternity leave. My brothers, who had been in business here since 1976, needed my help, so I joined the family business. I like it; I find it challenging.

AUTHOR   Did your families feel happy about your marriage?

HANNAH   My parents cut me off. They were embarrassed. 'What will the neighbours think?'

GREG   It took ten years before they agreed to meet me.

HANNAH   I went to Hong Kong during our honeymoon, but neither of my parents would see me. About three years later I again stopped in Hong Kong. I was not allowed to see my parents at their home, but I met my mother in coffee shops. Two years after that I tried a third time. On our way home to Australia, when David was a baby, we stopped in Hong Kong, and towards the end of our stay there, my father at last relented, and we were invited back to the house.

What maintained my sanity over the years was the realisation that my parents' ferocious behaviour was just an indication of their inability to bear emotional loss. As far as my father was concerned, his daughter had died.

GREG   Parents want to control daughters. I understood what was happening with Hannah's parents, because my father went through similar problems with a mixed-religion marriage. Perhaps the difficulties my parents had been through made them understanding about my marriage to Hannah.

HANNAH   Racism is present in all elements of Australian society — among the newcomers into Australia too. Younger Chinese are dismissive of Australians, saying Australians are slow, lazy and not smart. Chinese are unable to appreciate the humanity of Australians. They cannot see the good qualities of Australians, in giving people a fair go, in being relaxed and hospitable.

Since working with my brothers, I find I'm thinking more Chinese again. But getting close to my family has distanced me from Greg.

GREG   We have a lot in common. Our differences are not due to race, but more a different way of going about things. Perhaps the difference between academia and business.

HANNAH   It's more than that. Greg is a scientist by training and so he thinks like a scientist. I read Oriental literature, and my intellectual thought and research, and thus my current way of thinking, is of a very different kind.

I struggled through those first years when I was estranged from my family, and also the years of childbirth, the death of our second child, and my post-graduate studies, always believing it would get easier.

Coping with such stress, without the help of nearby extended family, strengthened the bond between us. So many shared challenges, as well as the joys of family life, make our marriage almost unassailable. But I find, to my dismay, that as our relationship matures, our stress has grown too, probably due to lack of time to communicate.

If we're tired and busy, I'll assume Greg will behave like my brothers. In similar circumstances Greg will expect me to behave like his sister. And, of course, neither of us do that.

My parents came to live in Australia six years ago, and since then they have had no problems accepting our marriage and Greg. My mother died here, and Greg was marvellous in accommodating a very heavy Buddhist ceremony.

GREG It's not just a matter of accommodating to different habits, or rituals, or even values, but expectations. There are customs that Australians live by that would come naturally to the girl next door, but Hannah would never adapt to them. And one thing I will never understand is the Chinese emphasis on food. They must push food onto you. Yet they don't think about many of the things and behaviours we regard as just common courtesy.

It creates continual irritation. You have to have a thick skin. If it's important to you that you continue with patterns of behaviour you grew up with, then you have to be strong. If it imposes too much pressure on your partner, then you have to compromise, because both have to be happy with the way you live your life together.

Communication is never as good as I would like it to be. It's very difficult. Hannah doesn't view things the way I do, but I don't view things as she does, either, even things we see on TV — we just come from such different backgrounds, and our training, too, has led us to different ways of looking at things.

HANNAH That's true, but we have a shared history now of what we have learned about ourselves and about each other, and that has given us strength, a sort of permanent bedrock that the boys, too, can rely on. Interracial marriage is a very big test of the commitment of the participants, and also on the support network. I don't think I'd have got through it without my brothers' support.

GREG Even discussing this is complicated because we were closer at the time when we were well away from both our families than we have been since returning to Australia.

AUTHOR Have the boys had difficulties?

GREG David never seemed to fit in at his Catholic primary school. Catholic schools are dominated by sport, while he's shy and bookish, a serious child. We knew there had been some taunting and at the end of sixth year, he didn't want to attend the farewell party. He now goes to a Uniting Church school and he's very happy there, though he remains a Catholic.

Alex is in the same school as David was, but Alex is different. He doesn't understand the implication of name-calling. He calls kids he doesn't like 'Chinky' and names like that, not realising that he is specifically singled out for these insults. So I suppose you could say, it doesn't hurt him, because he's unaware that he is the target.

Eventually these children will all fit into Australia. Society will homogenise, something like the old idea of assimilation. It's what has happened in America and some European countries over the last century or so. I think it's the only thing that will work.

HANNAH I disagree. Politicians now consider it acceptable for people to be culturally different, and to remain different.

GREG But kids are all going through the same school system. It's not that Australian culture is absorbing all these influences, but the whole Australian culture is shifting and embracing this new generation.

At their home in a leafy Canberra suburb I met Rebecca and her Malaysian Chinese husband, Carl.

REBECCA I was born in London of Jewish parents. My father was born in England and my mother, who was lucky enough to leave Poland at the age of twelve, met and married my father in England during World War 2. All of my mother's family in Europe disappeared during those war years.

My family and I came to Australia in 1963, and I met Carl at university in 1972. We knew our relationship was important, but we had not decided anything when Carl finished his studies and went back home to Malaysia. After much difficulty in getting a temporary visa, he returned for his graduation early in 1974. We married just a week or so before his visa expired, and Carl got permanent residence because of our marriage.

AUTHOR   How did your parents like your marriage?

REBECCA   Both my parents liked Carl, but my father was worried about what people would think. We took Carl to the synagogue, and everyone accepted him but he didn't want to become a Jew. I was glad because I'm not religious. In fact, we are quite similar in our religious convictions.

Initially my father did not want to be associated with our wedding, but after we said we'd have a party with paper plates, he relented. We married in a registry office and a week later my father gave us a reception. Then, to my father's horror, I learned how to cook and eat pork and seafood!

CARL   My family are atheists, but very tolerant. They welcomed my Jewish wife. Actually, Chinese and Jewish people are very much alike. Wealth acquisition, education and food — these are three very important themes that run through the lives of all Chinese and all Jews. Also, all Chinese and Jewish parents are very strict with children, especially teaching their children to value education, love of family, and investing for the future. Jewish people also have a very strong sense of identity, and so do the Chinese.

Our son, Dale, sparked a crisis with Rebecca's family. Her father wanted his only grandchild circumcised. But both Rebecca and I feel it's not necessary, so he was not 'done'. At first it didn't matter, but lately ...

REBECCA   Dale is fourteen now, and it has become very important. We used to go up for Passover. Now, my parents don't invite us. Dale can still choose to be a Jew, though. Even without circumcision, he could be a liberal Jew. It is his choice.

CARL   I haven't felt any prejudice since being in Australia. But there's a bit of racism in every society. There are people, including most Chinese, who are really prejudiced against dark-skinned people. Was the darkness of your husband's skin an issue? Would your parents have been as unhappy as they were, if you had married a fairer-skinned Asian?

AUTHOR   I'm not sure whether it was just the darkness of Josh's skin that was the issue, but perhaps it was.

REBECCA   To say that a certain face or skin colour conveys a set of values is a lot of hogwash. One might feel at home with Indians or other people brought up under British colonialism, and having the education and values that implies, in much the way that I feel that Carl and I have areas of similar values from the English influence on our childhood. Yet you might have more difficulty and sense of difference with, say, eastern Europeans or Muslim Albanians, who physically may look very like you, but have a totally different cultural background and set of social values.

10

ABORIGINAL INTERRACIAL MARRIAGES IN THE 1970s

You cannot have a rainbow with separate colours. In a rainbow all the colours have to mingle together.

<u>Walangari, Aboriginal artist and storyteller</u>

As Cynthia and her sons know, the darkness of one's skin does affect the way one is perceived and accepted in at least some parts of Australian society. The fairness of Sharmila's skin protected her from unpleasant name-calling by Australian students but also led Sri Lankans to treat her as an outsider, in contrast to the way her darker-skinned siblings were perceived and treated. The darkness of Cynthia's sons' skin attracted harassment and abuse at school. At least one Chinese Australian man suggested that the white wife of a dark-skinned man meets more prejudice than the white wife of a Chinese or similar Oriental.

Sometimes, though, it is more racial heritage than darkness of skin that brings discrimination. A light-skinned Aborigine told me he had often been mistaken for a Greek or a Palestinian. He spoke of how love affairs and relationships with women ended when parents learned that he was Aboriginal. 'Everything has been okay until I wanted to marry someone, and I told their families that I'm Aboriginal. Suddenly they say, "I'm not going to let my daughter marry a blackfella", even when they are actually darker than I am.'

In 1989 Aboriginal actor and television entertainer Ernie Dingo married a white woman. In an interview with Richard Guilliatt for the *Good Weekend* magazine, Ernie explained that the major problem

Sally faced was from her friends. It was all right that her boyfriend was Ernie Dingo — 'Y'know, the bloke from *Crocodile Dundee*' — but when Sally and Ernie were going to marry, the response was: 'Sally is going to marry an Aborigine!'.

In her book, *The Story of Our Mob*, Sally Dingo wrote: 'I think the reaction of my friends was not so much to do with race — it was that Ernie didn't quite fit the nice middle-class mould. He wasn't typically reliable as a nice young man should be. He did what he wanted'. And later: 'Because he … acts so effortlessly, a lot of people think of Ernie as a white man in a brown skin. But he's not and he never will be …'.[1]

Sally also wrote of the joy of the all-embracing welcome that she received from her husband's Aboriginal family. Similarly, Mayleah told me that the one thing above all else she loved about being Aboriginal was the all-inclusive nature of an Aboriginal family.

I spoke to Mayleah and Steve, her white Australian husband, in Katherine when they came to join Mayleah's brother for a few days' camping and fishing.

MAYLEAH   I'm from a big family, born on the Cherbourg Mission Station in Queensland, and we left the Mission in about 1967 and came down to Brisbane, to suburban Banyo. We were the first Aboriginal kids to go to the Nudgee school. Everything was new to us. We didn't have shoes or a bag to carry our books. We didn't know we needed them. At the Mission we'd all gone barefoot, and anything we needed was provided by the Mission school.

We must have seemed strange to the other kids, too. They noticed our speech. They said we spoke 'pidgin English' — and we did. The kids of Cherbourg still speak 'pidgin'. Those kids of today aren't being taught English properly, so they will be handicapped, just as we were. Our language brands us. It is not only the colour of our skin.

Coming to Banyo was the big stepping stone that gave us all a new start in life and we all thank Mum and Dad for that. It was hard for them, very hard, but they were determined to move us out into the mainstream. Dad came out of the Mission with nothing. The taxi driver who drove us from the station let us a house that he had for rent — a little two-bedroom place, with weeds growing up everywhere. He was kind and really looked after us for those first few months in Brisbane. The local Baptist church did too. They were incredibly kind. Without them, I don't know how we'd have managed.

STEVE   I'm from Sydney and I met Mayleah when I went up to Queensland for a holiday.

AUTHOR   How did your parents feel about you marrying Mayleah?

STEVE   Dad was a bit taken aback, and told me that it might not last. Mum was not happy about it. But I had no trouble with Mayleah's family. They opened their arms to me. Mayleah's uncle said of me, 'This is the blackest whitefella I've ever seen'.

MAYLEAH   Steve's father was wrong about us; our marriage has lasted. Steve and I have been married for twenty-four years.

STEVE   We've done well. We've just sold our own business — a big fencing business on the Sunshine Coast. We'd been there for eleven years and we were ready for a change when Manny, Mayleah's brother, told us about the opportunities up here. It is certainly different. Some of the communities here are fifty years behind the rest of Australia.

MAYLEAH   Hodgson Downs has 270 people, a third of them children. After primary school they come to high school here in Katherine, or go to the Aboriginal college. Because I know the difficulties caused by the poor language training at Mission schools, we've had a linguist out there at the community for some time.

STEVE   We call it Creole, or Aboriginal English, but it's really broken English and using it hinders people because it is so limited. We're lucky at Hodgson Downs that they still have their own language — Alawa — too.

AUTHOR   You're working in the community because you're Mayleah's husband, Steve, and you're white. How does that affect the people — and you?

STEVE   It's hard. I teach them work skills in the Community Development Employment program. We're working on several projects to improve the place, so they'll be proud of what they can do. But it's hard.

MAYLEAH   Even I am still an outsider there. They've never had a woman Administrator before, and some Administrators treated them like dirt. So it's been hard. I tell them: I'm here to help you. If you tell me to go, I'll go.

AUTHOR   Do you have children there with you?

MAYLEAH   We have three kids, grown up now. They're all still in Brisbane, living in our home there. The two boys are my colour, and our daughter, Shannon, is Steve's colour. At school no one believed the boys were her brothers. They'd ask Shannon, 'If you are Aboriginal, why aren't you dark?'. In the Aboriginal community all the children follow the mother.

AUTHOR   That can't always be so, Mayleah. Your brother tells me his son, despite being blond and blue-eyed like his white mother, is Aboriginal, because children follow the father.

MAYLEAH (LAUGHING AND GESTURING WITH HER ARMS SPREAD WIDE)   We want them all! After all, we're a dying race! We'll have them all.

STEVE   When Manny and I go into a river where there are crocodiles, he'll say, 'You go in first, Steve. There are more of you whitefellas!'.

MAYLEAH   Laughing and joking about skin colour like this is something that Steve's mother can't understand.

AUTHOR   Perhaps because to her difference in skin colour matters.

STEVE   I've had people in Sydney, or anywhere, say: 'You've married an Aboriginal. What is it like?'. I tell them that she's a beautiful person, that I love her and she's the mother of my children. But all we have to do is hold hands walking down the street, and you should see the looks! In Darwin, it's not the whites, but the Aboriginal people who look critically at us.

MAYLEAH   In Darwin full-bloods would not marry me! So they're surprised that I'd marry Steve.

John Taylor from the Centre for Aboriginal Economic Policy Research at the Australian National University, using the 1996 census data, showed that at least 64 per cent of indigenous couples are ethnically mixed, up from 46 per cent in 1986. This astonishing increase in the number of Aborigines who marry 'out' can be partly explained by the increase in part-Aborigines who identify as Aboriginals, and could also be linked to their move into cities and away from the bush where they are more likely to marry another Aborigine. Most Aborigines in Sydney are marrying 'out'; most in the Northern Territory are not. Another consideration is that most Aborigines in Sydney would already be racially mixed, and have only a tenuous link with the land, language and traditional life of their forefathers. Many more Aboriginal Territorians, however, are not racially mixed — at least not within the last few generations — and perhaps even more importantly, many still have their Aboriginal language and clear links with the land and traditional life.

Mayleah explained that Darwin's full-bloods would not marry her, but if such a marriage did occur, Mayleah would almost certainly find that she had much less in common with a full-blood tribal husband than she has with Steve.

MAYLEAH   Though I said we want everybody, our children are just as happy to identify as white Australians. They're happy to be either, or mixed, or just Australians. What I like about being Aboriginal, though, is that we seem to take everyone in. Whereas I couldn't walk into Steve's family place and stay.

AUTHOR   It's not necessarily a lack of love, Mayleah. Anglo-Saxon Australians respect one another's right to privacy; it's not thought polite to intrude. Everyone has the right to invite whoever they want into their home, but no one else has the right to come and stay except by invitation. I suppose it could be a hangover from every Englishman's home being his castle, and it's tied up with a whole set of traditions about the 'right' way to behave towards a guest under your roof, and indeed, 'right' ways for a guest to behave, too. In fact, many white Australians admire the openly expressed emotions of, say, Aboriginals or Mediterranean people, but hold back for fear of being thought 'pushy'. In their tradition 'right' behaviour puts a high value on restraint. Lack of restraint is almost akin to bad manners.

STEVE   I say: if you love them, accept all the differences. You know you've got to fit in with your spouse's family for your marriage to work.

Since that interview Mayleah has followed up her long-standing concern about speech education for Aboriginal children, and now works in the Indigenous Education Unit in Queensland, where she will work to ensure that the Aboriginal children in her care are not handicapped by their speech.

I spoke to another Aboriginal, Charles, in a coffee shop near his office in the cafe strip in inner suburban Sydney.

CHARLES I remember walking down this street, down near the park, a few months back. Kids sat there saying, 'I'm Irish', 'I'm Aboriginal', 'I'm Indian', etcetera, but in the big picture they're all Australian. I'm reminded of a pack of dogs. When they're all hunting together, they co-operate, but if something happens to one, they'll all turn and attack him.

AUTHOR We must believe that humans are different, or we are lost.

CHARLES We should be different, but our animal instincts come out. I remember sitting in the Davenport sandhills with my grandmother when I was very small, and she told me, 'It's a white man's world we live in, so whatever you do, don't go backwards'.

She wouldn't let us mix with the other Aborigines, so I didn't like being Aboriginal. Many of my people still believe that you can't be Aboriginal if you want to get on.

My mother is fair-skinned and she married an Irishman, an alcoholic who came and went while my mother worked hard to give us everything the other children had. I left home when I was twelve and went to live with an uncle. The idea was that I would finish high school — they were all at me to get an education. But I didn't have my mind set on school, so when I was called up to do national service, I did that instead — which was itself an education. I didn't go to Vietnam, but worked as a weapons instructor here in Australia. No discrimination in the Army. Even as an NCO, I didn't find any discrimination. One lad from the islands had trouble. Perhaps he behaved differently.

I married a non-Aboriginal girl who had grown up as a Christian, and we've brought our girls up to do unto others as you'd like others to do to you. It was the churches who took most of the Aboriginal kids away, in a bid to educate them and to give them a better chance.

After leaving the Army I worked in the building trade but I never forgot my grandmother's plans for me, so I went back to school and then, at thirty-eight years of age, I began first-year university with all those 18- and 19-year-old kids. It was one of the most difficult things I've ever done but if I had to do it again I would.

After studying for a few years (and keeping the family on a scholarship) I joined a department in charge of Aboriginal housing. I really got the job because of my building experience, though they wouldn't have considered me if I hadn't got myself an education. It's a funny old world.

I'm first of all an Australian, then I'm Aboriginal. The first Australians were Aboriginal people and all the people who have come here should only stay if they are willing to become Australians. Often they congregate in lumps, not contributing to Australia or thinking of it as their home. That is not good for Australia, nor for any of us who care about our country. But multiculturalism is set in concrete now.

AUTHOR I despair at the thought that the separateness in our society is set in concrete.

CHARLES I'm afraid it is, but I can't stop or change things that happened years ago. I try to instil that into my girls. 'Get on with life', I tell them. 'Don't muck around complaining about the difficulties.'

My elder daughter has a lot of friends who didn't know that she is, at least partly, Aboriginal. Her mother and I persuaded her to tell them. So she did, and they didn't care; they're still her friends.

AUTHOR After all, your daughter's mother is a white Australian, both her grandfathers and one grandmother are white, and the other grandmother — your mother — is half-white and half-Aboriginal. So if your daughter is happier to claim the 87-and-a-half per cent of her heritage that is white, why not? Does it matter if she wants to disregard — for the time being at least — the mere 12-and-a-half per cent that is Aboriginal?

CHARLES My sister did that. She claims only the Irish heritage of our father, and she married a German and lives in Germany, but I wanted my children to claim all their birthright, both black and white.

AUTHOR Identity is sometimes a worry when one has mixed heredity, and young people in particular often feel confused about it. This problem will get worse all around the world as people travel, migrate, settle elsewhere, intermarry. Maybe we'll need to develop an identity based only on where we live. We'll all be just Australians.

CHARLES I regard myself as Australian. I think the word reconciliation has a one-way slant that I don't like. People seem to believe that it is non-Aboriginal people who have to reconcile with Aboriginal people. But I believe it is a two-way thing. Both sides must make a move. That would be real reconciliation, but it's not happening.

Sometimes barriers could be breached by just a, 'Hey, I really don't know you. Could you tell me what's important to you?'.

AUTHOR We should be able to manage that.

Kayleen is Aboriginal, but so fair that she looks like any ordinary white Australian, while her husband Kevyn looks so like his ancestors, the Afghan camel drivers, that I asked him whether he had retained their devout Muslim religious practices.

KEVYN My grandfather was a Mullah. He had the mosque built in Marree, and my dad observed all the prayers and worship times there when I was a kid, but I'm not religious at all. Probably the only distinctively Afghan part of our lives now is the curries we eat.

The Khans married Scottish and Irish and Aboriginal women, and more recently they married daughters of other Afghans who had married here — a real mix. People take me for Greek or Italian, but I'd rather be known as an Afghan, or just an Australian.

AUTHOR Have you met much racism, discrimination?

KEVYN AND KATHLEEN Yes.

KEVYN Things have improved, though. When my mum was young, everyone was still very religious and pork was never touched. The white people of Marree used to hang pigs' trotters and pigs' heads and things on the fence near the railway line, just where my mother and her friends had to pass to get over the line if they were going to a dance … or anywhere else. It used to be called Ghantown. Hundreds and hundreds of Afghans lived there.

By the time I grew up and went to school in Marree there was no discrimination. We were all friends together. Compared to our parents we had a better education, and we got better jobs. I became a station master and mixed with everyone, though I didn't go to parties because I didn't drink. The police and everyone else treated us well, but our closest friends were mainly other Afghans and the Aboriginals in town.

AUTHOR   And dances? Did they have dances when you were a young man?

KEVYN   Yes, and we all danced together — everyone. Things had changed. Marree is a good town, good people. After we moved to Port Augusta I worked at the Power House and that was all right too.

It was only later when I went to work at the Commonwealth Employment Service — that was where I felt racism. My job there was to go out selling programs to the community, to get the disadvantaged client groups into employment. Maybe the town people would have been all right, but the CES people put me down ...

Kevyn hesitated. He found this difficult to talk about, so Kayleen stepped in to bridge the uncomfortable gap, picking up different threads of their story.

KAYLEEN   I grew up in Andamooka. The family dug for opals and worked as fencers for local farmers. There was no work for girls so I went off to Marree and worked on the trains. The trains changed there from standard gauge to narrow gauge, and there were always carriages to be cleaned. We all worked in together — whites, Aboriginals, Afghans. Country towns are different.

AUTHOR   Better or worse?

KAYLEEN   In some country towns, Aboriginals are a majority, and it's okay then. In Marree, it was good. It was only when we shifted to Port Augusta that the children experienced racism. At school, kids stabbed them in the back with pencils and called them 'boongs' or 'wogs'. We had never felt racism before — none of us. It shocked us.

AUTHOR   Are you telling me ...? I want to get this clear. You're both in your fifties and it wasn't until fourteen years ago, in Port Augusta, that you first noticed racism?

KAYLEEN   That's right.

KEVYN   The bloke I worked with there, in the CES job, used to introduce me as 'my little black mate'.

AUTHOR   Then, when you went back to see those employers to help your unemployed people, they respected you less because he had already diminished you?

KEVYN   Yes. He was senior to me, and I was new to the job. That was in 1987. After a few years, I left Port Augusta and came down to Adelaide, still with DEET, but in the Aboriginal Education Unit.

AUTHOR   What about you, Kayleen? Did you strike this sort of thing?

KAYLEEN   No. I'm white enough to be taken for an ordinary Australian. I'm much more than 50 per cent white, but I identify with my Aboriginal side because they're the only relatives I know.

When I apply for jobs identified as Aboriginal positions, they expect me to be dark, so I have to demonstrate that I know the culture. I never had rudeness, or any form of discrimination because although I had to prove I was an Aborigine to get the job, I am actually seen as an ordinary white Australian.

The children are all darker than me — taking more after Kevyn and the Khans.

Peter is the eldest, and Joanne, then Gavin. When Peter began his apprenticeship, peo-ple asked, 'Are you related to Imran Khan?'.

He'd say, no, he was part-Afghan and part-Aboriginal, and they'd jeer, 'You're not Afghan or Pakistani at all, you're just a black, a nigger!'.

Gavin copped a lot of racist remarks too, because he's the darkest in the family. It was the mix. He looked Aboriginal, but his name was Khan. Even my Aboriginal cousins say, 'He's just a nigger!', though they know he's Kevyn's son. It's as if they didn't know about Afghans being here, and intermarrying with us, and with white Australians — but of course they do know all that.

Even my daughter, Joanne, was called names. She mixes more with Asians than either whites or Aboriginals now. I suppose they felt mixed up, neither one thing nor the other.

KEVYN They'll learn to let that kind of stuff go over their heads. If you treat rudeness with kindness people don't know how to respond.

I used to run a Culture Awareness Course and people would say: Petrol sniffing is terrible! And I would say: Yes, it is. It's substance abuse — just like Adelaide people shooting up.

Then they'd say: Why do Aboriginal people go walkabout? And I'd say: In white society, if the government says 'Do national service', then you do national service.

They talked about smoke-signals and I talked about Catholics swinging their smoke-pots. When they talked about Aboriginals smashing their houses, I reminded them of the graffiti. It's just destruction, no matter who does it.

I don't think multiculturalism is working because the Australian culture is not chang-ing at all, though the government means well.

KAYLEEN I just wish everyone in the world was the same race and the same colour, and then there'd be no problems.

I explained to Gavin, Kevyn and Kayleen's younger son, why I sought his views on mixed-race marriage. The parents have a choice, I told him, they chose to marry across racial lines, but their children are born into it.

GAVIN I was only thinking the other day about this business of having no choice. It's only in the last few years that I've felt comfortable about my Afghan, and my Aboriginal, and my Irish and whatever. I now see that the most important part of me is that part which one can't attribute to coming from any cultural background, things like being kind or clever.

Everyone clings to stereotypes, too, particularly in regard to Aboriginals. They say, 'Oh you must be good at sports and art'. And I think, 'I wish I was'.

It's really odd that even I hold those stereotypes too. I have to remind myself that they are not true; that actually, I'm not well co-ordinated, and not at all artistic. I like to see myself as a good teacher, but some people, learning that I'm Aboriginal, think, 'You must have got here some special way'. And I find myself thinking, 'Maybe I'm not up to scratch as a real teacher'. Then I work three times as hard as other teachers, in a sort of continual justification to myself and other people.

AUTHOR Who are you, in your own mind?

GAVIN I'm an Australian. But I think of myself as a number of things. Maybe it's like being a schizophrenic. This facet of me is Aboriginal, but this other facet of me is Afghan, and then there is the part that is Irish and Scots and probably English as well. And I'm all of those things — not one or the other.

I have arguments with people who say, 'Are you quarter-caste? How much are you this or that?'.

It might be possible to quantify one's blood inheritance, but it's not possible to quantify one's identity. In the Aboriginal enclave at uni there was a big issue about who was an Aboriginal and who was a 'coconut' — black on the outside and white on the inside. That means people know you're Aboriginal, but you've betrayed that identity by taking on, for whatever reason, non-Aboriginal belief systems, thought systems, social systems, for example in the way that you dress, where you live, the way you speak.

AUTHOR   Wouldn't you say that every Aboriginal at university must have done that to a great degree?

GAVIN   Yes. To a degree. It then became a question of deciding what degree was acceptable.

AUTHOR   What you're saying is that by accessing education and professional employment, Aboriginals are necessarily becoming whiter inside — or that's how they express it?

GAVIN   Yes.

AUTHOR   Yet to succeed in Australia today, they have to do that.

GAVIN   That's right; to succeed in terms of non-Aboriginal culture means to reject those things that make up Aboriginality — or to put it on hold. For example, when I'm with Aboriginal people, the way I speak is quite different from the way I speak here. Adapting to where I am, who I'm with, making changes ... I do it all the time.

Attitudes have changed since Charles was a boy being told by his grandmother that he would never get on well in life if he played with Aborigines, or lived as an Aborigine. One can only suppose that there is some way those Aboriginal students at university who are still derisive towards colleagues they call coconuts —— those who speak, dress and live like white Australians — are somehow able to overlook the 'white' element in attending lectures, studying and sitting examinations. Perhaps there will come a time when Australia's Western culture will be valued for its intrinsic worth, and indeed, for its dominance in today's world, without Aborigines feeling that to partake of its riches somehow denigrates their own traditions.

Gavin and the Aboriginal enclave at his university may not have seen the article on John Moriarty, a successful Aboriginal artist and businessman who is reported in *The Australian Weekend Review* as saying, 'I don't go around with a red headband saying I'm an Aborigine. Nor do I walk around with a shamrock saying I'm half-Irish but I'm equally proud of the Irish as well as the Aboriginal — I'm very much a modern Australian'.[2]

GAVIN I think that interracial marriages can work, if both parties have a strong commitment to making it work. All of the people I have gone out with have been of non-Aboriginal background, and there has been that issue of identity, and the energy it takes to make adjustments from my partner's environment to mine — making changes that I just mentioned.

I broke up with one of my partners simply because of this issue. When we went out with my friends — Aboriginal friends from Murray Bridge — I went into this mode of speaking and acting to suit them, and she felt very uncomfortable.

If you asked me ten years ago I would have said that Australia is a very racist country, but I realise now that a lot of people in Australia have never thought about whether they're treating people unfairly. They just latch onto whatever they see in the media — stereotypes.

At least Pauline Hanson made people think about it.

AUTHOR If you had a magic wand, what would you wish for?

GAVIN I'd wish for people to use their brains and look logically at issues. Many of my colleagues put their training aside and respond only on a gut feeling. I certainly don't subscribe to the notion that we'll all be happy and everything will be wonderful if Australia ends up with a coffee-coloured people.

If we all contributed, Australia has the possibility of being a great nation, with its fantastic human and natural resources. We're so lucky, we can afford to address these issues, but if we are taken over by multinational companies, we're going to lose our identity.

On a very small scale, I've done what I could. I started off with a group of kids, and I've equipped them with skills to think for themselves, to use their own brains. I've been able to change these kids. I've taught them to respect themselves and others.

1980s — MARRIAGES BETWEEN CHRISTIANS

Be ye not unequally yoked with unbelievers for what fellowship
hath righteousness with unrighteousness?

2 Corinthians 6:13

Among the couples who allowed me to interview them, atheists and
Jews live happily together, Muslims, Zoroastrians, Hindus and
Christians adjust to their different ideas of God, while Buddhists
seemingly adapt to partners of any religious persuasion, perhaps
because Buddhism does not focus on any God figure at all. Many
couples assured me that they could be as relaxed or as strict in their
faith as they wanted to be, without insisting that their partner share
their beliefs. Padma, a Hindu, said of the place of religion in her
marriage to Peter, a religious Calvinist: 'It's never been a conflict. I
do what I do, and Peter does what he does'.

It seems, nevertheless, that a shared religious faith strengthens a
marriage and leads to a more consistent religious training for the
next generation. Lian finds herself as a young adult without a faith
at all, because each of her parents gave her just a taste of Buddhism
and of Christianity, in a loving effort not to exclude or diminish the
value of the other parent's religion. Decisions to wait and let the
child decide on a religion could well mean the child never becomes
centred in any faith at all, as Lian described the lack of structure or
guidelines in her own life.

For some couples, particularly Christians who choose missionary
work as their vocation, it is essential that both partners share the

same faith. They take Saint Paul's advice to the Corinthians, not to be 'unequally yoked', as a personal instruction.

Rex told me that he was living the hedonistic life of 'an ordinary young Aussie bloke' when he met the girl he wanted to marry. After a short while she told him a friendship was not possible because they were spiritually incompatible. 'She broke off our relationship for her God. I had never before met anyone with a personal relationship with God. I was curious and impressed, so I started to go to church and came to know the Lord myself. That was in July of 1980. We were married in 1981.'

Rex and Suan Lee live now in a home perched high on a hill with a bird's-eye view of Sydney's northern beaches, and together they run a Christian family ministry. They have two children.

SUAN LEE My ancestor was the fifteenth son of the emperor in the Wei dynasty, so I included Wei in the names of the children, to retain their links with that part of their heritage. I was born in a Christian Chinese family in Singapore in 1959 and came to Perth when I was twenty-one, in 1980. I was so filled with joy and awe at the spaciousness of Perth and the sense of freedom I found here, that I knew I could never go back to Singapore to live.

REX Me? Born in Australia; Scottish origin way back; grew up at City Beach in Perth. A good life. Well looked after, happy family, spent a lot of time on the beach. No spiritual aspect to my life. Went to university, but left after a year to travel around Australia. I worked at anything to earn my keep and petrol. The trip was an eye-opener. I drove back to Perth for Christmas 1979.

With the adventure out of my blood, I went back to university and met Suan Lee there. It was love at first sight. She was so different, a mystery; she fascinated me.

AUTHOR What did your parents think about your marriage?

REX Suan Lee's family accepted it; so did mine. We came to Sydney because of a job I was offered here. We wanted to go overseas as missionaries, but in the meantime we are raising our family and gaining more experience. We are missionaries to Australian families here — healing the broken-hearted.

I like the great diversity in Australia now, but I cannot understand why the government is discriminating against Christian practices. So many Australians, even if they are not regular churchgoers, hold onto Christian beliefs and ethics and behaviours and value them, and they are just sick of the continual denigration of our Christian heritage.

SUAN LEE The downside of tolerance is that it also means tolerance of immorality. Australians should be proud of our heritage, too. Some things that were done may not have been good, but all peoples have lived less than perfectly. We should just do what good we can now.

REX There are a lot of differences among people in Australia today. Different customs, different expectations, and many of them are cultural rather than racial. I learned about differences when I took a great deal of trouble to make a pendant for Suan Lee. It took me weeks of work and cost a lot of money, as I was still a student. When I gave it to Suan Lee, she did not respond in any way; she said nothing. I thought she didn't like it and I was so disappointed. She wore it for a time, and then stopped wearing it, all without comment.

SUAN LEE The Chinese way is not to thank people, and that comes across as a cool reception to Australians. I've learned to thank people profusely now when they give me things, because that's what Australians do.

Another example of the differences in social behaviour is that Chinese criticise a gift in order that others can contradict you and praise it. I remember I pointed out the faults in a beautiful table Rex had made me, and his parents were flabbergasted. I felt a sudden coldness from them, but I didn't realise why, until later.

AUTHOR One thing I had to learn when I lived in Singapore was to refrain from admiring babies or small children. It was so natural for me to admire these beautiful children, but my admiration was seen as a definite risk — it might draw the attention of an evil spirit!

SUAN LEE Yes, that's right. Some Chinese don't even call their child by the right name, but by an animal's name, in order to confuse the evil spirits.

REX How do Chinese express friendship, Suan Lee? How did I know that you were my friend?

SUAN LEE Chinese don't verbalise. They'll never say anything to indicate that they like you. But they might have you around for a meal.

AUTHOR Maybe that is one of the problems that we haven't addressed in the wider community. The vast difference in what is regarded as acceptable, well-mannered behaviour in different communities, and also the difficulty of reading unspoken messages between cultures.

REX Yes, Chinese never understand Aussies' humour, especially ironic or derogatory humour indicating a comfortable friendly relationship. Another thing — I grew up in a home where Dad was the traditional boss, too, and Mum ran around after everyone. Had I not married Suan Lee I would have been a bossy husband too.

AUTHOR Some men choose Asian wives particularly because they want a mild, easily-dominated person. Yet I must say that the Asian wives I've have met have been particularly strong.

SUAN LEE Yes. My mother rules the roost. My father is passive.

AUTHOR Do you feel Australian, Suan Lee?

SUAN LEE I am so proud of being Australian — right from the beginning. When I stepped into Australia and saw the difference, I couldn't go back. People in Singapore can be very materialistic and elitist; you're either in the rat-race or you're left behind. Even if I didn't marry Rex, I couldn't have married anyone from Singapore; I couldn't have married a traditional Asian, though I'm also proud of my heritage, my Chineseness.

There is such a wide choice of lifestyle here.

Yes, I'm proud and happy to be Australian. What seems strange to me, though, is that any minority is encouraged to follow his religion, express his culture, but anything which is seen as Anglo-Saxon Australian or Christian seems to be politically incorrect

— you feel as if you have to apologise for it. I'm a migrant and a Christian, and I feel I'm swimming upstream if I mention anything from the Bible. Yet if I spoke about Buddhism or Hinduism or Islam or anything else it would be welcomed. Australia is, or was, a Christian country. Why are we not celebrating that?

Shamini, a former Hindu from a Malaysian Indian family, and Ray were abroad, doing missionary work in Sabah, when the need for urgent, sophisticated medical treatment brought them home to Melbourne.

SHAMINI I came to Melbourne to do pharmacy in 1975 and met Ray four years later at a Christian fellowship meeting. He'd finished engineering and was doing theology at Ridley College. When Ray finished his theology course, we married and went out as missionaries, first to the interior of Sabah and then in Kota Kinibalu.

Although my family was not Christian then, Dad was open-minded about my marriage. He knew I came to Australia not only to study, but to learn about life, but Mum was not happy.

RAY After Shamini had told her parents about me, I went alone to Malaysia to ask for Shamini's hand. The relatives all had a look at me and they must have decided it could be worse. My family was no problem. I was already independent.

SHAMINI Ray's grandmother was rude and his mum, like mine, found it hard to accept that we were giving up well-paid careers to go out as missionaries. Ray's brother is a real ocker who just laughs at anything that isn't straight-down-the-line Australian, so I suppose he's had a lot of laughs at me. However, since Ray's illness, he's offered to help me with the garden.

RAY Just normal adjustment to marriage is a major thing to most people, so with different cultures, experiences, you're going to have extra difficulties. You're going to have parents in other countries; you're going to have relatives living with you for long spells. And you've also got a communication barrier. You have to expend effort to overcome that, or there'll be a problem.

People look at us strangely, still. They can accept Asians, but to marry them — that's going too far! Even in the church where I belonged when we were engaged, Sharmini didn't feel comfortable.

SHAMINI I prefer the Swanston Street church where we go now, because it is very multicultural.

RAY Very Asian, you mean. Australians are outnumbered many times over; it's Australians who feel uncomfortable there, and they leave.

AUTHOR That is a pity, because at some point the Asians are going to lose touch with the Australian community.

SHAMINI Yes. At the moment, it is good for mixed-race couples, but our children are Australian, and when they grow up, if they marry Australians, they will leave the church, because they will no longer be comfortable there.

RAY In an all-Asian situation, they want it all their way, and that is racism too. They get upset when Australian problems are talked about at church. The Chinese want the emphasis to be totally on them. For example, many ex-Singaporeans are very critical of the Australian government system and keep saying how wonderful Singapore is. But how wonderful is it when you don't have an opposition? When any one who protests has a lawsuit slapped on them? We've lived in Singapore. We know what it's like, but if I comment, they don't like it at all!

SHAMINI I have had very little trouble here in Australia but I have difficulty with the outspokenness of Australians, particularly young people. I even find it hard with my own kids. To me it seems to be a lack of respect. Australians just speak their minds. I guess because here in Australia they are comfortable about speaking their minds, even if they know their view is unpopular. Asians are more reticent. They might think the same, but they won't say it. They're not so comfortable with being open.

AUTHOR That contradicts what Ray just said about the Singapore Chinese at the church criticising Australia openly.

SHAMINI Both are true. We Asians will criticise things only in a situation where we know the majority is like-minded.

AUTHOR Perhaps that is a feature of immigrant thinking, when they don't yet feel at home.

SHAMINI There is another problem. A lot of people, for example our friends in the Swanston Street church, left their home countries twenty years ago, or more. Their children are now Australians and want to live Australian lives. But the Asian parents remember their home country as it was, and do not seem to realise that it has changed too. They try to force their Australian children to live what is really an out-of-date lifestyle.

Harvey and Nahtaw currently live in Esperance, on the long southern coast of Western Australia, until they set out once again to teach modern agricultural practice and Bible study to villagers connected with Baptist mission stations, in whatever country needs them. They were married in Nahtaw's home town of Chieng Mai in Thailand in 1986, and have two daughters.

HARVEY I went to Thailand in 1983 as an agricultural adviser and Nahtaw was working as an assistant in the mission there. After a couple of years we got married. We could go back and live there, but I like to work on a project to help the local people only until they can do it themselves. When I've taught them all I know, I might as well leave and go somewhere else.

Initially, as a Christian, I did not approve of mission work, but in the Baptist Mission the missionary is obligated to live among the local people and be directed by those local communities. We are there only to share our skills with them, so they can break out of their extreme poverty and have a better standard of living, so the children — well everybody, really — are healthier. It is our privilege to share their lives as Jesus would have us do.

NAHTAW My grandparents came from China, but I am not Chinese. I'm not Thai either, even though for two or three generations, we have lived in Thailand. I am a tribal person.

AUTHOR Are you saying that it doesn't matter what country you live in, you don't belong to that country, but only to your tribe?

NAHTAW Yes. We speak a different language. Everything is different. We always remain a tribal people.

AUTHOR Did your family like the idea of you marrying an Australian?

NAHTAW They knew Harvey and they liked him. We were all in the church together.

HARVEY They were my friends, quite apart from Nahtaw. I didn't live as a foreigner in Chieng Mai, but as one of them. There was no barrier between me and Nahtaw's family.

AUTHOR What about your family? Were they happy about your marriage?

HARVEY Well, my mum thought that whatever I did it was okay. She'd already met Nahtaw's people and Nahtaw on earlier visits. She came to the wedding in Thailand. Some of Mum's relatives were not too pleased, but I don't look for negatives, so perhaps that's why I don't see them.
   I've always been interested in different people, different countries. When I was young I really couldn't imagine myself marrying a white Australian girl. I knew all about Australian girls, I wanted to marry someone different!
   I think any marriage will work, but to marry across racial lines, it has to be in your nature. You have to be interested in different cultures. I think it's almost like a miracle, or the work of God, that brings two people of such different cultures as Nahtaw and I together, because our childhoods were so far apart — geographically and psychologically. There's no way one can actually plan for such a thing to happen. I know white guys who have married Asian women, and their characters suit the woman they chose. They wouldn't have found a partner to suit them in the country and culture where they were brought up.
   There's no doubt the church and church people made our life easier, though, especially when we first returned from Thailand.

NAHTAW When I first came here to Australia everyone from the church invited us to their homes. In the beginning Harvey's mother was there, helping me, making it easy for me. She invited all her relatives to meet me.

AUTHOR What about your children? Have they also had only positive experiences?

HARVEY At Kelmscott where we lived before there was no difficulty, but here, for a short time, the children had a fairly bad time.

NAHTAW When people don't know you, they feel you're different, and that happened when we first came to Esperance. With the children it was the same.

HARVEY In Zambia where our children went to school. about half the children were black, the rest white. They got on well with everybody, but their best friends were African.
   Here in Esperance there are very few Asians. The few Thais here have become great friends with Nahtaw, seeming not to notice the vast cultural differences between themselves and Nahtaw, which is almost as wide a gulf as the differences which separate them from Australians.

NAHTAW It's the food. We all cook up a party together. I have made lots of friends here — everywhere. In the street, at the school, not only in the church. Everyone is very nice to me. Their friendship to me is nothing to do with how I look, but everything to do with how I am. I have never had any difficulty yet.

AUTHOR I don't think you will have any difficulty ever, Nahtaw. Your exuberance for life and people disarms everyone. People you meet probably wonder why they hadn't noticed life was so good.

HARVEY Did you have opposition to your marriage?

AUTHOR Yes. My family was very much opposed. My brother still doesn't speak to my husband.

HARVEY Still?

AUTHOR Still. But of course we don't see him much. Perhaps he would change his mind if we lived next door, but we live 1000 kilometres apart, and since our mother died, I rarely go back.

NAHTAW You are very strong to marry with all your family against it.

AUTHOR Maybe just stubborn. It caused a lot of tears, a lot of heartbreak, and I did hurt my mother very badly. She felt utterly betrayed, and my father didn't come to my wedding.

HARVEY Wow! It's a wonder you didn't run away from everyone!

AUTHOR We did. We went to Singapore to live, planning never to return, but I was not totally cut off from my parents. Although they hated my marriage, they didn't hate me. They would never cut me off. They were good people, living for generations in the same country district where they knew everybody and everybody's family. They knew and loved their world and were very comfortable in it — and very uncomfortable with interracial marriage, which didn't fit into that world at all.
    It wasn't only my parents who hated my marriage, though. Many people in my life put intense pressure on me, to dissuade me from marrying Josh, including an ex-missionary who was then Warden of the university where Josh and I were students. I won him over, though, and later he presided at our wedding reception.

HARVEY The person who performed our wedding ceremony and his wife tried to persuade Nahtaw not to marry me. They'd worked with tribal people all their lives and thought that Western culture would destroy her.

NAHTAW The night before the wedding they came and said, 'If this is not what you want, it's not too late to change your mind!'.
    It was exactly what I wanted, so although they may have known tribal people for a long time, they didn't know this tribal person.

HARVEY In our case the white people involved were worried on behalf of the other, non-white one of the couple.

AUTHOR I think it's not the colour, but the gender that brings on advice and interference. It is the woman who people try to influence and control, no matter whether her skin is white or brown.

When we were newly-married and living in Singapore, my husband's niece, Gina, was a 7-or-8-month-old baby. I asked her mother whether she was crawling yet; I have never forgotten her mother's answer. 'I don't know', she said. 'She's never been put on the floor. The servant carries her all the time.'

Gina grew up living a very sheltered life: protected, guarded and guided by her family. Then she met Neil, the Australian she married. They now have two daughters. Neil's 90-year-old father, Merv, also joined our discussion.

GINA   Neil's sister, Jessie, had married a Chinese man and they lived in Singapore. Jessie was my friend at church there, and I met Neil's dad and mum when they were visiting and came to church with her.

NEIL   The following year I spent a holiday with Jessie, and Dad asked me to 'say hello to the little Indian girl' at the church, so when Jessie took me to church I said 'hello' to Gina. The next Sunday we went to another church and afterwards I said to my sister, half-jokingly, 'I missed out on seeing Gina this week'.

The following week, we went to Gina's church again and we talked there. Then Jessie invited Gina to visit us.

GINA   They lived quite a long way from the city, and the invitation was for Wednesday, the evening before Neil's flight back to Perth. I caught a bus all the way out to Seletar and Jessie put on a lovely dinner and then left us to talk. We talked and talked; we got on so well.

MERV   Jessie was a real matchmaker.

GINA   Then on Thursday morning, I was surprised to see Neil coming up the porch steps. We talked and talked for hours. I took him down to see Mum, who was teaching piano, and also introduced him to my sister. He still didn't go. Every time I reminded him that it was time to go, he'd say, 'Yes, I must go'. But he didn't go. He kept on talking.

NEIL   I had prayed to the Lord about giving me clear guidance if I was to meet the person for me while I was in Singapore. I did eventually leave, after I asked Gina if I could write to her.

AUTHOR   Was it a concern for you that Gina was Indian? That she was from a different culture, and she looked different?

NEIL   I don't remember that it bothered me at all, because she was a Christian and we got on so well, right from the start.

GINA   When I told my family doctor in Singapore I was going to Australia, he said it was the best thing I could do, and he was right. Coming to Australia was a sort of healing for me; I didn't know how I was ever going to become myself, or if I would ever marry at all. If I had married an Indian man, I couldn't have survived. I'd have been really stressed-out, just as I was stressed-out growing up in Singapore. That's why it was just so lovely and beautiful to meet Neil, and he was so quiet and gentle. It was so special; he was so different from anyone I had known. Just his quietness and gentleness, and the love and gentleness of his dad and mum, too. They helped me through to where I am today.

AUTHOR It's a delight to see how you have blossomed in your marriage, Gina. You are now the woman you should have been. You had no trouble — either of you — being accepted by the other's family?

GINA AND NEIL More than accepted. Welcomed.

GINA I was lucky. I fitted into Neil's family and the church very well. Even strangers were friendly because at that time there were not so many Asian migrants. I enjoy living in Australia, though after a few years I began to realise that there are differences. I find Australians quite reserved, though most are very friendly.

MERV I think talking about it like this is helping Gina and Neil clarify their thoughts — and mine too.

GINA In Singapore, I could never have managed a marriage like I have now. I don't wish to detract from Neil and his family, who have been so wonderful for me, but we are also linked into the church where we all have similar friends, similar goals, similar values. It's a wonderful loving community. And I have learned so much. I now speak, give talks to a whole congregation, rooms full of people! Imagine it, me! People who knew me in Singapore would never believe it.

AUTHOR What about Erica and Jodi?

NEIL Erica was teased a little bit, but it was not important, not too hurtful.

GINA Last year, when she started kindergarten, Jodi was called a brown girl, and she asked me why I am brown. I told her, adding that I don't get sunburnt, and neither will she. But no, Jodi protested, she was white. All of the children there at the kindergarten are white, you see, and she sees herself as one of them.

As you know, many of my father's family and most of my mother's family married Australians, English, Germans, Chinese — all sorts. I have uncles and aunts and cousins from all over, and all different races. It just hadn't occurred to me that I had to explain why I am what I am.

I think in Australia there will be more intermarriages, so perhaps I'll have to get used to explaining myself and others.

NEIL It doesn't matter where people come from, and race isn't the essential thing either. But it is important that Australia remains a Christian nation, trusting in God. In a sense, I feel we should accept anyone of any religion provided they treat people well. I would really like complete freedom, but I see what's happening in countries where Muslims are the majority, and so I fear that sort of thing happening in Australia.

I am wary of Christians forcing their values on others. Yet because I believe Australia should stick to its Christian values, then I've got to say that I like to see Christians come into Australia — the more the better. There is a danger that our established absolute values will be diluted. I recognise that many, perhaps most, Australians do not have a personal relationship with God, but I do think that the fact that our background and traditions are Christian has given us a tremendous strength and cohesion; we dare not let that break down. I know that migrants have their own moral values, and some of them are very beneficial to Australia, but the differences might cause a division.

AUTHOR Do you think of yourself as Australian, Gina?

GINA Oh, yes, all Australian. I can't think of myself ever living in Singapore again. I can visit, take a holiday, but I always long to come back home to Australia.

Derek came from the western district of Victoria to Melbourne after finishing school eighteen years ago. He married Roslin, an Iban from East Malaysia, in 1984. Derek runs his own re-stumping business and has practically re-built his and Roslin's large Victorian house in Richmond.

DEREK I met Roslin at the Swanston Street church, and later when a mate and I went over to help a friend working at a Bible college in East Malaysia, we dropped into Kuching to visit Roslin.

AUTHOR You must have been interested in Asians to go to that church in the first place.

DEREK Yes. For a long time back my family has had sympathy with Asia and Asians, mostly from listening to visiting missionaries. As a child I thought I might become a missionary in Borneo. Instead, as it turns out, I married a girl from Borneo.
    We billeted Asian students for weekends on our farm, too, while I was at high school. Then, when I came to Melbourne, those students took me to Swanston Street, with its mainly Asian congregation.

ROSLIN I spent a year, 1982, here, and I met Derek at the church but we were not special friends or anything. After I went home Derek and his friend had a working holiday at a mission not far away from my home, and later, turned up in Kuching. I acted as a sort of tour guide for them.
    We are not traditional Ibans, and I didn't grow up in a longhouse, but in the mission house where my father works.

DEREK Their grandparents do, though, and Roslin and her brother took us along the river to their grandparents' longhouse for the New Year celebration. That evening I fell sick — very sick. I had been bitten by sandflies. And Roslin nursed me. And so we got together.

AUTHOR How did your parents react to your proposed marriage, Roslin?

ROSLIN I'm their only daughter, among nine brothers, so Mum and Dad didn't want me to go so far away when I married.

DEREK Mum wasn't keen either, but both sets of parents accepted that it was our choice. Her parents insisted that Roslin come back here again before we married to see if she was sure she'd like it.
    We've been married for fourteen years, and it took a long time for us to learn to mesh together. Culturally, there have been quite a lot of difficulties. Though I had a fair bit of exposure to Asians, I still had a lot to learn. For instance, I thought Asian girls were all meek and demure. I learnt otherwise.
    Then there's the food. Roslin doesn't like Australian food, whereas I eat anything — even plain cold rice in Sabah. I try to eat local food wherever I am, because people accept you better, I think. But the very people who are glad when you are prepared to try their food are the ones who carry on and complain about our food when they come here.

ROSLIN I'm used to it now. Mostly I eat chicken, but I can now eat lamb and beef without any problem.

DEREK There are other things, too, but we've both adapted. For example, we let the children sleep in our room. We have a very big bedroom and the children like it, but I know that most Australians wouldn't do that.

There was a fair bit of tension during the first years of our marriage. We went through severe struggles, mainly caused, I believe, by cultural differences. We think differently, and communication was very, very difficult. For example … Roslin cooked up her first Australian meal and asked, 'How was it?' 'It was lovely', I said, 'but next time put some salt in the potatoes'. All hell broke loose because I was so direct. I should have praised the meal for a half-hour before getting around to mentioning the salt! Language itself is a problem, too. Although Ros speaks English, she doesn't pronounce the whole word. I thought I was going deaf, and then I realised Ros wasn't saying the endings of the words. And in English word endings are important. Also, when I'm talking, I expect feedback; a nod, or a yes. Most Australians do. This wasn't happening. I had to say, 'Did you hear me, or didn't you?'.

Things are getting better. I think I'm becoming a little more tolerant, and probably Ros gives me a bit more feedback now. We're both learning to cope with our differences.

Communication has been the biggest problem we've had to overcome, and communication means more than language. Another worry has been money, or the lack of it. When our finances were tough, everything was tough. I felt weighed down by the burden of providing for the family during that time. I worked every bit of overtime I could get, and at the end of three months, my bank account only had $100 more in it, even though I had a regular job all the way through. I remember getting mad when Ros bought a tin of milo she wanted. A tin of milo! It was tough. I can understand why some families are broken by the burden of worry.

I had a number of good friends from youth group days, even before I married, so I brought Roslin into that group. But one of the things that disappointed me was that when we were having real trouble in our marriage, the church people smiled, but didn't offer to help. So when newly married couples come into the church now, I tell them some of the difficulties that we had, so if and when things crop up to worry them, they'll realise they're not alone.

Derek was not alone in mentioning that fellow church members, while offering a smiling greeting, fail to offer more meaningful assistance to troubled fellow members. It could be put down to the natural reserve of Anglo-Saxon Australians (another trait mentioned often by migrants) that holds them back, lest they seem to be interfering. However, at Derek's church, the congregation was not comprised of white Australians, but overseas-born Asian Australians.

12

INTERRACIAL MARRIAGES IN THE 1980s

In any society there is always racism. In Singapore there is racism; in Malaysia there is racism, and in China. So, too, in Australia.

Dr Bernice Pfitzner

In 1984 the foreign press, particularly in Singapore, Malaysia, Thailand and other countries in Australia's neighbourhood, reacted strongly to Geoffrey Blainey's now famous speech recommending that migration be slowed. Most of the 'other' spouses in interracial marriages in Australia during the 1970s and 1980s came from just those countries whose leaders felt constrained to lecture Australia about racism. Migrants from these countries do not face the legal discrimination in Australia that is enacted against, for example, the Chinese in Malaysia. Richard Basham, of Sydney University, writes:

> In contrast to Australia, no Asian society genuinely prohibits racial discrimination in immigration or before the law. Indeed, racial discrimination is so deeply embedded in the moral premises of Asian society that it often goes unnoticed. While someone of Asian ancestry who is born in Australia can expect citizenship, the same cannot be said for someone of Caucasian ancestry born in Malaysia or Japan.[1]

Bernard, a Singapore Chinese, married Anglo-Celtic Australian Andrea in 1985.

ANDREA I was brought up as a Presbyterian, and there would have been a real fuss if I had married a Catholic. As it is, my mother thinks Bernard is great. We were married in Singapore and one of the old Chinese men at our wedding wouldn't shake my hand or my mother's.

Bernard's mother and I got on very well until I had our first child. She came to help, but her idea of helping me was to take over. I wanted to breastfeed. She didn't approve. That was out first clash. I was sad that it happened, and we have never regained the feeling we had before, though I have a lot of admiration for her.

Andrea was one of several Australian wives who found the long-time — usually six months or more — presence of her mother-in-law during and after childbirth overwhelmingly intrusive. Though Andrea realised the visit and advice and physical assistance were all offered in a spirit of helpfulness, she also felt bullied. Some mothers in a similar situation felt that they were forced to become a minor player in decisions about their children and home. Some, like Andrea, insisted that their rights as mothers were paramount. Others bore the intrusions during several successive childbirths, becoming increasingly resentful with each one. Australian husbands also complained, saying that during the intrusions of their mothers-in-law, they felt like strangers in their own homes.

BERNARD   I like being in Australia, but I enjoy Singapore too; my family is there. We holiday there a lot and we've even thought about going back to live.

ANDREA   Whenever he talks of going back, he talks of going back to live with his mother. If we'd decided to live that way, we should have done it years ago.

BERNARD   She has a big house and plenty of room, and we couldn't afford to buy such a good house in Singapore. In any case I enjoy being with my family. If I wasn't married, I'd probably have stayed in Singapore. With all the family connections over there it would be easier if I chose to venture into business.

Andrea and I met at university, and you wonder whether you'd have met other people, if you'd just done a different course. If I had married a Chinese woman, it would have been easier on my mother.

I sometimes wonder what it would be like to work in corporate Australia, if I had an Asian wife, too. I see Chinese friends who married Asian women, and they have no way of truly integrating with Australian families. Married to an Australian woman, I feel more comfortable mixing in Australian society. I think it's interesting and beneficial. I've become very Australianised. Really, it is better, all-round, for us to live in Australia.

However, I do believe that with increasing penetration of younger Asian Australians, corporate Australia will become more accepting of Asians at senior management level.

I've been here for twenty-two years and I've never had a taunt or anything unpleasant. I lived in Bathurst for the first three years, where they used to call me the Happy Honker. I came in after finishing my national service in Singapore, so I was more mature than most students, and I'm quite tall, too. Perhaps those circumstances helped me become Australian very quickly.

There have been little pinpricks, but never face-to-face. When I joined one company as their chief accountant, I was told that one of the employees would never work under a Chinaman. I decided to wait and see what happened. She didn't leave, and I heard no more about it.

ANDREA   We've all felt pinpricks. At the local doctor's surgery a man in the waiting room said, 'You wouldn't want to go out to Cabramatta now. All those power-points. You can't even let your dogs loose out there. They eat them'.

I pointed to my children sitting nearby and said, 'These are my children, and their father does not eat dogs'.

I try to make the children aware that they are of mixed race. Things like table manners have to be addressed, because Chinese table manners are quite different. I say, 'Don't open your mouth when you're eating'. They point out that Bernard's brother is eating with his mouth open. So I tell them there are two different ways, and they'll just have to learn both. Bernard has been giving our eldest, Julian, the educational push of the Chinese, with good results, too.

BERNARD   I think Australian children are imaginative and creative, but many of the kids who come to me for a job can't read properly, can't spell, can't write a proper letter. I want to make sure Julian can. It is a reflection of Australian parents, who let their children do what they like. In Singapore where education is so hard to get, it's valued more highly.

Wannapon met the Australian who is now her husband when she was tutoring in a temple night school in Bangkok. They married in 1983.

AUTHOR   Were both your families happy about your marriage?

WANNAPON   Not really. At first my parents were ashamed, as in Thailand only bar girls marry white men. My aunt persuaded them, by telling my mother that white men were more faithful, that a Thai husband might want more women. At the beginning John's family were not pleased either. They went to Thailand to try to stop our marriage, but they softened after meeting my family.

John and I get on very well, but there are some differences. I like it that he tells me his thoughts and feelings, but even though I know English, I cannot express my thoughts and feelings in English.

When John taught in Port Pirie, I did relief teaching there. Some kids were rude, making fun of my appearance. They made their eyes ... you know ... Asian. (Wannapon pulled her eyes into an exaggerated slant, and laughed a little self-consciously.)

John now teaches in Adelaide. It is better, but there's not much relief teaching here, so I started a little restaurant. It is not really successful as a business, but brings in some extra money for the family.

It's better for us to live in Australia. In Thailand, if they see me with John, they would think I am a bar girl.

Brenda, a Chinese Malaysian, met her husband, an Australian of Italian descent, at her first job. They are both accountants.

BRENDA   When I first came to Australia in 1974 as a HSC student at a local high school, I was very aware that I spoke with an accent. Getting to know fellow students was very hard. I felt like a square peg trying to fit into a round hole.

After finishing school, I went to Monash University, into the accounting department, where 90 per cent of the students were Asian. The class was full of black heads. I was not part of the minority there, and we were all here in Australia to concentrate on our studies and get our qualifications. We would be the first ones to grab the library books, and hang onto them until the day we delivered our assignments. Socialising or getting to know Australians was not a priority. The Asians kept with Asians, and the Australians mixed with Australians. If we were all in a room together, conversation would cease the minute formal greetings were done.

AUTHOR Yet when you met Vincent, you fell in love with him and married him!

BRENDA When I met Vincent, I was working in an office where the ability to communicate with fellow workmates was important. If I were to get anywhere in my career, I had to be able to relate to their idiosyncrasies. At university, getting to know these foreigners was not important.

AUTHOR By 'foreigners' you mean Australians?

BRENDA Anybody who is not yellow-skinned. Australians did not differentiate either. We were just Asians whether we were from Singapore or Malaysia or Hong Kong.

* * *

Brenda's university experience contrasts with that of Manjeet, a Sikh student who also came from Malaysia, and later married an Australian student she met at university.

MANJEET I was aware of Western culture before meeting Frank, and of course I could speak English. If you are able to communicate easily, then you're more acceptable to people. If you mix only with your fellow Asians and speak your own language all the time, only breaking into English when it is necessary — say in the lecture hall — then you've immediately built walls around yourself. The general Australian community is very aware of the walls you create by speaking in a different language. They naturally expect you, as the new kid on the block, to take the first step, and if you don't, then they assume you don't want to get to know them.

* * *

BRENDA During my first year at university, I had lived on campus, and in college I became friendly with a few Australian students. Later four of us flatted together — three Australian students and me. During the day I would be with my Chinese friends, and I would return to an Australian household at night.

AUTHOR But these Australian friends were students too. Not too different from the students in your class that you saw as so foreign that you couldn't speak to them.

BRENDA Yes, they were from the country and had the same aim as me — to get their degrees. With Vincent it was different too. He was genuinely interested in me and understanding of my culture. Actually, there is not much difference between our cultures. Having a close-knit family is of prime importance to Italians and also to Chinese. Initially, I did not feel comfortable with our relationship, though. We were looked upon as an oddity at first.

My parents were not unhappy; Vincent satisfied their expectations of an intelligent and hard-working son-in-law who had gone through university and had a professional qualification.

VINCENT My parents were not happy. They expected me to marry an Italian girl. It shocked me that my own parents discriminated against newer migrants. My father is very critical of the way the Vietnamese display their food on the footpath. Yet, when he first came here, the Australians didn't like the way Italians hung their sausages.

When I was a small child we lived in inner Melbourne suburbs, where there were a lot of migrants — Maltese, Italians, Greeks. I was just one of many. Then we moved to Springvale, which was predominantly English migrants then. It was there that I first became aware that I was different. I'd never been called names before.

Springvale has now been taken over by Vietnamese. I feel for the migrants who are aware that they're not welcome, and though I can understand why migrants cling together in huge groups, I wish they wouldn't. If they spread out they'd meet less hostility.

My parents have always stuck to the Italian section of Melbourne, so they don't really fit into Australian society, even after all these years. Yet they don't fit in when they go back to Italy, either.

We visit my parents and we all go with them to church on Christmas Day, but they are disappointed that we don't go to church regularly. Perhaps I will as I get older; most Catholics do.

BRENDA   Religion isn't an issue, even though I'm still a Buddhist. I visit the temple with the children on certain festive days and Vincent takes us all to church on Christmas Day, to make it extra special for the children. They are both having Bible study at their schools, and we are happy about that. We're bringing the children up as Australians.

VINCENT   We've been very lucky ... our life runs smoothly. Probably the only area of tension in our marriage is when Brenda's parents come out to visit us. They can't speak English, so I am unable to communicate with them. I try to understand, but I guess I get irritated because they stay for months. How many months, Brenda? Too long anyway.

BRENDA   Four or five months. Long enough to drive Vincent away from the house.

VINCENT   I end up feeling a stranger in my own house. I sometimes sit at the table with eight people, and they're all shouting in Chinese. On top of that, there's the Chinese attitude to food. For Chinese a meal is an exercise in eating. It is not, in any way, a social occasion. Real conversation doesn't play a part — only the eating and the discussion of the food. For Australians, and for Italians, a meal is an event, a social occasion. Not for Chinese; for them the purpose is to eat, just eat.

BRENDA   I love it when my mother comes and cooks Chinese, but after a while, I yearn for Australian meals too, so while my mother is here we often end up cooking two meals, or Vincent eats out.

Several Australian spouses interviewed mentioned what they saw as their Chinese partner's obsession with food, and said it caused a major difficulty in their relationship. One wife even felt that her Chinese husband's demands relating to food were a significant cause of the breakdown of their marriage. Only one Chinese wife recognised that 'the Chinese attitude to food' was different from that experienced in Australian homes, and she chose to develop an 'Australian way of thinking about food'. She was intrigued to discover that her young son, as he matured, was developing 'a Chinese attitude to food', with no encouragement from her.

'For the Chinese', wrote Diana Giese in *Astronauts, Lost Souls & Dragons*, 'food is life, in every sense of the word, a symbol of health, luck and prosperity. Every time Chinese eat a meal they are strengthening their body, mind and soul. In no other people has the preparation, cooking, serving, cultivation and preservation of food taken on such a dominant and pervasive role'.

Chinese cooking methods, if not their attitude to food, have infiltrated all our kitchens, though. According to a 1991 survey of eating habits, 65 per cent of Australians cook stir-fried meals twice a week.[2]

Suan Lee spoke of Chinese reticence in verbalising emotions, saying that instead of saying she liked someone, a Chinese girl might invite a new friend to have a meal at her house. To her, then, offering a meal was tantamount to offering friendship. Not so different from the old Australian custom of inviting someone who might become a friend to a Sunday family dinner.

Li Li came from Malaysia to study commerce at Melbourne University, and met her Australian husband, an earlier Melbourne commerce graduate, at a party given by mutual friends.

LI LI   I have never had any rudeness or racism from anyone. Nothing like that ever. Nothing worse than gentle teasing about my Malaysian accent by friends, workmates.

When I told my parents I was going out with an Australian my father seemed unperturbed, saying he wanted me to be happy. So I went home in 1979 to tell them all about Colin. For the whole of that three-week holiday my mother didn't speak to me. She was very prejudiced, quite racist and used emotional blackmail, trying to force me to give Colin up.

Colin and I were together for about five-and-a-half years before we got married in 1984. By then my mother had got used to the idea. They come to visit us now and I think at last they realise that we have a happy marriage.

COLIN   My family didn't mind at all. My mother had lived in India as part of a missionary family, so I guess she was used to mixing with other races. Li Li's family is very business-minded, very entrepreneurial, whereas I'm a true blue public servant. I can't get interested in money-making ideas, so we don't exactly hit it off.

LI LI   I always felt that Colin's parents welcomed me, but they are very reticent. They don't interfere.

It's true, my parents' antagonism towards Colin is mainly race, but they would have liked him to be a go-getter, a successful go-getter or maybe a doctor.

My father was a poor man, with no opportunities. But he made money at business and he gave us all every chance to have a good education. He offered to support us even if we wanted to go on and do a PhD, and some of my brothers did that. But my parents are still frugal.

AUTHOR   Did you have to make significant adjustments to cultural differences?

LI LI   Yes, we had major disagreements on a couple of things — money, and child-raising.

AUTHOR Chinese people have a reputation for being very good with money and very strict with children. Is that what you mean? And is it true?

LI LI Yes and yes. Both are true. I handle all the money matters, spending, investments, everything. I'm good at it.

COLIN Li Li keeps us on the straight and narrow and I appreciate her skill in this area, though I object sometimes because Li Li always wants to buy the less expensive thing — she's frugal, like her father. I tend towards the more expensive thing because you get what you pay for.

Li Li doesn't drink, either, and sometimes I begrudge the fact that I can't have a glass of wine as often as I'd like. And I would like to go out more. We never go out without the children, and I might go out only three or four times a year to a concert or something, alone.

I think Westerners, both men and women, are more inclined to want time to themselves.

AUTHOR You don't ever have a babysitter in to stay with the children so you can have a night out together?

LI LI No. If I go to a restaurant, I take the children. If friends invite us, I take the children too.

I am the strict one with children, too. I have named the children Su-Lin and Su-Kim according to Chinese custom because I wanted it to be obvious that, despite their surname, they were not ordinary Australians.

Our daughters learn Mandarin at Sunday classes and I teach them the Chinese way of behaviour and the correct forms of address. In Chinese families everyone is ranked. First Uncle, Second Uncle ... and when my children address them they must do it according to the rank. There are different formal titles for my mother's brothers and my father's brothers too. When my parents are here, in the morning my children must greet their grandmother and their grandfather with the Chinese title signifying the relationship each morning.

They learn the Chinese way right through. For instance, Su-Kim, the younger daughter, calls her elder sister by the Chinese word for 'elder sister'; she doesn't call her by her name, Su-Lin.

They do it only for my side of the family. For example they call Colin's brother Uncle Doug, because that is correct in Australian families.

I made a pledge when I was growing up that I would never marry a foreigner. In the beginning everything is lovey-dovey, but you should be aware that differences will crop up. I thought cultural differences wouldn't matter, but they do. If you want the marriage to last, you learn to adjust, you learn to cope.

COLIN Sometimes cultural differences are a good excuse to let things slide until life is really difficult. Li Li and I don't do that. I'm not prepared to dismiss things which irk me. We argue issues through until we come to a mutually satisfactory decision. I guess our discussions are not that different from those of any married couple, except we're probably discussing different issues.

LI LI I've come to accept that we are different, but the odd thing is that I no longer feel Asian. I'm not aware that we're an interracial couple until I see another interracial couple. I've been here so long that I belong. When I go back to Malaysia, though, I'm very aware that I'm in a mixed relationship. I feel people staring at us.

COLIN Nowadays, I'm only conscious of our difference when I have to introduce Li Li and the children to workmates. Then I'm pleased and proud; I see them as not only exotic, but as something infinitely desirable.

Jessie, who came to Hobart from Penang to train as a nurse, met her husband through the church.

WAYNE I was born in Melbourne forty-two years ago and have always been interested in Asian culture — probably sparked by having a short-wave radio set as a child. Most of the countries I could pick up were in Asia. When I was at university, many of the students were Asians, and they became my friends. I spent Sundays studying in the State Library, which had research material, and got into the habit of going over to the Swanston Street Church of Christ, which had a large Asian congregation. I soon got involved in the Overseas Christian Fellowship there.

Soon after starting work at Telstra they sent me to Tasmania for a month, and I went with an introduction to an Overseas Christian Fellowship member in Hobart — Jessie. My stay turned out to be not for one month, but six months, so we got to know one another very well.

JESSIE I come from a large Christian Chinese family in Penang and from the moment I touched ground in Hobart I have felt at home here in Australia. The Lord has been with me.

When Wayne came and lived near the nurses' home, we mostly went out in a group, and when he returned to Melbourne we all missed him very much. When my training time was up I went back home for three months' holiday, before going to England to do midwifery. While I was home in Penang, Wayne visited me.

WAYNE I was very conscious while I was in Penang that I might not be an acceptable son-in-law. To my astonishment and great relief, Jessie's dad asked me whether I planned to marry her, and indicated that there would be no problem.

I came back to Australia, and proposed by long-distance phone call to Jessie in England. We were married one year later, from her home in Penang.

My father had struggled to put me through my degree, so I really wanted them to like Jessie, too. I didn't like the alienation of families that I was seeing in Australia.

JESSIE Wayne's parents are very nice to me but they leave us to live our own lives, and we fitted right into Wayne's church.

WAYNE We've had no problems on the basis of race. Our major difficulty was when we found we couldn't have children, so we adopted our daughters from Korea. So far, the elder one, Leanne, has had no trouble at school here at Box Hill. The racial mix is good; there are other Asian children.

Jessie had an English education in Malaysia. I notice that the Chinese who had a traditional Chinese education have a different attitude, a different way of thinking, which perhaps makes adjusting to Australia, and an Australian marriage, far more difficult for them.

Peter has been interested in the project that led to this book from the beginning, and helped me with information about early mixed-race marriages. He has been a member of the local Presbyterian church all his life, and twenty years ago he stunned the congregation, which had long since labelled him a confirmed bachelor, by going on holiday and returning with Susan, his Malaysian Chinese bride, whom he had met a few months earlier while she was on a business trip to Australia.

PETER   We've been lucky ... our parents all approved. We married later than average so I think they were just glad to see us married at last with the prospect of grandchildren. Our son, John, has been enthusiastically welcomed by my mother of course, but also by the dynastically-minded Chinese family in Malaysia. I must say that surprised me, because I had become aware of the pride of the Chinese: that they really believe that they of the Middle Kingdom are the chosen ones, in much the same way that Jews do. But family feeling overwhelms that, and they welcomed our little half-Aussie John with real warmth.

Felix's Chinese family migrated from Indonesia to New Zealand because they couldn't afford to send the children abroad for education. It was cheaper for the whole family to move. Felix later came to Australia, where he met Louise.

FELIX   Indonesians get all the university places, so we knew we had to go abroad for education. Before the war, everyone had Dutch education, then for the last thirty years or so, Chinese education hasn't been allowed, so Chinese in Indonesia remain Chinese only racially. There's not much culture left, nor language. We had to change our name, too; take on an Indonesian name. We changed back when we migrated to New Zealand.

I was about nine when we went to New Zealand, and the kids and adults too went out of their way to help me learn English. Later, as more Asians came, there was a bit of name-calling. Since I've been in Australia, I've had no trouble at all. There are bastards in every race, but I think the only trouble in Australia will come from the ghettos where migrants all crowd together; they don't experience ordinary Australian life. They're not becoming Australian in any way, are in fact avoiding contact with Australians. There's racism there, much worse than any you'd see from Anglo-Saxons.

My father would have liked me to marry another Indonesian Chinese. He actually tried to get rid of Louise from my life. We didn't marry until after he died. My mother's different. She's not fussed about colour.

LOUISE   I never had any problems with Felix's mother. I never had any problems with his father either, until the old man came here to stay, and I realised he was trying to get rid of me. It was very uncomfortable. In fact Felix's father got what he wanted. I moved out, and I told Felix he had to choose — either his father or me. As you can see, my parents are fine. They're here at the moment visiting us. They were incredibly welcoming to Felix, but then, everyone likes Felix.

Felix's life has helped make him adaptable, flexible, able to fit in with various lifestyles. Other migrants who grew up in a country that they did not feel to be their own similarly seemed to find it easy to adapt to Australia and marriage to an Australian. Examples of this are Shamini, an Indian from Malaysia, and Bernie, a Chinese from Fiji.

13

1980s — MIXED-RACE FAMILIES IN DARWIN

There (in Darwin) you'll find every race, every mixture under the sun, and it's absolutely normal.

Suzanne Spunner, 1997[1]

Darwin, Australia's smallest capital, is also its most multi-racial city. With one quarter of the Northern Territory's population being Aboriginal, and people from all corners of the world, the domination of Anglo-Saxon Australians is less noticeable than in any other city in Australia. Bob Collins, a former Northern Territory Senator, long-time Darwin resident and himself married to a Tiwi woman from Bathurst Island, says Darwin is one of the better examples of a city where race is not an issue: 'Darwin has been interacting with Asia longer and better than anywhere else in Australia'.[2]

Although there is no questioning the multi-racial mix of Darwin's population, not everyone agrees that 'race is not an issue'.

My son Jeremy lived there for several years and we visited often, enjoying the variety of ethnic food as well as the cosmopolitan population, but we did notice the marginalisation of some groups. I asked my son what he had noticed about Darwin's multi-racial society.

JEREMY It's a very racist place up here. Most people here are super-conservative; some are rednecks. I often think I wouldn't like to be a Vietnamese person walking around Darwin, with people pointing you out, talking about you. Not active discrimination, maybe, but being waved off, dismissed. And everybody hates black. I definitely wouldn't like to be an Aboriginal working in Darwin. They are terribly looked down upon. Many of the Aboriginals up here are tribal people, who seem to fit nowhere once they come to town. There's a huge cultural vacuum.

I've never been asked if I'm quarter Aboriginal or anything like that. If I was, then I couldn't stay up here in the Territory and work. It would be a completely different world for us. It's an attitude that seems to be in the air. It's terrible ... terrible.

Francis, a dentist from Ghana, and his medical practitioner wife, Moira, have been disappointed by the prejudice that Francis has met in Darwin, and are now weighing the possible advantages of moving to Ghana.

MOIRA I was born in Brisbane in 1954 and grew up as the youngest in a large extended Irish-Australian family. My mother died when I was ten, and I was sent to boarding school. When I was fifteen my father died, and only then was I told that in fact my mother had been my aunt. She had taken me, the illegitimate daughter of her youngest sister, into her family.

I had very little contact with my natural mother, and none at all with my natural father. A couple of years later, still feeling abandoned and rebellious, I went to Queensland University to do medicine, and there I met Francis.

FRANCIS I come from northern Ghana. After first-year science at the University of Ghana my application to study dentistry in Germany was mislaid, so I counted myself lucky to be included among twelve students accepted to study dentistry at the University of Queensland. Two of us were sent to repeat first-year science in Townsville early in 1972.

When I entered Coles cafeteria there, all the kids started away, crying, and mothers grabbed them, saying, 'It doesn't matter, darling'. It was noon, and the place was filled with mothers and small kids, and none of them would sit within five tables of me.

I met Malaysian and Singaporean students, and I began to realise what racism was about, but the real problems began when I moved down to Brisbane to begin second-year science. We were told the second-year quota was filled. The other chap packed his bags and went home, but I was stubborn. For the third time I did first-year science. During the later years of the course I was sometimes failed, while students who had done much less well not only passed, but got distinctions. Chinese and Malaysians had the same treatment, but they told us they were treated a bit better after we came along.

In desperation, I threatened to go to the press, then transfer to another university. Immediately two tutors were taken off assessing our work, because they had been so blatantly racist.

By the time I finished my course, the old Dean had retired, and I was off to Papua New Guinea even before the results came out.

MOIRA My much older, macho brothers expressed distaste at the thought of my marriage to Francis, and my sister was concerned about any children we might have. But Francis and I have a lot of common attitudes and values, despite our different cultural background. We have both been through strict Catholic boarding schools and we both have become non-practising Catholics.

Though we were in love while still at university, we decided not to marry straight away. We felt a time apart would enable us to be sure of our feelings. When I graduated in 1977, I came up here to Darwin to do my internship, and the following year, after Francis graduated, he went to work in Papua New Guinea.

When Francis arrived here in Darwin to join me in September 1979 the hospital superintendent suddenly told me they didn't want me to continue my residency, even though I had had good reports for all my terms. They later changed their minds and asked me to stay, but we headed off for jobs in Bouganville and then England.

We planned to stop in Ghana on the way back, but political instability there prevented that. However, Francis and Bridget did have a short holiday there. When we finally got back to Brisbane, Francis couldn't get a job, but he was offered a job here in Darwin. We were quite keen to come back, as we thought it a better place than Brisbane to bring up a mixed-race child.

FRANCIS Bridget's school is very multi-racial, and teachers here are well aware of the difficulties inherent in multiculturalism, whereas down south everyone pretends there is no problem.

My job was with the public health service, and I went out to Katherine on regular dental service trips. The other dentists advised taking a good book and a fishing line because Aboriginals never came to consult them; it was like a holiday, they said. But when I went out on clinics, so many patients came to see me that I had to hold the plane back so I could finish the work.

AUTHOR You weren't the fearsome white authority figure.

FRANCIS Perhaps I treated Aborigines differently. There is an undercurrent of racism in Darwin society — people think it's okay to be rude to anyone of another race or colour. Senior people in the dental department discriminated against me, too, and eventually I took my case to the Equal Opportunity and Human Rights Board, and left the department. I now have a private practice.

Here comes Bridget. When we were in London we joked that she would be worth one hundred cows.

MOIRA Our Bridget has always identified with her African heritage, and because of the amazing power of the media, she also identifies with black Americans — the music, the clothes, the hairstyles. It could be worse, I suppose. There are not many female role models for a part-African girl to model herself on in Darwin.

Moira and Francis's daughter, Bridget, is fourteen, with tight-curled hair and skin like dark honey. She joined us on the shady verandah of their home.

AUTHOR Bridget, your mother tells me you liked your holiday in Ghana; felt at home there.

BRIDGET Yes and no. Maybe I don't fit in anywhere.

AUTHOR Do you feel you have to pretend to fit in?

BRIDGET Yes.

AUTHOR How would you describe yourself?

BRIDGET I'd say half-African and half-Australian.

AUTHOR Some of the young people I've spoken to call themselves 'half-and-half'.

BRIDGET Half-caste?

AUTHOR   Sometimes.

BRIDGET   That's used a lot with Aborigines here and that's what some people think I am. When I go into a classroom, they expect me to be a thick Aboriginal trouble-maker.

In school you see all the Aboriginal kids hanging around together and all the Chinese kids hanging around together, and the Portuguese, too, in groups. Then the others just fit in.

AUTHOR   What about the ordinary white Australian kids?

BRIDGET   They just fit in. Everyone else only mixes and makes friends with those like themselves. And there's no one like me, so I just fit in where I can, mostly with ordinary Australian girls.

FRANCIS   My idea of multiculturalism is that people should be encouraged to accept that they are now Australians since they are in Australia, but they should not forget their origins.

AUTHOR   Do you think of yourself as Australian, Francis?

FRANCIS   Yes, I have a stake in Australia now. Bridget is Australian, so I must be too. But I don't barrack for Australia against the West Indies at cricket.

Lucinda and Donald Tay lived in Darwin during the 1980s, and re-located to Canberra in the early 1990s while Donald did post-graduate training in public health.

DONALD   I see startling differences between Canberra and Darwin. In Darwin, no one takes any notice of your race, as there are so many different races there. I think Darwin has less racism, more tolerance than anywhere else I've lived.

In Malaysia, when I was a boy in the sixties, there were race riots in Ipoh. Chinese people were being killed down the road from our house. There was a curfew, and we lived behind locked doors for weeks. I was delegated to protect the family should anything violent occur, and we kept a big stick beside the door, which would be my weapon if the mob should come our way. Thankfully, the riots passed, but many people were killed. The newspapers were banned from telling the truth about what exactly happened, but rumours and articles in smuggled foreign press told us the story.

I remember, when asked why I wanted to stay in Australia by the immigration officer, I replied, 'Why would I want to go back to a country where there is no tolerance for my people?'.

I did experience some racial intolerance in Brisbane when I was studying medicine — by some of the tutors — and one weekend when I was on duty, a patient in hospital refused to let me see him. He didn't want to be attended by a Chinese doctor. When my colleagues heard about it, they refused to see him. I was pretty impressed by that support.

Australia is a good and peaceful place to be, and I've never regretted staying. I could not see myself returning to Malaysia, a country where I could not have studied medicine because of strict quotas on medical training based on racial grounds. I feel I owe Australia everything. By natural instinct I have not mixed with a lot of Malaysians, but have mixed with Australians and people of many other cultures.

After graduation I worked for two years in the Ipswich hospital where I met Lucinda, and in 1982 we married. I think it needs a mature person for an interracial marriage to work, and it's important to work out the differences and focus on the positives. I'm constantly surprised to see how 'normal' interracial marriage is now.

The world is getting smaller, and one way to break down barriers is with interracial marriages. We saw a lot of that in the Northern Territory with Australians marrying Aborigines, and the children were absolutely marvellous. Mixed-race marriages should be encouraged in the interests of racial harmony in such a mixed society as ours.

LUCINDA I was born in Toowoomba into a farming family, and because I was a nurse and had worked away from home, my parents were happy with whatever I did. Our daughter did have a few unhappy times when she was small, but she's grown up to be proud of who she is. When she was training at the Institute of Sport, the physios would compliment her on her beautiful smooth olive skin, and she would say, 'That's because my dad is Chinese'.

Katherine, south of Darwin, seemed to have many young Filipina and Thai women in a substantially male population. Many of the Asian women had come to join members of their family already in Australia, and some were there as 'mail-order' brides. One Australian spoke at length about the happiness of his marriage to his Thai wife. He felt the more Asian wives that came to marry Australian men the better, as it would instil the go-ahead business practices of Asians into what he saw as our moribund economy. However, he was saddened by the rough way many Asian women are treated in the Territory, saying his wife only escaped this when she came here as a teenager because she was an expert in martial arts.

No discussion of mixed-race marriage in Australia can ignore the so-called 'mail-order brides' of the late twentieth century. Research quoted by Justice Elizabeth Evatt in 1995 revealed that though more Filipinos migrated to the United States and Canada, the number of Filipina spouses marrying Australian men was four times greater per capita than those marrying American and Canadian men.

'Why', asked Evatt, 'are Australian men so eager to seek out relationships which are riddled with structural power imbalances — such as age difference, isolation, language difficulties, economic dependency and race?'.

Robert Drewe's image of bars in nearby Asian countries — as filled with dainty and delectable women waiting to be picked off like ripe fruit by any visiting Westerner[3] — is not too far, I believe, from the dreams of many Australian men.

One man I met took an aggressive stance as soon as he learned that I was writing this book. 'You Australian women are to blame', he said. 'You are so independent; you want to run your own lives. Asian women are content to stay home and look after us.'

As can be seen from the many Asian wives I interviewed, this is not always true. Many Australian men like Derek and Rex fell in love with beautiful young Asian women, believing the stereotype that they are all modest, dutiful, and 'content to stay home and look after us', only to find, after marriage, that their wives are strong and independent. As John Burge said, there is a supposition that Asian wives are very submissive. This is not true; often Asian women are better able to handle themselves than Australian women, or indeed, men. Men such as Derek and Rex, and John himself, see the unexpected strength of their wives as a bonus, but not all Australian men do.

There are many complexities, but two conditions existed to produce the phenomenon of mail-order brides. Until well into the twentieth century there was a gender imbalance in Australia. Fewer women meant there were many lonely men, often living in isolated places, where Australian women were not available. These men, and those lonely for other reasons, yield to the temptation of acquiring a wife without the usual demands of long-term courtship. In nearby countries there are many women desperate to get away from the poverty of their homeland, to find a way to a more comfortable life, and in doing so relieve the economic plight of their families. The stated aim of many of these young women is to find a white/European husband, because they are seen as less domineering, more likely to be happy with one woman and also richer than Asian men.

Filipinas, in particular, have been painted as exploiters, and there are certainly some who plan only to get a marriage certificate safely in their handbag, squeezing or enticing as much money as possible from their target/husband before abandoning him. Equipped with permanent residence in Australia, and all its social service benefits by virtue of the marriage, the wife, and as many of her family as she can sponsor, then move into one of the fast-growing Filipino centres in a big city.

This is not the whole picture. By far the greater number of needy Asian women (Filipinas and others), while openly planning to snare an Australian husband in a bar, through a pen-pal magazine, or through a private introduction, sincerely hope that it will lead to a 'proper' marriage — a loving relationship and a settled family life with children, where the woman expects to play her part in contributing whatever she can as wife and mother.

Australia is not the only Western country targeted, but it has several advantages. It is in the same part of the world, the population is English-speaking (and most of the potential mail-order brides have at least a rudimentary knowledge of English) and, most importantly, Australia opens its doors to migrants of all kinds and has a generous social welfare system. Once a woman finds a husband here, she can sponsor, over a few years, the rest of her extended family; for many years the welfare system looked after her family members too, until they found work. This is changing somewhat as rules are tightened on family reunion visas.

In this situation both men and women see what they want to see. Many Australian men have found the warm, submissive, loving wife of their dreams, and many women have settled happily into the more comfortable conditions in Australia, bringing their siblings and parents when possible, and finding happiness with their Australian husbands and children. These are the good-news stories, and they do not find their way into the newspapers. None of this process differs very much from sending shiploads of women from England and Ireland to Australia in the nineteenth century to provide wives for lonely colonists — but there was, and still is, a darker side.

Sex tourism, during which planeloads of men descended upon the bars and discos of Manila and Bangkok, was probably the worst aspect of this 'trade' and it no longer takes place — or at least not so blatantly. Private agencies offering a free return trip to the Philippines for men who wanted to return with a bride, thrived for a while. These agencies were pressure-cooker marriage bureaus and the foreign brides had little protection from exploitation.

Alongside these wife-shopping sprees, quieter, more personal arrangements were being made by men who sought their brides in a fairer, less manipulative way. The men answered advertisements placed by women in so-called 'pen-pal' magazines. A correspondence followed, enabling the prospective bride and groom to get to know one another — or know as much as one can ever know from letters. Many of the matches made in this manner have been successful; some have not. But from these unions enough Asian mail-order brides have come to Australia to allow new marriages to be made by personal introduction.

Once a woman from the Philippines or similarly poor country is married to her Australian husband, she will introduce her husband's friend to her sister or her cousin at home by mail or telephone. A correspondence follows, and sooner or later, if he is interested, the Australian will travel to meet the woman and decide whether to pursue the matter further. If the man wishes to continue the relationship, he might marry at once, or return home, continue the correspondence and make plans, perhaps even returning for another visit before sponsoring the woman on a fiancée visa. The sponsored woman is able to enter Australia on a fiancée visa that is valid for six months, giving her time to assess both her husband-to-be and her future life in Australia, before committing herself to marriage. This is a much more civilised way of going into an arranged marriage, and success and happiness are more likely to result.

One of the worst outcomes of this whole pattern of arranged marriages arises when an Australian man manipulates for his own ends a vulnerable young woman who risks everything to improve her family's lifestyle. He might become a serial sponsor, and sometimes, a serial husband. Finding the first wife not to his fancy, he sends her away, gets an easy divorce, and does it all again. Some men have had three, four and up to seven Filipina fiancées or wives. The discarded wives stay in Australia, for that was always their aim. Some have children, either children from previous marriages or children of their Australian husband. Even welfare benefits provide a better lifestyle than they had in the Philippines.

Government agencies and Filipino groups in the bigger cities have set up committees to protect women from men who want commitment, and often servitude, for the cost of an airfare from the Philippines, with no emotional involvement. Australian Embassy staff are briefed to warn women who apply for fiancée visas: applicants are shown videos of realistic life in Australia to counteract the glossy brochures and the tales they have heard. Unfortunately this appears to be to no avail. Embassy staff report that even when a young woman is warned that her fiancé has married and discarded other overseas wives — that she is not the first and probably will not be the last — she will not let go of her dream to escape the poverty of her homeland. Some of the young women who have come to Australia on fiancée visas have been treated cruelly, even violently. About twenty have been killed; murdered by their husbands.

In the 1980s a young Sinhalese Malaysian girl from a caring and well-respected family advertised for a husband in a 'pen-pal' magazine. Her father's salary had been suddenly reduced as he neared retirement and his position, though carrying respect and status, carried no superannuation entitlements. The family faced a sudden reduction in living standards, as there is no old-age pension in Malaysia. The oldest daughter was studying at university on a scholarship, her future professional salary already ear-marked to educate the younger children. The second daughter, though pretty and gregarious, did not do well at school despite extra tuition.

A marriage could be arranged, according to Sinhalese tradition, but she would not attract a high-salaried groom, despite her beauty, since the family could afford no large dowry and she could never earn a good salary. She decided to risk finding a husband herself for, in her eyes, all Australian men were wealthy and they did not expect a dowry. Her advertisement attracted several answers, and after exchanging a few letters and photos, she chose a good-looking young farmer.

All the evidence suggests that the husband and wife both tried to make the marriage work. She tried to please him, but she could not become accustomed to the isolation of his farm, and though the husband was initially impressed by her beauty and sweet ways, her ignorance of the modern world and her inability to fit into the social life of the nearby country town disappointed him.

Her family expected her to send money home, pressing her in every letter to help them, but she was not educated or equipped to earn money in Australia, and her husband had no money to spare. Everything he made was needed for ordinary living expenses and to finish and furnish the house he had built for her. In desperation, she stole from his wallet to satisfy her parents' demands. He found out and called her a thief. Lonely and depressed, and now shamed by her husband's anger and disgust as well as her inability to help her family, she failed to provide the companionship her husband needed.

Eventually, he met and fell in love with a local girl — a girl who was unaware of his marriage — and seven years after his marriage, he asked his wife for a divorce. She would not agree. She could never go home as a discarded wife; it would bring shame on her parents. Unable to think of any other way to solve the tangle his life had become, the young husband murdered his wife, and went to prison for a life sentence. Three close, loving families, each well-respected in their communities, were destroyed.

Even the happy stories of marriages that are consummated before the bride and groom really know one another often show up cultural differences that may be seen as interesting and charming at a distance, but call for difficult adjustments when considered full-time and close-up. Since the main reason a Filipina (or other Asian) woman seeks to marry a stranger from a comparatively affluent country is to help her family rise from poverty, this will be her major priority as soon as the wedding is over. I am told that in poor Filipino families the wife holds the purse strings, and it is her responsibility to stretch the small amount earned as far as possible. If she handles the money wisely, then the husband is happy to accept just a small allowance for himself. So the young Filipina wife from a poor family expects to handle her Australian husband's money, and since she knows it will be a comparatively large amount, she feels confident that she will be able to syphon off a considerable sum to send to her family in the Philippines without her husband knowing. This is rarely possible.

Australian husbands usually keep tight control of their money, perhaps allowing a minimal housekeeping allowance, but keeping to themselves all decisions regarding large spending. It is virtually impossible for the wife to send money home without her husband's consent, except by stealing it from his pockets. And it is seen as stealing, whereas in other cultures it might be seen as sharing household money. If the marriage is secure and the relationship good, then the husband may be generous, but Asian families are often large, and many marriages are strained when there seems no end to the demands on the Australian husband's pocket from his just-acquired extended family. The husband is likely to raise questions as to where his wife's loyalty lies.

The lack of separation between work and play is another area of friction. Unlike Australians, Filipinos, in particular, seem to play all the time, even while they are working. Filipinos can never understand the concept of solitude ever being a happy, or even a satisfactory, state. They are used to having people around them all the time, and tired Australian husbands are confronted with what seems like a party every night of the week. The Australian husband's need for quiet contrasts with the Filipina's need for company, and the Australian husband sees the crowd of his wife's friends constantly filling his home as an invasion of his privacy. While many husbands appreciate the warmth and loving spontaneity of their Filipina wives, some put the worst possible interpretation on their wives' demonstrative friendliness towards others — seeing them as flirtatious towards male friends.[4]

Luz, a Filipina married to an Irish Australian, Tom, referred constantly to loneliness — the need for the constant company of her fellow countrymen and women — as a feature of Australian life; this mirrored her husband's main irritation — the noise and frequency of Filipino parties.

Irish Tom had come to Australia in 1950, lived a quiet life with quiet friends, and visited his pub regularly. He bought himself a pleasant house in a quiet Adelaide suburb and continued his lifelong habit of attending church regularly, but his local Catholic church was changing. By 1980 the congregation included a large number of Asians, mostly Filipinos. One of them, noticing the ageing bachelor, suggested that as he was lonely and needed a wife, she could send for her niece, Luz, as a suitable wife for him. Tom says he was too busy with his job and his mates at the pub to be lonely and he did not need a wife. But after a while, Tom visited the Philippines and met Luz and her family.

TOM I returned, and nominated her to migrate. It took nine months. We got married here, when I was already old enough to be a grandfather and Luz was nearly fifty. I only wanted a very small wedding but all the people from work came, and from the church too — all the Filipinos.

LUZ We had a nice wedding. Everybody came and gave us presents. But at home a wedding is a big day for the whole family. A woman gets married only once in her life. Afterwards, for the first time in my life I'm alone. Here, I'm so lonely. Also, we argue sometimes. I want something, he wants something else. I work for eight years, too, but really I want a baby. Maybe I'm too old.

I was so lonely when Tom was at work. The streets are empty. I'm happy, but I'm lonely. The food is good, everything is good, but I'm lonely; I don't even see the neighbours. I know all the Filipinos here. They are my friends. I don't know many foreigners.

AUTHOR Foreigners? You mean Australians?

LUZ Yes, Australians.

TOM Luz is a good cook. She has taught me about food and introduced me to fish. I still think there's nothing as good as lamb, and Luz cooks it beautifully with spices and things.

I retired a few years ago but there are things to fill in the days. We go bushwalking on Tuesdays and Thursdays, and we go line-dancing on Wednesday mornings and Saturday afternoons. I still go to the pub and I still have the same friends I've had for years.

Things are all right, but Luz and her people live differently. The parties are never-ending, and the music loud and the laughing and talking — well, you'd have to hear it. I don't like that sort of thing. Some of the Filipino men can't speak English, so there's not much company there for me while she's with her girlfriends. I don't join in much, but I have to go with her because I have to drive her there and bring her home.

INTERRACIAL MARRIAGES IN THE 1980s AND 1990s

What is culture? It's a nebulous concept, something that
changes wherever you are.

Sivanandan, quoted in *Colour of Love*[1]

A Dutch astronomer married a well-known Indian classical dancer in
Canberra in 1994. Peter spoke of their marriage just after the birth
of their daughter in 1997.

PETER   First question — any marriage? Any marriage is hard. A marriage to someone
who is obviously different is easier, frankly, for me, because the differences are so obvious you can address them up-front. I met Padma at a party. There she was, this beautiful brown-skinned woman in a room full of Australians and she was totally
unselfconscious, totally at ease with who she was. Her self-confidence and her acceptance of her difference was very appealing.

    I am a mathematical scientist, an introvert. I keep things inside. I have great diffi-
culties with personal relationships. So any relationship is hard for me. Differences have
to be loud and clear for me to even see them. A more sensitive person might be aware
of small differences and make allowances and adjustments, as everyone in a relationship has to. But I need those large, glaring differences before I can begin to make
allowances. For example, Padma eats with her fingers. It is a bold difference that can't
be ignored. More seriously, Hinduism is not at all like Calvinism. The
differences are huge.

Two years later Padma and Peter and their baby daughter left Australia
to live in Holland, where a son was born. From there, Padma wrote of
the experiences of living within an interracial marriage in Australia and
in Holland, two countries that have different ways, both legally and
socially, of coping with relatively recent large-scale Asian immigration.

PADMA Peter and I started living together in Canberra in 1992, and we married in 1994. Three years later our daughter, Isha, was born. In 1999 we left Australia to live in the Netherlands and in 2000 our son, Aditya, was born in The Hague.

Peter has lived and worked in disparate places and cultures — such as the USA, South America, South Africa, England and Australia. Being European, he understands the weight of heritage and history in cultural concepts. He does not treat difference in a superficial way.

I was born into a Malayali family (belonging to the state of Kerala) but grew up in the Telegu-Urdu ambience of Hyderabad and in the cosmopolitan city of Madras. I studied in a Catholic convent school and had girls from all over India as my friends. I have been dancing professionally, in the Telagu dance style, since the age of nine. When Peter and I began living together, I was conscious that I was breaking a cultural code and that the parents of my students were somewhat uncomfortable. It is to their credit that they respected my dance skills so highly that they overlooked this trespass. There were many sighs of relief when we were finally married. My family seemed to accept Peter openly, and Peter's family also seemed polite and gracious. We both had busy careers with little time to introspect on culture and such things. All this changed when our daughter arrived.

First, I had to stop working. Even in Indian traditional dance, one works within structures that are almost universal, at least in art. Now I had to bring up a child, and all my resources were specifically Indian. I found then that there is no more profound way to define a culture than through birth and motherhood, through the machinations of developing a 'family'. Suddenly there seemed to be a chasm between Peter and I. Despite all our urbane veneer my instinct was Indian and Hindu, and Peter's was Dutch and Calvinist. Neither of us understood this sudden divide since we had got along so well intellectually.

Suddenly, the families also found this chasm. My mother, who came to help with the baby, clashed with Peter. She could not understand Peter's need to be actively involved with caring for the baby, for in India fathers have an entirely different role. My mother made a horoscope for my daughter, much against Peter's wishes, but in India the grandchildren belong as much to the grandparents as to the parents.

Then Peter's mother came and could not understand my need to interact with the baby. These were just superficial things of course. The whole battle was about degrees of ownership. Which family? Which culture? Which religion? Every gesture from either side was riddled with controversy.

My dancing has been concerned with cross-cultural concepts. I realise now how little of reality art touches. I wonder if cultures can ever cross equally, if there ever can be a dialogue between Occidental and Eastern cultures.

I fiercely advocated assimilation when I was in Australia. I thought that people should not hang onto the superficial notions of India like the saree and the dot on the forehead, as they are reduced to empty symbols. Now I live in the Netherlands, which has made assimilation an art form, and I see how efforts to create a supposedly universal Dutch population can rob the immigrants of their self-esteem. They form the underclass here, gathering in ghettos that are regarded suspiciously by the Dutch people. Even if they speak Dutch, and even if the official 'Bureau for the Newcomers' certifies them as Dutch, the native Dutch will still say in hushed tones, 'But they are not Dutch'.

There is a glass ceiling everywhere. It is slightly higher in Australia. Here the ceiling is visible even before one begins the journey. This society is more honest and more mature. It lays down before you the terms on which it wishes to engage with difference.

There is no pretence of equality. In Australia, all the rhetoric about cultural diversity does not translate into reality.

A cross-cultural marriage is a mini-universe. There, also, such political things have to be actively negotiated. I realise that as long as I live in a Western world, it will not be an equal dialogue. Maybe it will not be equal even in India. People from the 'third world' are so well trained in adapting to the ways of their diverse Western conquerors that it is second nature to us to bend in the wind.

Every act in an interracial marriage is a self-conscious one. When I take Isha to the prayer room to sing songs to the Hindu gods, I am aware also of the Calvinist side that we had to ignore to do this. When the children are named, my matrilineal history weighs upon me to fight the Dutch system and to include my surname in my children's names.

A cross-cultural marriage takes one back to the fundamentals again and again. Almost every day, I face the questions — Who am I? Who are the children? It is exhausting. I do not know what Peter thinks, but if I have another chance at life, I would like to be born an illiterate woman in a remote village in India, and never leave that village for the rest of my life!

In her deep unhappiness, Padma sees the rift between her and Peter widen as she spends more time with her children and less time in the cultural world that she and Peter enjoyed when they were childless. But many of the interviewees, as different physically as Padma is from Peter, remarked on how comfortably the other's culture fitted in with that of the Australian spouse, a consequence of an English-language education that included so much that is included in Australia's heritage too.

Visually, Michael and Rashda are 'mismatched' too. Physically they are not unlike Padma and Peter, but Rashda regards herself as an Englishwoman in every way, albeit an Englishwoman with a good tan, so she feels confident about adapting easily to her Irish husband and to Australian society. Religion, as with Padma and Peter, is the one glaring difference, for Rashda is Muslim and Michael is Catholic.

MICHAEL In 1986 I came for a visit to Australia and liked it. A company in Melbourne offered me a job, then sponsored me. After a year I came to Sydney where I met my current employer, and I have worked as a real estate agent since 1992.

RASHDA I came to Australia for a working holiday, too, in 1988. I'd just qualified as a barrister in England and decided to take a year off before beginning my job there. When I got to Sydney I met Michael, but when the year was up I went back to England to practise law, because my career was all arranged. Over the next two or three years we tried to keep up the relationship by phone, visits, letters, and in the end we got married in America in 1991.

When I became pregnant, the question that concerned both sets of parents was: what religion will the child be, for my parents are Pakistani Muslims. So will our child be Christian, a Catholic? Or will she be Muslim?

MICHAEL We have worked that out. We christened Rabia to appease my family, and we intend sending her to a Catholic girls' school. Though I haven't been inside a church for a long time, I do appreciate the church's code of ethics.

RASHDA Here in Sydney I have felt no tension. Even walking down the street together, I have never been aware of anyone looking askance. A lot of the deciding factors in favour of coming to Australia were lifestyle, jobs, weather and those things, but we also looked at where we wanted to be in ten years' time.

Because of the profession I am in, the relaxed, informal way of doing business here was a stark difference to what I was used to. But I like it very much — to be able to concentrate on what you're doing without reference to what university you went to, or your school, or where you live.

I've not been aware of any animosity. I had an interesting conversation on the phone with a client, and he came to see me a couple of days later. One of his first comments was, 'I thought you'd be ...'. I knew he wanted to say 'English', but he quickly substituted 'taller'.

Perhaps Australia will be able to claim that it is a truly multi-racial country, with the maturity to accept and enjoy the diversity of its multi-racial population, when such a client can acknowledge unselfconsciously his surprise that Rashda is a dark-skinned Englishwoman, not the fair-skinned one he had imagined from hearing her voice.

MICHAEL We've had so many good experiences. I think the greatest challenge is that we don't have any family support in this country, and that has become important now we have a child. Yesterday we talked to a Lebanese guy who is marrying an Anglo-Australian, and the biggest issue was the size of the wedding! They didn't even think of the culture mix.

RASHDA We've made so many friends, to whom it doesn't matter. We went to a wedding of an Australian woman and an American-born Chinese. He'd worked in London and he just didn't like what he saw in England. He's successful enough, he could live anywhere he wants, and they're going to stay here.

My siblings have all married Pakistanis, but I don't think we'll strike problems we can't resolve. Michael and I are very much alike.

John Pilbeam, an Australian diplomat, met his Jamaican wife, Yvonne, during a posting to her home country. They speak of a similar education, a similar British colonial history behind them and even a shared religion to sustain them. Yvonne lives in Canberra with their children and teaches school, and when I visited John was home on leave from his posting in Korea.

AUTHOR Did your family approve of you marrying John?

YVONNE They thought he was a nice young man, and because we're both middle class, we have a lot in common, more in common than if either of us had married out of our class. We've never had any discrimination because of the circles we move in.

JOHN We have had a very similar education and we share the cultural baggage which goes along with that. It's Shakespeare, all the inherited British Empire stuff and the Saturday cryptic crossword. The upbringing we've had is very similar despite the fact that we look so different.

Caribbean middle-class culture is very open to foreign influences, and there are bits of Australian middle-class culture that are very like that. You don't have to explain the basis of things before you talk. Whereas in Korea, where I'm currently stationed, I'm always having to explain why Australian culture is as it is.

YVONNE In Jamaica, African culture is strong in what one expects from one's family. Jamaicans are exuberant, too. I miss that, because Australians are reticent.

JOHN I enjoy the exuberance — once removed. Yvonne is more passionate about her religion than I am, too. Yvonne opened my life up to a wider world.

AUTHOR What do you feel about the future of your children?

YVONNE We live in a good economic area here in Canberra, so we have no problems. Whether or not the level of feeling that Pauline Hanson articulates has increased among the Anglos, I don't know. But it is the perception of the minority that it has. I don't feel Australian though, and my children will have to adapt.

JOHN Growing up here in Australia will be good for them. I don't know whether they'll necessarily spend their lives here, though this is where they call home. We'll encourage them to go out into the world, and we'll equip them with all the skills to cope with that.

Sonali and Douglas are another white Australian/dark wife marriage. After more than twenty-five years in Australia, Sonali, despite being brought up in Colombo within an almost monocultural society, fits into her marriage and Australia's business world very well, and feels herself to be, in every way, Australian.

SONALI I was born in Colombo, the third of four sisters, and had just left school when my mum died. After about four years, Dad got married again and I wanted to get away, so an aunt who was aleady in Australia sponsored me. Three days after I arrived — that was in 1974 — I got a job as a receptionist. It was difficult at first. Though I spoke English well, it was not Australian English and I was dealing with the public eight hours a day. It was the best training I could have had and after six months I joined the public service and began studying at night.

Douglas saw me organising a Sri Lankan dance display and we became good friends, and stayed just that for five years. After we married, I left the public service and joined Douglas in his construction business. It was just picking up when Douglas became desperately ill. We knew it would take years for him to get back to work again, so we sold the business and I looked for a job in private enterprise, hoping to work hard and win rapid promotion, because I was now the sole breadwinner.

It worked. Slowly, of course, very slowly. Our lives seemed to go by as if in a dream. Slowly Douglas's health picked up, and slowly my promotions came. I became known in the firm as the girl who would tackle any job and fix it. I am grateful that my hard work was recognised and rewarded, and now I'm a senior manager. At work I met very little racism, even when my job was comparatively lowly — a couple of drunks, now and again an ocker-type ignorant comment. Otherwise I'm respected because of the job I do, particularly these last few years. I feel the same as you and all the others. We're all equal in God's eyes.

DOUGLAS   Of course, people are just people. No matter what colour their skin. Sometimes we're at a party where everyone else is Sri Lankan and I don't even realise I'm different until someone asks why I'm there.

AUTHOR   Have you had any negative reaction, Douglas, concerning your marriage to Sonali?

DOUGLAS   Yes. Friends have turned away and Dad is a bit of a racist.

SONALI   Douglas's brother is a great friend to me, though — both him and his wife. They're my age — we're all sixteen years younger than Douglas.

My father never met Douglas, but he wouldn't have minded our marriage at all. He'd been through it all himself. Dad's from an old Sinhalese family and he was disowned when he married Mum because, though Mum's father was Sinhalese, her mother was Irish. Grandma was an Irish schoolteacher in Java when she met Grandpa there. They fell in love and married and he took her back to Sri Lanka.

I have Sri Lankan and Malaysian, and Australian friends, too, but I have met some odd rebuffs. I've always been a Catholic — blame my Irish grandmother! But here, after we were married and built this house, we joined the Anglican church. I worked in the vestry and in various ways helped the church and its congregation. When anyone was sick or needed help, I cooked dishes for them, made cakes. We even gave a good chair, which we were actually still using, to a congregation member who had a car accident, because we thought it would make his life a bit more comfortable.

But when Douglas got sick, and remember he was sick for years and years, not one of the church people came and asked me if we needed help. Not the vicar, no one from that fairly big congregation. They all live nearby, so I see them around occasionally, and they still come looking for their donation.

AUTHOR   I find that shocking.

SONALI   When they see me, they ask, 'How is Douglas?' as small talk, but that is all. Maybe I'm too independent. Maybe I frightened them off. I don't know, but I certainly felt the rebuff.

DOUGLAS   Or maybe they discount helping Sonali, because she's not one of us! No matter what she does, no matter what she gives for the church and its people, she can never be 'one of us', so she's not even considered as a worthy recipient of their good works, even when we so desperately needed it.

SONALI   Now I occasionally go to St Xaviers church in the city, and if I want to go to church here, I go to the Catholic church. I don't become involved anywhere.

Australia doesn't need any more migrants. Probably didn't need the ones it's got, but we're here now. No immigrant group should band together to make Australians feel uncomfortable. For example, I don't think the ethnic associations should be exclusive. If Australians who are interested were welcomed to join, then there would be more understanding. I want a community that is mingled and a community where I will be comfortable. Everyone wants that.

When I spoke to Paula and Athol, another culturally similar couple despite vast differences in appearance and skin colour, they were living together and already regarded their relationship as permanent. They have since married.

PAULA My grandparents moved from South India to Singapore; my parents were children of the British colonial system. Singapore was not corrupt, but because I didn't share the philosophies of that society, I left in 1979. I enjoy being in Australia. I've worked with Aboriginal people for the last fourteen years, and that's where I met Athol.

I've always had an interest in different cultures, possibly because I feel I've never had a culture of my own. I've felt like a gypsy, because I knew Singapore wasn't where I really belonged. I am of Indian heritage, but I don't speak the language, practise the religion or embrace the culture. Only the cuisine is left!

ATHOL My father is English and my mother is an Australian of several generations. I have worked in various Aboriginal administrations for ten years.

AUTHOR How have you two been perceived here in Brisbane?

ATHOL Walking down the street, I find myself watching people's faces. A lot of people stare, and I'll look at Paula, but she charitably thinks they're looking because we're an attractive couple. I don't think it is entirely that.

I became more aware after Pauline Hanson, and I am particularly conscious when I see National Front people. I almost wait for something to happen. But it never has.

People are interested in our relationship, too. White Anglo-Saxon men with exotic fancies look at us, and they might be thinking, 'Gee, that's something we've never tried — a dark, exciting, native woman'. They mightn't admit to it, even to their mates. It might remain just a private fantasy. But with you, with a white woman with an Asian husband, they'll look at you as, 'That's one of ours we've lost!'. That's how men think, but I don't know about women. Do they think like this? Do you think like this?

AUTHOR No. I don't think women, Australian women anyway, look on the men in their lives as property. Perhaps as a prize — so such a notion would only be entertained if you were already attracted to the man who was 'lost'. I think there is a man/woman difference. Women don't look on all men as a pool of possible mates. As you must know, women are afraid of many men, don't trust even more, and find a good number of the rest repulsive.

ATHOL Men do. The mail-order bride phenomenon would accentuate this property angle. I have met some of those women, and they're treated as chattels. Such husbands are often the worst bigots, more racist than the obvious ones.

PAULA I think one's upbringing is important in interracial marriages. Although I present as Asian, or non-Caucasian, my thinking and my education are very Western. There's a lack of congruence between my inside and my outside self. So Athol and I are a better match than we at first appear to be.

There are many Aboriginal people who question why non-Aboriginal persons go into the Aboriginal industry. Racism is fairly common among minority groups, and among Aboriginals there is a lot of racism. Recently I was roundly abused by an Aboriginal work colleague. She said, 'She's not Aboriginal, she's not even an Australian'.

I'm not Aboriginal and I'm not white. While there is some sort of affinity to me, there is also suspicion. Aboriginal people who are still struggling with their own Aboriginality and identity tend to be much more discriminatory towards non-Aboriginal people than traditional people are.

ATHOL A lot of the people we work with are in mixed-race marriages.

PAULA Aboriginal men see having a white wife as a status symbol. Since opportunities for Aboriginal people have improved, Aboriginal men have climbed the ladder, and the wives of their early years may no longer be appropriate consorts. The more multicultural we are the happier we'll be about mixed relationships and coffee-coloured children.

AUTHOR You've spoken almost entirely about the intolerance you've encountered from Aborigines. Have you had any discrimination from the wider Australian community, Paula?

PAULA Hardly at all. Perhaps at pubs I felt I was served slowly or ignored sometimes. Maybe it wasn't race, though. I think now that we didn't dress the way we should have, to get the service we wanted.

Dark-skinned Australian-born Shara is the daughter of a Sikh from Malaysia and a Christian Tamil from Singapore who came to Australia as students over thirty years ago, married and stayed here to raise their family. Shara laughed when I asked if she would allow me to interview her and her fiancé. 'We don't fit your book', she said. 'We're both Australians.'

Her friends know that, but most Australians would question it until she spoke, whereas with her fiancé there would be no question. Shara's attitude, her joyful acceptance of her Australianness, was similar to that expressed by Briony Lim, and of course they were both born here of Asian parents who were themselves happy to embrace Australia's culture. Briony and Shara will bring the wok-cooking, the family togetherness, the curries and the colour of Indian rituals to enliven their Australian homes, and thus enrich us all.

SHARA You know where I come from, and you probably know that in Indian families, the mother usually does all the work in the home, even if she goes out to work as well. I think Australian husbands are much more helpful. I'm lucky Jonathon does most of the cooking, and we share the housework.

Mum likes Jonathon; he always gets special treatment, and she's very excited about our wedding. Can you believe, even after spending most of his life in Australia, Dad still talked about arranging our marriages? He wants us to have the full Punjabi wedding. If we do that, it will be just to make Dad happy.

JONATHON My father's great-grandparents and both of my mother's great-grandparents came out in the nineteenth century from Wales, Scotland and Ireland. We probably wouldn't be having this discussion about what sort of wedding we'll be having if I was marrying another Anglo-Saxon. But Shara and I haven't noticed many differences in our thinking, our lifestyle. No more than any two people would find.

SHARA That's because I'm Australian too. Of course I'm Australian. And quite apart from the worry about housework, I don't think I'd be able to get along with an Indian husband. I've noticed Indians — ones who grew up in India, or even Singapore or Malaysia, are different. Their ideas about things, about what is important in life, are very different. I just know I'd never agree with their ideas. Whereas Jonathon and I are both Australians.

A few months later, Jonathon and Shara were married in a simple garden ceremony.

Navaratnam is a young Indian man who came to Australia as a teenager with his family from Singapore.

NAVARATNAM   We are all here now — all my family. When my uncle came, none of us realised how good it would be here, because Australia is criticised in Singapore, but it shouldn't be. We all came from Singapore where the Malays and Indians don't get the promotions or the jobs. There is constant discrimination there, in everything you do, but they won't admit it.

I like Australia. I fit in well here. Until I look in the mirror I forget I'm an Indian. Only once have I had any trouble, and that really concerned my Australian wife.

We were having a meal in a restaurant when a man walked past and jiggled my wife's chair. He apologised, then noticed me. He became belligerent. 'All you black guys come here and take our white women' — all that stuff. Then he took a swing at me, which just clipped me, but I'd already reacted and I knocked him out.

All the people gathered around us, reassuring us that it wasn't my fault, offering to stay and tell the police how it was. Then the policeman came and he walked me through the whole business. It was a bad incident, but a lot of good came of it. We saw that people had been helpful to us when we needed them. They saw that I wasn't the cause of the fight so they were prepared to support me to the police even against another Australian.

I think the government's idea of Australia getting closer to Asia is a good thing, because Australia doesn't have any traditions.

Do so many migrants really choose to come to a land without traditions? Our democratically elected parliament, universal franchise, equality of all citizens — or even visitors — before the law, the separation of powers and the general lack of official corruption — these things, and our good fortune to be situated in a temperate climate, are why people come to Australia to live. The structures in our society are not perfect; they can be adapted and improved, but I doubt that Navaratnam or any Australian, old or new, would want any of them replaced with those existing in Singapore, China, India, Indonesia or any other Asian country.

Perhaps it is because our traditions, those we inherited from Britain and Ireland, are so deepy entrenched and universally shared that we have been able to come full circle from an Anglo-Celtic society where 98 per cent of our citizens shared the same culture including religious faith, language and many social behaviours, to being one of the most diverse nations on earth. An old-time favourite national poem has been adapted by 'Anon' to read:

I love a sunburnt country
A democratic country
Where, safe from fear's attacks Earth's children are all equal —
Brave yellow, browns and blacks.

The people who come to share our country and the structures of our society may, under multiculturalism, choose to share our culture, too, or keep their own. This has lead to questions about Australia's cohesiveness as a nation in the future. Richard Basham, an anthropologist from the University of Sydney, adviser on Asian culture to the New South Wales police and member of an interracial family, feels that Australia's traditions are safe and national cohesiveness assured despite its racial diversity:

> Far from being pessimistic about Australia's racial future, I hold out great hope for it. I cannot but be reminded of my family's return to Australia from a trip to Thailand late one night in January. Exhausted, the three of us, my Thai-born wife, my Eurasian, Australia-born teenage daughter and I, with my distinctive American accent, approached the immigration officer and handed him our passports. After stamping them he handed them back to us with a warm and genuine smile and said: 'Welcome home'.[2]

MODERN MARRIAGES OF THE 1990s

Australia, to be a nation worth living in, must be monocultural as
well as multicultural. It must possess shared values as well as
different values.

Geoffrey Blainey, 1984

Sakura and Ron served me Japanese tea in a thin porcelain cup with
no handle, and I burnt my fingers. Someone cleverly invented handles for cups, with just this situation in mind. Perhaps I was just
demonstrating the undue impatience of a Westerner; I should have
waited calmly for the tea to cool.

RON   Returning home after an 18-month stint in Hong Kong, I found I myself sitting
next to Sakura, who was travelling from Tokyo. We talked on the long flight and afterwards we corresponded for a year or so. I invited Sakura to spend her next holiday with
me. She came for a week. I was living at a beautiful place on the coast and I proposed
to her there. She accepted, but at the end of the week, she returned to Japan.

I visited Sakura in Japan about three months later, and she told me that while she
was happy to marry me, she was not happy to live in a quiet little town on the coast, no
matter how beautiful. She wanted to live in a city.

Sakura's mother, who doesn't speak English, was bitterly opposed to our marriage.
Through Sakura, she asked me the most extraordinary questions, such as whether I'm
already married? What income I earn? Have I got AIDS?

I can understand a mother's concern, but what she put me through was quite chill-
ing. I met her father only briefly on that visit and I've never told my family what happened. Well, I sold up and moved to Melbourne, and we were married here. My parents
came for our wedding, and so did Sakura's parents, but they showed no signs of soft-
ening towards me — and still don't after eight years.

SAKURA Ron's family did welcome me, but I couldn't understand them at first. When I first came, my English was not good. I was working as a typist on a word processor and I was treated as a dumb person when I did not know some of the English words. People swore at me. They expected me to know every single word!

Learning English is an enormous task. But I studied, and I have just finished my degree. Now I have a job teaching, so things are better now.

RON I was very happy when Sakura scored a job among several Japanese-speaking people. I had seen how difficult she found it, how isolated she felt because she never tried to fit in or assimilate in any way.

SAKURA For me our marriage was a part of growing up; I always wanted to be independent, not trapped at home with children. If I'd married a Japanese man, I'd be a proper Japanese wife, getting up early making breakfast. I wouldn't have been able to study like I have here, or pursue an academic career, so I do appreciate what Australia has given me, but I have found that since coming to Australia I have begun to like my parents and also Japan much better. I go back every year, and mentally I am much closer to Japan now than I used to be.

RON I accompanied Sakura to Japan a couple of years ago, and it was ... well ... memorable. For most of our time there, I was confined to the bedroom in Sakura's parents' house. Meals were served to me in the bedroom, and I was told that it wouldn't be a good thing for me to move around in the living room, because the father was ill and me moving around would disturb him.

SAKURA They don't understand English, so it is difficult for them to have someone there who doesn't speak Japanese.

RON I really don't want to visit them for any extended time again, although I'm extremely oriented towards Asia and all things Asian. I like their food, their culture, their people. I enjoyed learning about Chinese culture while in Hong Kong, and even learned to speak Cantonese. I like many Japanese things, but I've never met anyone like Sakura's parents.

Sakura and I are fairly compatible, though; I don't think we've had too many conflicts. My only disappointment is that Sakura has not embraced my family as much as I would have liked her to, though they are continually welcoming.

SAKURA To be straightforward, I must say I find it hard to harmonise with Ron's family. I can't get on with people who have focussed ideas, and they seem not to understand my position. Ron is exceptional, and my friends are also flexible.

RON We've both been very busy, too; both studying for the last three years. Even getting married was not an easy thing to do. We're both very private people. We don't go partying. We have very few friends.

SAKURA Ultimately every choice is personal, not a cultural or racial choice. Some Japanese girls tend to marry English or American or Australian men because they are learning English and such a marriage will help them with their language studies.

Months later, Sakura wrote to tell me that she and Ron had separated.

Saemi was working as a translator for an Australian film crew in Tokyo when she met the Australian who became her husband.

SAEMI I've been here for eleven years, but I lived in Sydney for four years when I was a child, and I remember, even then, being very happy and content here. It must have to do with the environment and the psyche of this continent. I may be genetically Japanese, but culturally and socially and philosophically I'm very Western, and I will be living the rest of my life in Australia.

AUTHOR What did your very conservative Japanese parents think of your marriage?

SAEMI They didn't want to know about it, so I just hopped on a plane and came. After our daughter, Malina, was born, they mellowed. I take Malina back to Japan to see them, and so she can learn something of Japan. When she was a baby I used to speak to her in Japanese so she'd know the sound of the language, but now she is at school it's English 100 per cent of the time. I'm happy about that because I want Malina to identify with this country, not with where her mother came from. It's important that she feels firmly rooted here. This is where she belongs.

My husband thinks Sydney is the best place on earth, and I agree with him. His family lives here in Sydney, and they are amazingly warm and close to me and to Malina. Even his uncle, a farmer who fought in World War 2, has no ill feelings towards me. He is generous and hospitable, to me and to everyone in the welcoming Australian country way.

AUTHOR Have many of your attitudes had to change for you to fit so comfortably into Australia?

SAEMI Changing the physical location of where you live requires a lot of adaptation. It took two years for my physical body to fit into this air, this water and food. Then, of course, my spiritual being had to change too. Some of the changes were conscious, some were unconscious. In Japan there are many unspoken rules and expectations that you have to know and obey. Here it is much freer, so I can be more direct.

Pauline Hanson has voiced some of the concerns that people were afraid to voice, and I think it is important that it comes out in the open and is discussed instead of burying it underneath to fester. It's okay for Australians to feel a bit insecure, even afraid about all these changes in their society. I think Australia has the right ingredients — people from all over the world — but fear is bred when the future is unknown.

AUTHOR What would your advice be to a young interracial couple?

SAEMI Interracial marriage is not just a little harder. It's much, much harder. It requires an enormous amount of commitment, an enormous amount of work. A common background, even a common language, helps. That said, interracial marriage is great fun! It gives you a chance to create your own rules. It's a great opportunity to re-evaluate yourself and your partner and both backgrounds. Decide what you want to keep and discard those you don't. And, above all, remember that being different can be a positive thing.

Within James and Tomoko's Canberra home, their 11-year-old daughter happily telephones Tokyo and chats to her maternal grandmother in Japanese, while she and her younger sister also maintain a close relationship with their paternal grandmother in another Canberra suburb.

JAMES   We met here in Canberra in the seventies and saw each other a few times. Then when I went to Japan in 1980, I looked Tomoko up.

TOMOKO   Living together just happened. My parents were living in another part of Japan, and though they were not happy when they learned that we were together, they didn't make a fuss.

One adjustment I had to make was that James is very laid back, perhaps all Australian men are ... and lacking in physical precision, perhaps?

AUTHOR   You mean clumsy?

TOMOKO   Yes, in such things as not opening a sliding door correctly. I should get used to it, but it does sometimes stress me.

JAMES   Living in Japan was far more stressful for me!

TOMOKO   Yes, of course. You were going from this free society into a structured society. Adjustments to Australia are very easy, especially for a woman, after Japan. Here, I feel I have become a pretty laid-back person too.

When John Burge, a public servant in Canberra, married Heckyung, immigration officials treated their marriage as if it were a suspected marriage of convenience.

JOHN   I'm a fifth-generation Australian, grew up in Melbourne in a traditional home, the eldest of six children.

HECKYUNG   I'm Korean. I learned English all through my school years, and came to Australia in 1985 to study English at the University of New South Wales for one year. Back in Korea I worked as an executive secretary at General Motors. Later I came back here for a holiday. That's when I met John.

JOHN   We had to go through difficult and time-consuming immigration procedures — quite a bit of inconvenience. Though we decided to marry while Heckyung was in Australia, she went back to Korea, and I had to sponsor her out here. It took about six months. We had to provide copies of love letters, etcetera. It seemed intrusive at the time.

The Korean family is very patriarchal. When Heckyung's father agreed to our marriage, the rest of the family fell into line. My parents welcomed it. We were married in the chapel of Trinity College at the University of Melbourne in January 1991. Before that we had had a Korean wedding, which was essentially introducing the families to one another.

I try to keep up those Korean traditions which are important to Heckyung. For instance, when the children are one hundred days old there is a big party, and again when the child is one year old.

HECKYUNG   John's family are wonderful. I love them and they love me.

When Patrick was a baby I was on the way back from the shops with the pram when about six little kids all walked past, saying, 'Ching Chong'.

I was very angry, so I asked, 'What did you say?'.

And they went, 'Ching Chong' again.

I said, 'I saw you. Come here'. I was very bossy and a little boy came and I said, 'That's very insulting, don't ever do that'.

He said, 'I won't do it again. I'll never do it again'.

I work as a guide in Parliament House. I give pamphlets and directions to many people, Australians and overseas visitors. Most people are very friendly towards me. But some are very cold. Some people seem to be shocked at being told about Parliament House by me.

AUTHOR   What about you, John? Have you noticed any displeasure or criticism of your marriage?

JOHN   No, never any displeasure. There's been a good deal of interest in Korean culture and background. Nothing adverse from friends and colleagues. But sometimes hurtful things happen.

My son Patrick was on a children's ride when he was about three and I overheard a woman say, 'You might want that half-caste child to fall off, but don't push him'.

I let it pass, and I wish I hadn't. It made me angry, and … no, I was more than angry, it hurt me terribly, and made me feel so protective towards Patrick — as if I wanted to protect him from all of life's hurts to come.

You see, even though I'm a man and in my own country where I should feel strong and confident, I'm not so willing to tackle offensive behaviour as Heckyung is.

Apart from that one comment there has been nothing said to or about Patrick. At the pre-school there are children from Africa and lots of other places. I don't think there will be any problems.

I'm enjoying finding out about Korean traditions, except for the food. I do have some difficulties especially with their national dish, kim chi, which is a sort of pickled cabbage. To me, it is truly dreadful. Heckyung seems to be adjusting well, too, though she finds it difficult when Australian males call one another names like 'bastard'. She cannot see that it is affectionate.

AUTHOR   That's a man/woman difference, Heckyung. Australian women don't do that, and Australian men don't usually use that language in front of women, though that may be changing. There are two languages; there are some words and phrases, expressions that women don't use.

HECKYUNG   I think I still must improve my communication skills. It is so important in interracial marriage where home languages are different. I want to make it easy for us.

I am happy here. Korea is more of a man's country. There, it is difficult for a woman to get a good job. Women are not seen as any good there. I'm happy here, very happy here.

JOHN   There is a supposition that Asian wives are very submissive. It's not true, and often they are more able to handle themselves than Australian women — or indeed men! Look at the way Heckyung handled those rude boys.

Briony, an Australian-born Chinese doctor, and her Australian architect husband, Matthew, had invited a friend, Phyllida, to meet me. Phyllida had brought her little son, Shann, and was glad to talk about her marriage to an African and the turmoil it caused in her upper north shore middle-class Australian family.

BRIONY   I was born in Australia of two Chinese parents who came here as teenagers and met at high school. They went back to Hong Kong after they graduated to marry, and then returned as migrants. So I was born and brought up here in Australia in an

English-speaking Chinese family. My dad lectures in computing. My mum did a law degree, but mostly stayed home while we were small, then went back to work after being out of the workforce for nearly twenty years.

AUTHOR   It's interesting that your parents did not continue to speak Chinese to one another at home.

BRIONY   They came so young, when there were not so many Chinese around, and they just got into the habit of speaking English. When Mum writes to her mother in Hong Kong, she struggles with a Chinese dictionary for hours, just to get a letter written and I don't know enough of the language to teach my children anything at all of it. In Hong Kong when I try to speak Chinese, people there know that inside I'm not Chinese.

I'm happy to be Australian. Having been born and brought up here, how much more Australian can you get? All my friends are Australian; some of them are Australian-born Chinese, but they are all English speakers, and like me they feel that they are Australians.

The only Chinese I have is what you see — my face. I'm Australian, but I feel enriched by having Chinese culture behind me, even if it's receded until it's only vaguely in the background. The only difference I can think of is that I cook my steak in a wok!

I have hung on to my name of Lim, too, for several reasons. When I speak over the phone I sound totally Australian, so people get a surprise when they see me and realise that I'm Chinese. That clearly places me in the minds of the people with whom I'm in contact.

AUTHOR   It also reminds people that some Australians have Chinese faces.

BRIONY   Yes. Mum told me that when they decided to come to Australia, they knew any children they might have would probably marry Australians, and they had no problem with me marrying Matthew.

AUTHOR   Did you ever feel discriminated against, or teased?

BRIONY   Teased a bit at school, but more for my glasses than my race. There were only a very few Chinese children in my school. My friends were Australian, and the occasional 'Ching Chong' would be the same pleasant teasing that I got for glasses, but not nearly as often. Other children were teased about glasses too, or anything else. It didn't matter. We never separated ourselves; we never spoke Chinese or made ourselves different; we were always part of a group of Australian kids. There might have been the occasional reference to slanty-eyes, but so rarely, and anyway, I accepted the fact that I looked different, just as a red-haired child accepts the colour of her hair.

When I married Matthew my parents were happy and so were my friends. I did feel uncomfortable with Matthew's parents at first. Whether it is because I'm a town girl and they are country folk, I don't know. Or is it because I'm Chinese? Since our daughter was born, we have a better reason to be friendly, and they live close by now. I suppose you could say we get on quite well, but there's no doubt there is some strain.

MATTHEW   I grew up in the country; a farming family. Mum wanted us to go to a better school, but Dad had vowed he would never send his children away to school because he had been a boarder at Geelong Grammar and hated it. They sold up and moved to the city so my sister and brother and I could finish school here. I met Briony's brother at school. We remained friends at university, and I met Briony through him.

Mum has great expectations of her children, and perhaps Briony didn't fit the pattern of the ideal wife that Mum had imagined for me. Even though we now have Alison, their granddaughter, they don't embrace the situation, they just grin and bear it. My sister went to China and subsequently ended up married to an Indian in Hong Kong. Our parents' response to that was disgraceful. Awful. Racist. Ugh! My sister had to choose.

BRIONY Your mother's attitude to me improved after your sister married. Maybe she thought, Briony's not so bad after all!

PHYLLIDA My parents' reactions were similar, though they didn't go as far as disowning me. They have travelled the world, been exposed to all different cultures, and are extremely tolerant of everyone else, but not in their own family!

It didn't matter what kind of a person Samuel was. That was not the issue. They used emotional blackmail, threats, anything to try to persuade me not to marry him. My husband says of Pauline Hanson that at least she says what she thinks. He believes most Australians think like she does.

Samuel is Ugandan. I met him when I was holidaying in Kenya. Later he came out to visit me. My flatmate refused to have him in the house, so I had to move out. Samuel went back home after his holiday here and then returned a year later, and we lived together for a year before we married. During all that time my parents went into complete denial. He was always introduced as 'a friend of Phyllida's from Africa, who is visiting for a while', even though every time Mum rang up, Samuel answered the phone. My parents were so difficult that in the end I gave them just a week's notice of our marriage. We had a very quiet wedding.

My mother, a Protestant, had married a Catholic and that was just as bad at that time, so you'd think she would have related to what she was putting me through. It seems to me that most people are happy to meet other races, but not to have them in their family.

MATTHEW I think racism is related to intellectual capacity. My brother uses words like 'Chink', 'Abo', 'Black'. He won't eat with us because he won't eat rice. He won't eat anything except the standard English/Australian food.

PHYLLIDA My mother is like that too. She finds it difficult even to love Shann — a small child. My sisters' children are very fair and lighter built and she can't keep her hands off them. With them she's the storybook cuddly grandmother. But not with Shann.

BRIONY Matthew has a very open mind about how Alison is brought up. I really like the idea of raising my children in an extended family situation. We're lucky we have both sets of parents nearby.

MATTHEW The extended family idea is okay, but I'm not sure whether my parents will ever participate. They don't want to interfere. Briony's family do interfere, but I recognise that it is their way of helping.

PHYLLIDA Shann does not have two sets of loving grandparents, though. He really doesn't have any close grandparents at all! My stepfather calls Shann a half-caste. He thinks it's funny.

My mother realises how she has hurt me, and I've got to say that I know my marriage has hurt her too. Everything is not rosy yet. We're trying to organise for Shann to be christened, but it's never convenient, so we haven't had it yet.

BRIONY Matthew's parents are nearly as bad. We have to invite them, and they say, 'Oh we'll see what we're doing'. Then they ring up on the day and say they have something else on.

AUTHOR Have you lost friends, or anything like that?

MATTHEW Yes, I have lost some friends. The intellectual level of some people ...

PHYLLIDA I don't think it matters how educated people are.

BRIONY That's right. In medical school, racial groups still congregate, particularly the Malaysian Chinese, but others too.

PHYLLIDA I wish I had met Samuel's parents when I was in Africa, but I didn't. Shann is the eldest son of an eldest son, of an eldest son, etcetera, and there is a lot of pressure for us to go back there. But it's a third world country. I'd be happy to go back and stay a while, but I don't want to live there, nor do I want to bring Shann up there.

AUTHOR What cultural adaptations do you and your husband have to make?

PHYLLIDA Food! Samuel does most of the cooking. He eats lots of meat, mostly beef and goat, in casseroles and barbecued. His Catholicism is very strong, too; probably stronger than mine.
We socialise mainly with other mixed couples. Samuel feels more comfortable with them because even walking in the street, or in the train, Samuel still attracts attention. He's very dark and he wears dreadlocks. I was sensitive to racism when Samuel and I were first going out. When people said things, I would cringe.
Soon after Samuel came here to Australia, an acquaintance who had married a Jamaican told me that it was wonderful when they first married. They mixed with lots of people who were also in mixed marriages. But she warned me that a mixed marriage is much more difficult. She said that of the fifteen mixed-race couples who had been their friends, only two couples are still together.

MATTHEW In a relationship the woman needs more support. If the woman loses her family's support, then it's very difficult. Briony has the support from her family. But with Phyllida, it is her only family.

PHYLLIDA My family is waiting for my marriage to fail, though they'd never dare say it to me. Every marriage has problems, but in my situation I can't go to my mother and sound off. No way!
Samuel and I don't discuss how he feels about my parents, or any racism he might meet from them or from anyone else. I spent such a long time protecting him from racism but I couldn't go on. Now he deals with it in his own way. We don't discuss it.
I hope that by the time Shann is twenty people will be more open and will talk about their feelings, though I fear they will still be racist. That will be an ongoing issue for the next fifty years, possibly more.
African-Australian children are so noticeably different from their peers that they're often angry and lost. Visiting Africa might help them feel as if they belonged somewhere, but I'm not sure about Shann, because although my husband was born in Uganda, his sense of identity is not strong, for he has lived elsewhere for many years.

AUTHOR Perhaps he'll feel Australian one day.

PHYLLIDA I was overwhelmed by the hoo-haa that migrants have to go through to become American. They are indoctrinated that they are lucky to become Americans; they go to a special school to learn the history and wow, they come out feeling so patriotic. If we worked on the same principal, that though migrants may keep some elements of their old culture, they must become Australian, then I'm fairly sure they would be proud to be Australian, and it would improve our society as a whole.

Samuel comes from a patriarchal society, and nothing will change that. Even though I work much longer hours, I still have to shop, totally look after Shann, do most of the housework. When I get home, even from a late shift, Samuel often hasn't fed Shann, let alone toiletted him. Once he wanted me to take Shann with me to work on a late shift at the library, just because he didn't want to push the stroller up to the shops to buy supplies.

I'm sure being married is always difficult, and much more difficult with no family support, and with a different language and culture. If you love the person enough ... but be prepared for difficulty. It has been much more difficult than I ever imagined it could be.

Some months after this interview, Phyllida and Samuel separated.

One young Australian man and his Chinese-Japanese wife lead what seems to me to be a very cosmopolitan life, within and outside Australia. Stewart's house perches high above the road winding around Sydney's northern peninsula, and after climbing dozens of steps we reached his living room and peered through the leaves of an overhanging gum tree to gaze across the blue of Pittwater. A surf-lover, Stewart builds his life and his livelihood around the surfing beaches of Australia, Bali and Japan. He spoke of his life with Mari, who at the time of our interview was in Japan.

STEWART My parents are happy about Mari and me. They've become used to me bringing home overseas friends, and Mari's English is good enough for her to communicate comfortably in social situations. The sorts of things my parents may express concern about are children, schools, etcetera.

I think we can face any difficulties when they come up. A friend in Mona Vale has been married to a Japanese woman for twelve years and they have four kids. The irony is that he has to work in Japan, which separates him from his Japanese wife and the children. They still live here because they want the quality of life that they get here, and the schooling. They didn't want the children to go through the rigid Japanese system.

I don't even think of Mari as Japanese. In fact she's not; she is only one-quarter Japanese. Her mother is half-Japanese/Chinese, and her father is Chinese. Mari was born and brought up in China until she was ten, when she came to Japan with her parents. Soon afterwards, however, her parents split up and her father returned to China.

Mari is accepted as Japanese within her peer group, but she would face prejudice in marriage. They have a caste system, and for those who are concerned about such things there is a public registry where you can check up on castes. There is no way a leather-worker could mix with a noble in Japan.

I can't think of a better lifestyle than the one we have: travelling between Japan and Indonesia and Australia constantly and teaching wherever we stop. I love it. I've met families who always travel, just like us, and their children benefit tremendously. But if we have children and need to stop somewhere, then we could well stay in Japan, or indeed China. The kids could be at least bilingual, even trilingual.

Mari and I don't have problems here in Sydney. In the country areas of Western Australia, up in Geraldton and Carnarvon, we had some unpleasant experiences which varied between heckling, name-calling, suggestions that Mari was a Filipina bride, and some ordinary old, country larrikinism.

AUTHOR   What about you two as a couple in Japan?

STEWART   We spent eight months living together in a small town and not once did we notice any discrimination. We have only occasional conflicts within our own relationship, and we can never work out whether they arise from differences in language or culture, or whether it is just the differences between two individuals.

At the moment we're working on improving the public face of our marriage. No matter where we live each of us must be able to cope with all the daily necessities, so the burden will not fall on one at any time.

AUTHOR   So you have to learn to function in Japan as well as you do in Australia?

STEWART   Yes, but I already know Japan well. This is my tenth year of going there, and every time I learn something new. My father might come with me to visit Japan this year. He seems to be a little uncomfortable about it; his generation and his family still remember the war.

I wonder about this multicultural thing Australia is moving towards. If the aim was to promote social cohesion, it would be good, but actually I think it is dividing Australia. The danger of multiculturalism is that we are going to keep people behind that fence of multiculturalism. Multicultural devotees will prevent some Australians from being recognised as Australians. We should forget all about one ethnicity or another. Everyone should be Australians. Though differences will probably all wash out in a couple of generations.

Stewart and Mari now have a small daughter. I hope she does not slow them down too much.

CONCLUSION

I love its culture. I love its diversity. Australian culture
tends to absorb all cultures and transform them.

Kim Beazley, 1999

There are interracial marriages in Australia today that call for no more adaptation than if one married the boy or girl next door. Some couples, such as Herb and Eileen, and Shara and Jonathon, have so much in common culturally that the difference in their skin colour, or slant of the eyes, is of no importance at all. Their marriages are interracial, but not intercultural to any important extent. As another wife pointed out, all couples have some adapting to do, as we each have a unique culture that we carry around, shifting, sloughing off, as well as absorbing, borrowing and growing as we see fit.

Paula (an Indian from Singapore), Sonali (a Sinhalese from Sri Lanka) and Yvonne (a Jamaican of African descent) all referred to the shared culture and shared interests that help to make their marriages work. Even Jamaica and Australia seemed culturally similar, not only because of the shared interest in cricket that Pauline mentioned, but because we have all inherited the residual trappings of British colonialism — Christianity and the English language and those pieces of knowledge dragged along with the language such as Shakespeare, English-based nursery rhymes and stories. As Yvonne's Australian diplomat husband said, 'You don't have to explain the basis of things before you talk. Whereas in Korea … I'm always having to explain why Australian culture is as it is'. Such a background also provides familiar structures of society, including the rule of law with separation of law-makers and law-keepers, the same rules of behaviour on which local customs can be superimposed, and the bulwark of state and church-run education.

Rebecca, whose mother fled Poland and married in England where Rebecca was born, shares the language and all the structures of daily life with her husband because, although Chinese and an atheist, Carl came from British-influenced Malaysia. Because of that, Rebecca says, she has more in common with him than with people more closely related to her Polish background. Carl also pointed out that food, education and the accumulation of money are of great importance to Chinese and Jews, giving them even more in common. Australian-born Chinese Herb also pointed out these similarities between Chinese and Jews.

From the evidence — anecdotal though it was — that emerged from these interviews, it seems that Wayne and others may be correct in saying that Chinese who have a Chinese education find it far more difficult to adapt to marriage with an Australian, and perhaps to the Australian environment in general, than those who have had an English education. This has more to do with the ideas, values and what one might call the peripheral knowledge that an English education hauls along with it, than a fluency in the language itself. Wayne's wife, Jessie, came from Penang, where what remains of English colonialism is almost certainly stronger than in the rest of Malaysia. Jessie's father happily welcomed Wayne as a potential son-in-law, because he had worked with Englishmen and liked them. In sharp contrast, the great majority of Chinese fathers in Singapore and Hong Kong did not like white men, were suspicious of their motives and were adamantly opposed to their daughters marrying Australians.

There are still cultural differences between Lawrie and Pat after thirty-five years of happy marriage, because Chinese-educated Pat is still strongly Chinese in many ways. Throughout their marriage each has adapted and changed their life expectations in ways that may not have diminished the cultural gap, but lessen any disturbance to the even tenor of their life together. Lawrie has turned to study and further education, which Pat finds more easily understandable than, say, Lawrie's former involvement in sport. And though love overcomes high hurdles Pat still feels deprived of the Chinese culture in which she grew up.

Paula spoke of feeling gypsy-like and rootless in Singapore, claiming that there is no congruence between her Asian outer self and her western European inner self that fits seamlessly into Australia's culture and into her marriage with her Australian husband. It could be that people who, like Paula, grew up in a culture not truly their own, find it comparatively easy to adapt to the mixed cultures of an interracial marriage and to Australian society. Navaratnam, too, felt excluded from Singapore's society, and Donald had similar feelings towards Malaysia, which he felt had rejected him, while Felix had moved from Indonesia as a small schoolboy to fit into New Zealand and then Australia. They all fit easily into Australia's lifestyle.

The stress Padma is going through has nothing to do with the fact that she is a lithe, dark-skinned Indian dancer and her husband is a blue-eyed, fair-haired, fair-skinned northern European. It has everything to do with the conflict between her age-old Hindu traditions and the certainty of Dutch Calvinism. The chasm that yawns between India's history and Holland's tests the adaptability of this couple now.

Padma's insight, 'that there is no more profound way to define a culture than through birth and motherhood', would be endorsed by many Australian wives (and husbands) trying to cope with what they see as an invasion of their home and family by Asian in-laws, particularly at the birth of a child. The estrangement between Andrea and her Chinese mother-in-law began when the mother-in-law tried to impose her will and defeat Andrea's desire to breastfeed her first child. A husband said bitterly of his Thai in-laws: 'They speak in English only when they want something'. Vincent flees the house and eats out during his Chinese in-laws' long visits. Another husband felt that he became a stranger in his own home during the six months his Filipina mother-in-law was in charge after the birth of his first child. Even now, years later, he says, 'I married Mary-lou but really I married her family too'. By contrast, Gideon, the first-generation Australian who lost most of his relatives during European wars, sees his wife's numerous family relations as a definite plus.

Australian parents are very much aware that they must not interfere in their adult children's lives. The result, if their child marries into another culture where the parents are more intrusive, is that the Australian spouse's parents, unwilling to appear to be pushy or competitive, drop into the background and are seen in contrast with the all-enveloping Asian family as cold and uncaring. This misunderstanding is hurtful to the Australian spouse and his or her family, and they are likely to drift further and further apart.

Many 'other' partners have little knowledge of how Australian families function, what they hold dear. Traditional laid-back undemonstrative Australian reserve is mis-read as coldness, as lack of affection. Several Chinese women referred to the closeness of Chinese families with the clear implication that Australian families were not close. Bernie regarded Chinese families as closer than Australian families, even though she had first-hand experience of her own birth-family giving babies away and was herself offered as a gift. She also pointed out that, as a girl, she was not going to be educated, while her Australian husband's parents had made exceptional sacrifices for the benefit of all their children.

When a Vietnamese woman married an Australian country man whose family had rarely, if ever, met an Asian before, they welcomed her as a daughter-in-law, made her feel at home, complimented her on her cooking and much more. Her own family of refugees and migrants were not pleased about the marriage, saying such things as, 'How can we communicate with him?' and 'Australians are different. You won't be happy'. She vehemently denied that these opinions could suggest that her family was racist and said, 'My husband's family are good and supportive, and very loving. I cannot think of another Australian family which functions like this. To have a supporting family must not be normal in Australia, but Vietnamese families are supportive'.

Thoughtful interviewees remarked that though Australians take an interest in the different traditions of the migrant — or ethnic — population, most new citizens take no interest in Australia's traditions, seeming to be unaware of them or, like Navaratnam, believe that Australia has no traditions.

Despite the often-mentioned existence in Australia of different cultures existing side-by-side, many Australians change their daily lives to fit in and understand their spouse's in-brought culture, just as some 'other' spouses make every effort not only to adapt to, but to adopt Australia's cultural traditions. Suan Lee, descended from a powerful Imperial family, happily abandons Chinese customs in favour of the prevailing Australian practices because she feels that she is now an Australian. Her 'we' includes all Australians, whereas so many migrants, even after many years of citizenship, still refer to ordinary white Australians as 'foreigners'. This attitude was most astonishing in a Singapore Chinese former member of an Australian parliament, who more than thirty years after marrying a white Australian says she still sees us not as Australians but as 'white persons'.

Children attending ordinary Australian schools absorb Australian culture from their peers, but there is often conflict suffered when they have to cope with two cultures, and have to make up their own minds which will be appropriate in a given situation. Gavin still feels this pressure as an adult, making him feel 'somewhat schizophrenic'. Mothers like Andrea recognise the difficulty children have in bridging two cultures. Teaching her children table manners, Andrea pointed out that there are two rules of courtesy to be followed in mixed-race families. Children of interracial families growing up in Australia see their parents as different from their mates' parents, unless they are as unobservant as our second son, who tells me he noticed that his father and I were of different skin colour only as he approached adulthood. On the other hand, our daughter, throughout her childhood was extremely fussy when choosing a home-cooked biscuit, scone, pikelet or the like. In her teens she volunteered the reason. 'Daddy always took the well-browned ones and you liked the white ones, so I thought the ones in between would be just right for me!'

Lian seems to be caught between her Australianness and her Chineseness, and she sees no advantage in developing her feeling of belonging to this country. 'I'm a citizen of Australia', she says, 'but I am not an Australian', and her tone suggests that she does not particularly wish to be. What have we done to our sense of Australia as a proud, cohesive nation that a child of a dinkum Aussie like Lawrie can be born here, grow up and be educated in Australian schools and universities and yet feel that she is not Australian?

On the other hand, fiercely Australian Katy's desperate worry is her skin colour (actually the palest ivory), which she feels is responsible for the problem that has dogged her all her life — her peers do not accept her as Australian. If the necessity of accepting different races were to be as loudly broadcast in Australia as the acceptance of many cultures is, then almost certainly Katy and other Australian citizens with one overseas-born parent who gifted them a different skin colour or shape of face would not be angered and hurt by people questioning their Australian identity. Acceptance by one's peers as just another Australian should not depend upon one's face.

The mothers of Lian and Katy are both Malaysian Chinese women who retain a very strong sense of their Chinese identity, to the extent that Katy's Australian father says that they live a very Chinese life within the context of this country. Fears such as those of ivory-skinned Katy — that she is not seen as the Australian she is — do not dog Briony Lim. Born in Australia of two Chinese parents, Briony is totally, unequivocally Australian. Hearing her voice — so very Australian — and seeing her face — indisputably Chinese — no one can ignore the fact that Australia is a multi-racial nation. The same could be said of dark-skinned Shara, born here of two Indian parents, who laughingly told me, 'Jonathon and I don't fit your book … we're both Australians'.

It will be interesting to see whether Li Li's daughters (both still at primary school) grow up with the strong sense of being Australian claimed by most of the children of mixed-race families to whom I spoke. Li Li, more than any other 'other' wife of an Australian husband, keeps alive Chinese relationship rituals within their home, making sure that her daughters know and practise all that would be expected of them if they had grown up in a strict Chinese home in

Malaysia. Li Li's insistence on instilling the Chinese behaviour patterns in her daughters may mean that Li Li is confident that they are Australians, as she feels herself to be, and these rituals are just to remind her daughters of their heritage — rather like my daughter telling stories to her children of where her father comes from.

The Australian columnist Frank Devine wrote that the word 'multiculturalism' was a 'Canberra contrivance aimed at camouflaging the fast growth of Asian immigration'. Perhaps it was, because every effort seems to have been made to avoid the words 'race' or 'colour', even though, as I learned, one's race or skin colour is of no importance in that most intimate of relationships: marriage. Differences in culture, though, do matter and need to be addressed and accommodated. In fact, in our efforts to avoid the words 'race' or 'multi-racial', we have blurred the meaning of 'multicultural' until it no longer makes sense. Luke Slattery, in an article in *The Australian*, quoting the head of a modelling agency, wrote, 'People can now open a magazine and see somebody who looks like their culture'. Really? If we mean race, why can't we say it? In the same article the interviewee did use the forbidden word. Slattery quotes her as saying, 'We're such a multicultural race here'.

She was speaking about models and their facial features. Is there such a thing as a cultural or multicultural face? Surely she meant, 'We're such a multi-racial population here', because culture is not only irrelevant but indiscernible in a photograph, particularly a fashion photograph. The meanings of the words have been fudged over the years since 'multicultural' became a fad-word and 'race' became taboo.

A committee reviewing multiculturalism in 1978 reported: 'We are convinced that migrants have the right to maintain their cultural and racial identity and that it is clearly in the best interests of our nation that they should be encouraged and assisted to do so if they wish'. It went on to say that this 'ethnic identity should be interwoven into the fabric of our nationhood by ... multicultural interaction'. This is an interesting statement. Leaving aside the encouragement to maintain one's racial identity — as if anyone could change it — the rest seems to say: we would like you to keep the culture of your previous domicile and we will help you do that, but yours, and all the other different cultures, must also be interwoven with Australia's culture.

It was a dream of 1978, and it has helped Australia become an interesting, exciting and diverse nation, but 20-plus years on it must be clear to those who love Australia that the incoming cultures show very little evidence of interweaving. A little of the religion, mostly through intermarriage, and much acceptance of ethnic food has changed Australia and made it a more cosmopolitan place, yet one still has the feeling that most Australians, newcomers, as well as those who have been here for generations, see great divisions between Australians of different backgrounds. The most heart-breaking of these is seen in school grounds, where the colour of their skin divides the children, as Bridget so vividly described of her Darwin school.

One of the side-effects of the encouragement by governments of all political flavours to migrants to retain the culture of the country they left has been that many long-time Australians feel their own culture to be denigrated. An example of this is one husband's statement that his children are Australian and should be brought up as Australian, when his wife's Chinese family wanted to take them back to Hong Kong to be brought up as Chinese.

Dr Bernice Pfitzner, a Singapore Chinese who studied medicine here, married an Australian and worked as a general practitioner in Australia for over thirty years before being elected to the upper house of South Australia's parliament, believes that it is now time for non-European migrants to enrich Australia's culture in much the same way that years ago the great influx of European migrants added some elements of their culture to the mainstream Australian culture under the name of assimilation. Though those European immigrants became Australians, they did not join the existing Australian culture, but became part of a new and different Australian culture that they enhanced.

Vincent speaks of his parents, who came from Italy in their youth but would no longer fit in Italy because Italy's culture has changed since they left. Because they had clung to the large Italian community in Melbourne, they do not really fit into the Australian culture either. Other interviewees, and particularly their children, remarked upon the way many migrants cling to what is an out-of-date version of their original way of life. Since transported culture dies away from its base, would it not be more sensible for incoming migrants to embrace the culture of their new homeland and enhance it by adding their own culture to the mainstream, actively contributing to and taking part in a growing living culture instead of clinging to a dying one?

If there are fears from incoming citizens that their inherited culture will be lost, swamped by Australia's mainstream, it should be pointed out that by adding it to Australia's culture, it will live. It will change, of course, as the years go by, just as that original culture is changing back in their former homeland, but the greatest change will be seen in Australia's culture. Under multiculturalism, many interviewees see different cultures existing side by side in Australia and believe that the mainstream culture is not changing.

Some interviewees expect the divisions within our society to disappear within 'a couple of generations', but it has already taken very much longer than the changes that took place after the enormous influx of Europeans after World War 2. It is likely that this time would be shortened if newcomers of all races were encouraged to embrace Australia's culture, while keeping constant and precious those things that they feel they could not live without, and incorporating them into the wider Australian culture.

Becoming Australian, though, should not mean totally relinquishing one's former culture. In the interviews, there were many examples of happy adjustment to Australia and to an interracial marriage by people who saw themselves as a fully integrated part of the Australian community, yet, as one would expect, they spoke of retaining cherished cultural activities from their former homes. After five generations Russell Jack, a dinky-di Australian with a Chinese face, and his Australian wife, who is descended from the second fleet, live a very Chinese life in their home in Bendigo. Their son, killed in an accident, was buried according to Chinese rites and Joan has already renounced Christian burial and opted for a Chinese funeral when her time comes. Russell remains proud, though, to speak of his 'Aussie grit' and plays a vital part as an Australian in the Australian community.

Back in 1959 Sir Macfarlane Burnet said Australia's population mix should include many genes to allow the best selection for a vigorous and intelligent population. People like my grandchildren fit seamlessly into the Australian population, but in addition to their majority Anglo-Celtic genes they have input from their Sinhalese great-grandfather and their South Indian Telagu great-grandmother. From them, all my grandchildren, even the blond, blue-eyed ones, have gained resistance to the onslaught of the Australian sun — surely an important plus.

Benjamin, the small son of Daniel and Betsy, has inherited the Anglo-Saxon and the Australian Aboriginal genes of his father and the Chinese genes of his mother — a spread from three continents at least! Sir Macfarlane Burnet would be happy and astonished that the Australian gene pool encompasses such a racially wide variety only fifty years after his speech advocating genetic diversity for Australia's future caused such a furore. We should take the concept that Australians (new and old) can be of different racial origin out of the closet and openly acknowledge that the multi-racial nature of Australia's population is its major feature, as indeed it is.

If all Australians were encouraged to embrace multi-racialism as, for the last twenty years, we have been urged to embrace multiculturalism, then there would be no one referring to a 3-year-old child as a half-caste. Australia's open recognition — dare I say celebration? — that it is a multi-racial nation would encourage people to accept, even welcome, people of different races, different skin colours as an integral part of our nation — a step that has not been achieved under the difficult-to-define label of multiculturalism. The inclusive acceptance of other races — people who are noticeably different physically — as well as people of other cultures may have been the intended outcome of the multicultural policy, but it has not happened.

Perhaps it would be better if we could re-define ourselves as cosmopolitan, a light-hearted, cheerful word that means many races as well as many cultures. Under that umbrella, we could ignore the differences in culture among fellow Australians and learn to adapt one to the other until we saw this great simmering stew that is Australia as a population where each individual could follow those habits and customs, those rituals, those cultural behaviours that pleased each one, as long as it was within the law of the land and did not offend one's neighbours. Each person living permanently in Australia would be an Australian (without an adjectival tag) and would be thought of as Australian, even though he or she may look African or Mongolian and follow the precepts of Mohammed or Buddha or any other belief. Since our population includes people of many different traditions, why should we not adapt to all our neighbours' differences, accepting them not as a different culture belonging somewhere else, but as the preferred customs of some Australians, as part of the richness of cosmopolitan Australia's culture?

We have so hidden the multi-racial nature of our society that for some time even police reports were not allowed to specify the 'race' to which a suspect or a victim belonged. By hiding the idea that there are many different racial groups in Australia, we have driven underground the acceptance of racial differences within our country, as if it is rude or unkind (or even racist!) to say to Briony that she is an Australian with a Chinese face, as she happily calls herself, along with Herbert and Thomas and others. They are all examples of multi-racial Australia, their Australian culture affected just a little by their parents' cultural heritage, as it should be. Briony cooks her steak in a wok and Shara contemplates the brilliant spectacle of perhaps having a traditional Sikh wedding.

We are a multi-racial nation and we should flaunt it. One's race only signifies the genes one inherited; it is nothing to be ashamed of, nor yet anything to be inordinately proud of. It is a given; it does not indicate where one lives, how one lives, where one's loyalty lies, nor one's faith, attitude to life, character or indeed, one's culture.

If Australia was openly multi-racial, then children with Chinese faces would not feel different. They may be teased as Briony was — or Herb seventy years ago — just as red-haired children, overweight children, or children with glasses are sometimes teased. But they would not have their identity as Australians questioned in ways that caused such childhood pain to Katy and Anton. Why do we not tell all the children of Australia that, whether their skin is black or white, whether their face is Chinese or African or anything else, they are as 'dinky-di' Australian as anyone else? Why do we not tell them that the colour or shape of their faces matters not at all; that to be Australian all they have to do is understand and be part of our infinitely varied and constantly changing culture, our language, our history and our loyalties, and share, too, a selection of the pastimes, including those that though ancient may be new to Australia, habits, and passions that are available to us all?

Within a marriage race is not a problem. Interracial marriages within a shared culture are just marriages. Only when there are two very different cultures within the marriage do extra adjustments have to be made. Difficult decisions have to be reached with regard to children, education, faith and various behaviours within the family. Sometimes the stresses are so great that the marriage breaks down, but most mixed-culture couples continually adjust their expectations, changing their way of life to suit their partner, until a unique culture, unique to that family, evolves. As Japanese-born Saemi says, 'Interracial marriage is great fun! It gives you a chance to create your own rules … Decide what you want to keep, and discard those you don't'.

Over the last 200 years Australia's interracial families have absorbed customs and habits from this continent's first culture along with old-time British traditions that have been loosened and adapted to become uniquely Australian. Now they are being interlaced and expanded with languages, religions and traditions from a score or more incoming cultures. Those that fit and improve our way of life will stay, the others will be sloughed off, just as we have sloughed off inappropriate English ways over the last 200 years.

NOTES

PREFACE
1   Gerard Henderson, 'Populate or Perish', in the *Sydney Morning Herald*, 18 January 2000.
2   Graham Leech, 'A Nation Gripped by Madness?', *The Australian*, 25 October 1996, p 13.
3   Billie Livingstone, 'The Paternal Side', *Imago*, No 3, Vol 3, 1995.

1 INTRODUCTION
1   Item in the *Colonial Times* quoted in RV Hall's chapter 'Racism and the Press' in F Stevens (ed), *Racism: The Australian Experience*, A&NZ Book Co, Sydney, 1971, p 155.
2   GB Barton, *History of New South Wales from the Records*, Charles Potter, Government Printer, Sydney, 1889, p 476.
3   Eric Rolls, *Sojourners*, University of Queensland Press, St Lucia, 1992, pp 32–33.
4   Manning Clark, *A Short History of Australia*, Penguin, Melbourne, 1963, p 116.
5   Eric Rolls, *Sojourners*, pp 142–44.
6   A Yarwood, *Attitudes to Non-European Migrants*, Cassell, Melbourne, 1968, pp 48–68.
7   F Bandler, *Welou, My Brother*, Redress Press, 1984.
8   'Parallel Lines', quoting from a 1901 edition of *The Bulletin* in *The Australian Magazine*, 26–27 April 1997.
9   'Progress', quoted in RV Hall's 'Racism & the Press', in F Stevens (ed), *Racism: The Australian Experience*, 1971.
10 Edgar Penzig in a letter to *The Australian*, 17 August 1998.
11 Denis O'Brien, in an article in *The Australian*, 22 January 1986.

2 INTERRACIAL MARRIAGES FROM 1788 TO 1900
1   AC Palfreyman, 'The White Australia Policy', in F Stevens (ed), *Racism: The Australian Experience*, Sydney, 1971.
2   Andrew Markus, *Fear & Hatred*, Hale & Iremonger, Sydney, 1979, p 14.

3   Andrew Markus, *Fear & Hatred*, p 15.
4   Andrew Markus, *Fear & Hatred*, p 18.
5   Andrew Markus, *Fear & Hatred*, p 92.
6   Alan Sharpe, *Colonial New South Wales, 1853–1894*, Harper & Row, Sydney, 1979, p 153.
7   Andrew Markus, *Fear & Hatred*, p 18.
8   Robert Travers, *Australian Mandarin — The Life & Times of Quong Tart*, Kangaroo Press, Sydney, 1981.
9   June Owen, *Heart of the City, a history of the Sydney City Mission*, Kangaroo Press, Sydney, 1987, p 53.
10 Quoted in Alison Broinowsky's *The Yellow Lady: Australian Impressions of Asia*, Oxford University Press, Melbourne, 1992, p 46.
11 *The Boomerang*, Bathurst, 25 February 1888.
12 Quoted in AT Yarwood's 'Attitudes to Non-European Migrants', in FS Stevens (ed), *Racism: The Australian Experience*, Sydney, 1971.
13 Yu Lan Poon, 'Two-Way Mirror: contemporary issues as seen through the eyes of the Chinese language press, 1901–1911', in S Fitzgerald & G Wotherspoon (eds), *Minorities, cultural diversity in Sydney*, State Library of New South Wales, Sydney, 2000.
14 Pamela Raikowsky, *In the Tracks of the Camelmen*, Angus & Robertson, Sydney, 1987.
15 Winifred Steger, *Always Bells: Life with Ali*, Angus & Robertson, Adelaide, 1969.
16 Michael Ciglar, *Afghans in Australia*, AE Press, Melbourne, 1986.
17 WS Weerasooria, *Links between Sri Lanka and Australia*, Government Press, Colombo, 1988.
18 Keith Butler, 'A Suitable Boy', *Good Weekend*, 11 December 1999.

3 INTERRACIAL MARRIAGES FROM 1901 TO 1950
1   *Commonwealth Parliamentary Debates*, Vol 14, p 5233.
2   S Encel, 'The Nature of Prejudice', in F Stevens (ed), *Racism: The Australian Experience*, Sydney, 1971.
3   Edward Foxall, *Coloraphobia*, quoted in *There Goes the Neighbourhood*, Australian Institute of Multicultural Affairs, Macmillan, Sydney, 1984, p 102.
4   Douglas Lockwood, in *The Front Door — Darwin 1869–1969*, Rigby Ltd, Adelaide, 1968, p 121.
5   Marion Lake & Farley Kelly (eds), *Double Time Women in Victoria — 150 Years*, Penguin Books, Melbourne, 1985, p 337.
6   Quoted in *The Australian*, 9 April 1997.
7   WS Weerasooria, *Links between Sri Lanka and Australia*, Government Press, Colombo, 1988.
8   RV Hall, *White Australia's Darkest Days* in *Racism: The Australian Experience*.
9   Alison Broinowsky, *The Yellow Lady: Australian Impressions of Asia*, Oxford University Press, Melbourne, 1992, p 40.

4 INTERRACIAL MARRIAGES IN THE 1950s
1   Sir Macfarlane Burnet, Director of the Walter and Eliza Hall Institute of Medical Research, speaking of Asian Colombo Plan students at the Citizenship Convention, January 1959.
2   Digest of 1950 Citizenship Convention quoted in John Lack & Jacqueline Templeton, *Bold Experiment — a Documentary History of Australian Immigration since 1945*, Oxford University Press, Melbourne.
3   From Army newspapers issued to BOAC troops serving in Japan.
4   From Army newspapers issued to BOAC troops serving in Japan.
5   'Bridging the Cultural Gap', a profile of Rhoda Roberts, by Kelly Burke, in the *Sydney Morning Herald*, 4 March 1998.

6   The *Sydney Morning Herald*, 21 January 1959.
7   The *Sydney Morning Herald*, 23 January 1959.
8   The *Sydney Morning Herald*, 22 January 1959.

5 INTERRACIAL MARRIAGES IN THE 1960s
1   Janet Penny & Siew-Ean Khoo, *Intermarriage*, Bureau of Immigration & Multicultural Research, 1996, p xiv.
2   *The Weekend Australian*, 14–15 December 1996.
3   Reported in the *Age*, 23 January 1964.

6 1960s MARRIAGES WITH MIXED-RACE CHILDREN
1   M Ciglar, *Afghans in Australia*, AE Press, Melbourne, 1986.
2   Steve Sailor, article in the *Australian Financial Review* 10 October 1997.

7 INTERRACIAL MARRIAGES IN THE 1970s
1   Prime Minister John Gorton in a speech in Singapore in 1971.
2   A Huck, 'Chinese in Australia', in 'Prejudice & Zenophobia', in Stevens (ed), *Racism: The Australian Experience*, 1971.

8 1970s MARRIAGES WITH MIXED-RACE CHILDREN
1   Louise Williams, from Indonesia, the *Sydney Morning Herald*, 31 October 1996.

10 ABORIGINAL INTERRACIAL MARRIAGES IN THE 1970s
1   Sally Dingo, *The Story of Our Mob*, Random House, 1997.
2   *The Australian Weekend Review*, 19–20 April 1997, p 12.

12 INTERRACIAL MARRIAGES IN THE 1980s
1   Paul Sheehan, 'Gang Buster', profile of Richard Basham in the *Sydney Morning Herald*, 9 August 1997.
2   Alison Broinowsky in *The Yellow Lady: Australian Impressions of Asia*, Oxford University Press, Melbourne, 1992, p 216.

13 1980s — MIXED-RACE FAMILIES IN DARWIN
1   Suzanne Spunner, in 'Top Enders Living Our Future' by Sue Neales, in *Good Weekend*, 22 February 1997.
2   Suzanne Spunner, in 'Top Enders Living Our Future'.
3   Robert Drewe, *A Cry in the Jungle Bar*, Picador, Sydney, 1988.
4   Information kindly supplied by Dr Rogee Pe-Pua, of the Social Work Department, at the University of New South Wales.

14 INTERRACIAL MARRIAGES IN THE 1980s AND 1990s
1   *Colour of Love* is a British Race Relations publication.
2   Paul Sheehan, 'Gang Buster', profile of Richard Basham in the *Sydney Morning Herald*, 9 August 1997.

BIBLIOGRAPHY

Ata, Abe W (2000) *Inter-Marriage between Christians and Muslims*, David Lovell
   Publishing, Melbourne.
Australian Population and Immigration Council (1977) *Immigration Policies and
   Australia's Population*, AGPS, Canberra.
Bandler, Faith (1984) *Welou, My Brother*, Redress Press, Sydney.
Bandler, Faith (1989) *Turning the Tide*, Aboriginal Studies Press, Canberra.
Blainey, Geoffrey (1994) *A Shorter History of Australia*, Random House, Sydney.
Blue Eyes and *A Class Divided*, produced by Denkmal Film GM&H, videos
   screened by SBS in November and December 1997.
Bo Yang (1991) *The Ugly Chinaman*, Allen & Unwin, Sydney.
Bowditch, Jim (1993) *Whispers from the North*, NTU Press, Darwin.
The British Institute of Race Relations, *Colour of Love*, London.
Broinowsky, Alison (1996) *The Yellow Lady: Australian Impressions of Asia*, Oxford
   University Press, Melbourne.
Caltabiano, NJ (1985) 'How Ethnicity & Religion Affects Attitudes towards Mixed
   Marriages', *Australian Journal of Sex, Marriage & Family*, Vol 6, No 4.
Ciglar, Beryl & Michael (1985) *Australia: A Land of Immigrants*, Jacaranda Press,
   Brisbane.
Ciglar, Michael (1986) *Afghans in Australia*, AE Press, Melbourne.
Clark, Manning (1963) *A Short History of Australia*, Penguin Books, Melbourne.
de Lepervanche, Marie M (1984) *Indians in White Australia*, George Allen &
   Unwin, Sydney.
Dilke, Charles (1985) *Greater Britain*, Methuen Haynes, Sydney.
Dugan, Michael & Szware, Josef (1984) *There Goes the Neighbourhood —
   Australia's Migrant Experience*, for the Australian Multicultural Institute,
   Macmillan, Melbourne.
Dunn, Michael (1984) *Australian and the Empire — from 1788 to the Present*,
   Fontana, Sydney.
Dutton, Geoffrey (ed) (1966) *Australia and the Monarchy*, Sun Books.
Ethnic Studies Journals, especially Vol 2, No 3, 1978.
Falk, Barbara (1978) *Personal Identity in a Multicultural Australia*, Buntine
   Oration, Australian Council for Educational Research, Canberra.

Fitzgerald, Shirley & Wotherspoon, Garry (eds) (1995) *Minorities — cultural diversity in Sydney*, State Library of NSW Press, Sydney.

Giese, Diana (1997) *Astronauts, Lost Souls & Dragons*, University of Queensland Press, Brisbane.

Lack, John & Templeton, Jacqueline (1995) *Bold Experiment — a Documentary History of Australian Immigration since 1945*, Oxford University Press, Melbourne.

Lake, Marilyn & Kelly, Farley (1985) *Double Time, Women in Victoria — 150 Years*, Penguin Books, Melbourne.

Lippmann, Lorna (1973) *Words or Blows — Racial Attitudes in Australia*, Penguin Books, Melbourne.

Lockwood, Douglas (1968) *The Front Door — Darwin 1869–1969*, Rigby Ltd, Adelaide.

Markus, Andrew (1979) *Fear & Hatred — Purifying Australia & California 1850–1901*, Hale & Iremonger, Sydney.

Nile, Richard (ed) (1994) *Australian Civilisation*, Oxford University Press, Melbourne.

Owen, June (1987) *Heart of the City — the first 125 years of the Sydney City Mission*, Kangaroo Press, Sydney.

Penny, Janet & Khoo, Siew-Ean (1996) *Intermarriage — A study of migration and integration*, Bureau of Immigration, Multicultural & Population Research, AGPS, Canberra.

Poole, ME, de Lacey, PR & Randhawa, BS (1985) *Australia in Transition: Culture and Life Possibilities*, Harcourt, Brace & Jovanovich, Sydney.

Price CA 'Ethnic Intermixture in Australia', *People & Place*, Vol 1, No 1, and Vol 2, No 4.

Raikowsky, Pamela (1987) *In the Tracks of the Camelmen*, Angus & Robertson, Sydney.

Rivett, Kenneth (1975) *Australia & the Non-White Migrant*, Melbourne University Press, Melbourne.

Rolls, Eric (1992) *Sojourners*, University of Queensland Press, Brisbane.

Sharpe, Alan (1979) *Colonial New South Wales, 1853–1894*, Harper & Row, Sydney.

Sheehan, Paul (1998) *Among the Barbarians*, Random House, Sydney.

Sri Lankan Journal for Women's Liberation, (December 1994), Vol 4, Voice of Women, Colombo.

Steger, Winifred (1969) *Always Bells — Life with Ali*, Angus & Robertson, Adelaide.

Stevens, Christine (1998) *Tin Mosques and Ghantowns: A History of Afghan Camel Drivers in Australia*, Oxford University Press, Melbourne.

Stevens, FS (ed) (1971) *Racism: The Australian Experience, Vol 1 Prejudice & Xenophobia*, Aust & NZ Book Co, Melbourne.

Travers, Robert (1981) *Australian Mandarin — The life & Times of Quong Tart*, Kangaroo Press, Sydney

Yarwood, AT (1968) *Attitudes to Non-European Immigration*, Cassell, Melbourne.

Weerasooria, WS (1996) *Sri Lankans in Australia*, Government Press, Colombo.

INDEX